Torquemada a:

Spanish Inquisition

A History

Rafael Sabatini

Alpha Editions

This edition published in 2024

ISBN : 9789357961806

Design and Setting By
Alpha Editions
www.alphaedis.com
Email - info@alphaedis.com

Contents

PREFACE

The history of Frey Tómas de Torquemada is the history of the establishment of the Modern Inquisition. It is not so much the history of a man as of an abstract genius presiding over a gigantic and cruel engine of its own perfecting. Of this engine we may examine for ourselves to-day the details of the complex machinery. Through the records that survive we may observe its cold, smooth action, and trace in this the awful intelligence of its architect. But of that architect himself we are permitted to catch no more than an occasional and fleeting glimpse. It is only in the rarest and briefest moments that he stands clearly before us, revealed as a man of flesh and blood.

We see him, now fervidly urging a reluctant queen to do her duty by her God and unsheathe the sword of persecution, now harshly threatening his sovereigns with the wrath of Heaven when they are in danger of relenting in the wielding of that same sword. But in the main he must be studied, not in his actions, but in his enactments—the emanations of his relentless spirit. In these he is to be seen devoutly compassing evil in the perfervid quest of good.

Untouched by worldly ambitions, he seems at once superhuman and less than human. Dauntless amid execrations, unmoved by plaudits, sublimely disdainful of temporal weal, in nothing is he so admirable as in the unfaltering self-abnegation with which he devotes himself to the service of his God, in nothing so terrible and tragically deplorable as in the actual service which he renders.

"His history," says Prescott, "may be thought to prove that of all human infirmities there is none productive of more extensive mischief to society than fanaticism."

To this day—four centuries after his passing—Spain still bears the imprint of his pitiless work, and none may deny the truth of Rosseeuw St. Hilaire's indictment that, after Philip II, Torquemada was the man who did most harm to the land that gave him birth.

<hr>

The materials for this history have been gathered from the sources cited in the appended bibliography, to all of which the author acknowledges his profound indebtedness. In particular, however, are his thanks due—as must be the thanks of all men who engage in studies of the Spanish Inquisition—to the voluminous, succinct, and enormously comprehensive works of Juan Antonio Llorente, a historian of unimpugned honesty and authority, who wrote under circumstances peculiarly advantageous and with qualifications peculiarly full.

Juan Antonio Llorente was born at Logroño in 1756, and he was ordained priest in 1779, after a university course of Roman and Canon law which enabled him to obtain a place among the lawyers of the Supreme Council of Castile—*i.e.* the Council of the Inquisition. Having graduated as a Doctor of Canon Law, he discharged the duties of Vicar-General to the Bishop of Calahorra, and later on became the Commissary of the Holy Office in Logroño—for which it was necessary that he should prove that he was of "clean blood," undefiled by the taint of Jew or Moor or heretic.

In 1789 he was appointed Secretary-General to the Holy Office, an appointment which took him to Madrid, where he was well received by the King, who gave him a canonry of Calahorra.

A profound student of sociological questions, with leanings towards rationalism, he provoked a certain degree of mistrust, and when the Liberal party fell from power and dragged with it many of those who had held offices of consequence, the young priest found himself not only deposed, but forced to meet certain minor charges, which resulted in his being sent into retreat in a convent for a month as a penance.

Thereafter he concerned himself with educational matters until the coming of Bonaparte's eagles into Spain. When that invasion took place, he hailed the French as the saviours of his country, and as a consequence found himself a member of the Assembly of Notables convoked by Murat to reform the Spanish Government. But most important of all, from our point of view, is the fact that when the Inquisition was abolished, in 1809, he accepted the charge of going through its vast archives, and he spent two years and employed a number of amanuenses in copying or making extracts of all that he considered of account.

He held various offices of importance under the French Government, so that when this was finally expelled from Spain, he, too, was forced to go. He sought refuge in Paris, and there he wrote his famous "Historia Critica de la Inquisicion de España," the crystallization of his vast researches.

It was a very daring thing to have done, and, thanks to the royalist and clerical Government, he was not suffered to remain long unpunished. He was inhibited from hearing confession or celebrating Mass—practically unfrocked—and forbidden to teach the Castilian language in private schools. He hit back by publishing "The Political Portrait of the Popes," which earned him orders to leave France immediately. He set out in December of 1822 to return to Spain, and died a few days after reaching Madrid, killed by the rigours of the journey at his advanced age.

Although his "Critical History" displays at times a certain vehemence, in the main it is concerned with the sober transcription of the musty records he was privileged to explore.

The Spanish Inquisition has been the subject of much unrestrained and exaggerated writing, expressing points of view that are diametrically opposed. From such authors as Garcia Rodrigo, who laud its work of purification, misrepresent its scope, and deplore (in our own times) the extinction of that terrible tribunal, it is a far cry indeed to such writers as Dr. Rule, who dip their pens in the gall of an intolerance as virulent as that which they attack.

The author has sought here to hold a course that is unencumbered by religious partisanship, treating purely as a phase of history the institution for which Torquemada was so largely responsible. He has not written in the Catholic interest, or the Protestant interest, or the Jewish interest. He holds the view that on the score of intolerance it is not for Christians to cast a stone at Jews, nor Jews at Christians, nor yet Christians of one sect at Christians of another. Each will find in his own history more than enough to answer for at the bar of Humanity. And when achievement is measured by opportunity, each will discover that he is entitled to fling at the others no reproaches which the others are not entitled to fling at him.

If the Spanish Inquisition is here shown as a ruthless engine of destruction whose wheels drip the blood of mangled generations, yet it is very far from being implied that religious persecution is an offence peculiar to the Church of Rome.

"She persecuted to the full extent of the power of her clergy, and that power was very great. The persecution of which every Protestant church was guilty was measured by the same rule, but clerical influence in Protestant countries was comparatively weak."

Thus Lecky, whom we quote lest any should be tempted to use anything in these pages as a weapon of unchristian Christian partisanship. Let any such remember that against Torquemada, who was unfortunately well served by opportunity, may be set the bloody-minded John Knox, who, fortunately for humanity, was not; let him ponder the slaughter of Presbyterians, Puritans, and Roman Catholics under Elizabeth; let him call to mind the persecutions of the Anabaptists under Edward VI, and the Anabaptists' own clamour for the blood of all who were not re-baptized.

CHAPTER I
EARLY PERSECUTIONS

In an endeavour to trace the Inquisition to its source it is not necessary to go as far back into antiquity as went Paramo; nor yet is it possible to agree with him that God Himself was the first inquisitor, that the first "Act of Faith" was executed upon Adam and Eve, and that their expulsion from Eden is a proper precedent for the confiscation of the property of heretics.[1]

Nevertheless, it is necessary to go very far back indeed; for it is in the very dawn of Christianity that the beginnings of this organization are to be discovered.

There is no more lamentable lesson to be culled from history than that contained in her inability to furnish a single instance of a religion accepted with unquestioning sincerity and fervour which did not, out of those very qualities, beget intolerance. It would seem that only when a faith has been diluted by certain general elements of doubt, that only when a certain degree of indifference has crept into the observance of a prevailing cult, does it become possible for the members of that cult to bear themselves complacently towards the members of another. Until this comes to pass, intolerance is the very breath of religion, and—when the power is present—this intolerance never fails to express itself in persecution.

Deplorable as this is in all religions, in none is it so utterly anomalous as in Christianity, which is established upon tenets of charity, patience, and forbearance, and which has for cardinal guidance its Founder's sublime admonition—"Love one another!"

From the earliest days of its history, persecution has unfailingly signalized the spread of Christianity, until to the thoughtful observer Christianity must afford the grimmest, the saddest—indeed, the most tragic—of all the paradoxes that go to make up the history of civilized man.

Its benign gospel of love has been thundered forth in malign hatred; its divine lesson of patience and forbearance has been taught in murderous impatience and bloodthirsty intolerance; its mild tenets of mercy and compassion have been ferociously expounded with fire and sword and rack; its precepts of humility have been inculcated with a pride and arrogance as harsh as any that the world has known.

It is impossible to deny that at almost any time in the history of Christianity the enlightened pagan of the second century would have been justified of his stinging gibe—"Behold how these Christians love one another!"

It may even be said of the earliest Christians that it was largely through their own intolerance of the opinions and beliefs of others that they brought upon themselves the persecutions to which through three centuries they were intermittently subjected. Certain it is that they were the first to disturb the toleration which in polytheistic Rome was accorded to all religions. They might have pursued their cult unmolested so long as they accorded the same liberty to others. But by the vehemence with which they denounced false all creeds but their own, they offended the zealous worshippers of other gods, and so disturbed the peace of the community; by denying obedience to the state in which they dwelt, by refusing to bear arms for the Empire on the plea of "Nolo militare; militia mea est ad Dominum!" they provoked the resentment of the law. When driven, by the beginnings of persecution, to assemble and celebrate their rites in secret, this very secrecy became the cause of further and sharper proceedings against them. Their mysteriousness evoked suspicion, and surmise sprang up to explain it. Very soon there was levelled against them the charge from which hardly any cult that celebrates in secret has been exempt. It was put abroad that they practised abominations, and that they engaged in the ritual murder of infants. Public opinion, ever credulous where evil is the subject, was still further inflamed against them, and fresh and greater disorders were the result. Thus they came to be denounced for atheism, insubordination, and subversion of public order.

The severity dealt out to them by a state hitherto indifferent—through the agnosticism prevalent in the ruling classes—to the religious opinions of its citizens, was dictated by the desire to suppress an element that had become socially perturbative, rather than by any vindictiveness or intolerance towards this new cult out of Syria.

Under Claudius we see the Nazarenes expelled from Rome as disturbers of the public peace; under Nero and Domitian we see them, denounced as *hostes publici*, suffering their first great persecution. But that persecution on purely religious grounds was repugnant to the Roman is shown by the conduct of Nerva, who forbade delations and oppressions on the score of belief, and recalled the Christians who had been banished. His successor, the just and wise Trajan, provoked perhaps by the fierce insurrection of the Jews which occurred in his reign, moved against the Nazarenes at first, but later on afforded them complete toleration. Similarly were they unmolested by the accomplished Adrian, who, indeed, so far approved of their creed as to have notions of including Christ in the Roman Pantheon; and they were left in peace by his successor Antoninus, notwithstanding that the last was so attached to the faith of his country and to the service of the gods as to have earned for himself the surname of Pius.

With the accession of the philosopher-emperor Marcus Aurelius, who was rendered hostile to the new doctrine not only by his own stoical convictions, but also because politically he viewed the Christians with disfavour, came the next great persecution; and persecution was their portion thereafter for some sixty years, under four reigns, until the accession of Alexander Severus in the third decade of the third century of the Christian era.

Alexander's mother, Julia Mannea, is believed to have been instructed in the new doctrine by Origen, the Alexandrian, although her conversion to Christianity and her ideas upon it do not appear to be greatly in advance of those of Adrian, for she is said to have included an image of Christ in the group of beneficent deities set up in her *lararium*.[2]

For twenty years the Christians now knew peace and enjoyed the fullest liberty. Upon that followed a period of severe oppression, initiated by Decius, continued by Valerian and Aurelian, and reaching something of a climax under Diocletian, in the dawn of the fourth century, when the Christians endured the cruellest and most ferocious of all these persecutions. But the end of their sufferings was at hand, and with the accession of Constantine in 312 a new era began for Christianity. Constantine, upheld by the Christians as their saviour, in admitting the inevitable predominance which the new religion had obtained in rather less than three hundred years, was compelled to recognize the rights of its votaries not only to existence but to authority.

Legends surround the history of this emperor. The most popular relates how, when he was marching against Maxentius, his rival for the throne, desponding in the consciousness of his own inferior force, there appeared at sunset a fiery cross in the heavens with the inscription ΕΝ ΤΟΓΤΩ ΝΙΚΑ— IN THIS SIGN YOU CONQUER. And it is claimed that as a consequence of this portent, whose injunction he obeyed, he sought instruction in Christianity, was baptized and made public avowal of that faith. Others maintain that he was reared in Christianity by his mother, St. Helena—she who made an expedition to the Holy Land to recover the true cross, and who is said to have built the Church of the Holy Sepulchre in Jerusalem; whilst others still assert that Constantine did not receive baptism until at the point of death, and that throughout his life, whilst undoubtedly favouring Christians, he continued in the pagan religion in which he had been educated by his father.

The truth probably lies midway. During the early years of his reign Constantine not only pursued a middle course, according religious liberty to all sects, but, himself, whilst leaning strongly towards Christianity, retained his imperial dignity of High-priest of the polytheistic Roman cult, and the title "Pontifex Maximus," which later—together with so much else of pagan origin—was appropriated by the Christians and bestowed upon their chief bishop. But in 313-14 he refused to celebrate the *ludi seculares*, and in 330 he issued an edict forbidding temple-worship, whilst the Christian Council of Nicæa, in 325, was held undoubtedly under his auspices.

From the very moment that the new religion found itself recognized and invested not only with civil rights but actually with power, from the very moment that the Christian could rear his head and go openly and unafraid abroad, from that very moment do we find him engaging in persecutions against the votaries of other cults—against pagan, Jew, and heretic. For although Christianity was but in the beginning of the fourth century of its existence, not only had it spread irresistibly and mightily in spite of the repressive measures against it, but it was already beginning to know dismemberment and divisions in its own body. Indeed, it has been computed that the number of schisms in the fourth century amounted to no less than ninety.

Of these the most famous is that of Arius, a priest of Alexandria, who denied that Christ was God Incarnate, accounting Him no more than divinely inspired, the first and the highest of the sons of men. Although already denounced by the Synod that met at Alexandria in 321, so great had been the spread of this doctrine that the Œcumenical Council of Nicæa was convoked especially to deal with it. It was then condemned as heretical, and the Articles of Faith were defined and set down in the Nicene Creed, which is recited to this day.

Other famous heresies were the Manichæan, the Gnostic, the Adamite, the Severist, and the Donatist; and to these were soon to be added, amongst others, the Pelagian and the Priscilliantist.

Perhaps the Manichæans' chief claim to celebrity lies in the fact that the great St. Augustine of Tagaste, when he abandoned the disorders of his youth, entered Christianity through this sect, which professed a form of it vitiated by Sun-worship and Buddhism.

The other heresies—with the exception of the Pelagian—were, in the main, equally fantastic. The Gnostic heresy, with its many subdivisions, was made up of mysticism and magic, and founded upon Zoroastrian notions of dualism, of the two powers of good and evil, light and darkness. To the power of evil it attributed all creation save man, whose soul was accounted of divine substance. The Adamites claimed to be in the state of original innocency of Adam before the fall; they demanded purity in their followers, rejected marriage, which they urged could never have come into existence but for sin, and they expelled from their Church all sinners against their tenets, even as Adam and Eve had been expelled from Eden. The Severists denied the resurrection of the flesh, would not accept the acts of the apostles, and carried purity to fantastic lengths. The Soldiers of Florinus denied the

Last Judgment, and held it as an undeniable truth that the resurrection of the flesh lay entirely in reproduction.

The Pelagians were the followers of Pelagius, a British monk who settled in Rome towards the year 400, and his heresy at least was founded upon rational grounds. He denied the doctrine of original sin, maintained that every human being was born in a state of innocency, and that his perseverance in virtue depended upon himself. He found numerous followers, and for twenty years the conflict raged between Pelagians and the Church, until Pope Zosimus declared against them and banished Pelagius from Rome.

From Constantine onwards Christianity steadily maintains her ascendancy, and her earliest assertion of her power is to bare the sword of persecution, oblivious of the lofty protests against it which she, herself, had uttered, the broad and noble advocacy of tolerance which she had urged in the days of her own affliction. We find Optatus urging the massacre of the Donatists— who claimed that theirs was the true Church—and Constantine threatening with the stake any Jew who should affront a Christian and any Christian who should become a Jew. We find him demolishing the churches of the Arians and Donatists, banishing their priests and forbidding under pain of death the propagation of their doctrines.

The power of Christianity suffered one slight check thereafter, under the tolerant rule of Julian the Apostate, who reopened the pagan temples and restored the cult of the old gods; but it rose again to be finally and firmly established under Theodosius in 380.

Now we see the pagan temples not only closed, but razed to the ground, the images broken and swept away, their worship, and even private sacrifice, forbidden under pain of death. From Libanius we may gather something of the desolation which this spread among the pagan peasant-folk. Residing at a distance from the great centres where doctrines were being expounded, they found themselves bereft of the old gods and without knowledge of the new. Their plight is a far more pathetic one than that of the Arians, Manichæans, Donatists, and all other heretics against whom there was a similar enactment.

It is now, at this early date, that for the first time we come across the title "Inquisitor of the Faith," in the first law[3] promulgated to render death the penalty of heresy. It is now that we find the great Augustine of Tagaste—the mightiest genius that the Church has brought forth—denouncing religious liberty with the question, "Quid est enim pejor, mors animæ quam libertas erroris?"[4] and strenuously urging the death of heretics on the ground that it is a merciful measure, since it must result in the saving of others from the damnation consequent upon their being led into error. Similarly he applauded those decrees of death against any one pursuing the polytheism that but a few generations earlier had been the official religion of the Roman Empire.

It was Augustine—of whom it has been truly said that "no man since the days of the Apostles has infused into the Church a larger measure of his spirit"—in his enormous fervour, and with the overwhelming arguments inspired by his stupendous intellect, who laid down the principles that governed persecution, and were cited in justification of it for nearly 1,500 years after his day. "He was," says Lecky, "the most staunch and enthusiastic defender of all those doctrines that grow out of the habits of mind that lead to persecution."[5]

So far, however much persecution may have been inspired by the Church, its actual execution had rested entirely and solely with the civil authorities; and this aloofness, indeed, is urged upon the clergy by St. Augustine. But already before the close of the fourth century we find ecclesiastics themselves directly engaged in causing the death of heretics.

Priscillian, a Spanish theologian, was led by St. Paul's "Know ye not that ye are the temple of God?" to seek to render himself by purity a worthy dwelling. He preached from that text a doctrine of stern asceticism, and forbade the marriage of the clergy. This at the time was optional,[6] and by proclaiming it to be Christ's law he laid himself open to a charge of heresy. He was accused of magic and licentiousness, excommunicated in 380 and burnt alive, together with several of his companions, by order of two Christian bishops. He has been described as the first martyr burnt by a Spanish Inquisition.[7]

It must be added that the deed excited the profoundest indignation on the part of the clergy against those bishops who had been responsible for it, and St. Martin of Tours hotly denounced the act. But this indignation was not provoked by the fact that men had suffered death for heresy, but by the circumstance that ecclesiastics had procured the execution. For it was part of the pure teaching of the early Church that under no circumstances—not as judge, soldier, or executioner—should a Christian render himself the instrument of the death of a fellow-creature; and it was partly through their rigid obedience to this precept that the Christians had first drawn attention to themselves and aroused the resentment of the Roman government, as we have seen. Now, whilst at no time after the Church's accession to power was this teaching observed with any degree of strictness, yet there were limits to the extent to which it might be neglected, and that limit, it was considered, had been exceeded by those prelates responsible for the death of the Priscilliantists.

The point, apparently trivial at present, has been insisted upon here, in view of the important and curious part which it was destined to play in the procedure of the Inquisition.

The Church had now come to identify herself with the State. She had strengthened her organizations; she had permeated the State with her influences, until it may almost be said that the State had lost its capacity for independent existence, and had become her instrument. The civil laws were based upon her spiritual laws; the standard of morality was founded upon her doctrines; the development of the arts—of painting, sculpture, literature, and music—became such as was best adapted for her service, and, cramped thereby into confines far too narrow, was partly arrested for a time; sciences and crafts were stimulated only by her needs and curbed by her principles; the very recreation of the people was governed by her spirit.

And yet, whilst influencing the State in its every ramification so profoundly that State and Church appeared welded into one disintegrable whole, she kept herself independent, unfettered, and autonomous. So that when that great Empire of the West upon which she had seemed to lean was laid in ruins by the invading barbarians, she continued upright, unshaken by that tremendous cataclysm. She remained to conquer the barbarian far more subtly and completely than he had conquered. Her conquest lay in bringing him to look upon her as the natural inheritor of fallen Rome. Soon she entered upon that splendid heritage, claiming for her own the world-supremacy that Rome had boasted, and assuming dominion over the new nations that were building upon the ruins of the shattered empire.

CHAPTER II
THE INQUISITION CANONICALLY ESTABLISHED

For some seven centuries after the fall of the Roman Empire persecutions for heresy were very rare and very slight. This, however, cannot be attributed to mercy. Although some of the old heresies survived, yet they were so sapped of their vitality that they were no longer openly flaunted in defiance of the mother-Church, but were practised in such obscurity as, in the main, to escape observation.

Fresh schisms, on the other hand, do not appear to have sprung up during that spell. Largely this would be due to the clear formulation of the Catholic theology by the various œcumenical councils held in the years that followed upon the Christian emancipation, and by the intellectual breadth of these doctrines, which were entirely adequate and all-sufficient to the intellectual capacity of the time. But this state of things could only have endured at the cost of arresting man's intellectual progress. A certain restraint and curb undoubtedly was exerted, but definitely to check the imaginative and reasoning faculties of man has never been within the power of any creed, and never can be. It was in vain that the Church sought to coerce thought and to stifle the learning that struck at her very foundations and discovered the error of the cosmic and historical conceptions upon which her theology was based; in vain that she entrenched herself within her doctrines, and adhered rigidly to the form she had adopted.

Upon this uncompromising rigidity of the Catholic Church much censure has been poured. The present aim is a cold survey of certain features of history, and in such a task all polemical matters should be avoided. Yet it may be permissible to say a word here to elucidate rather than to defend an attitude that has been unduly abused.

It is admitted that the unyielding policy of the Church was one that militated seriously against intellectual evolution, and on that account it is to be deplored. But let the unbiassed mind consider for a moment the alternative. The admission of error is the commencement of disruption. Where one error is admitted, a thread is drawn from a weft whose threads are interdependent for the stability of the whole. Who has yielded once has set up a precedent that will be urged against him to make him yield again, and yet again, until he shall have yielded all, and, having nothing left, must suffer an imperceptible effacement.

When all is considered, there is an indisputable dignity in the attitude of a Church which, claiming that what she teaches rests not upon human knowledge but upon divine inspiration, refuses to cede one jot of her doctrines to man's discoveries; holding—and incontestably, so long as the premise is admitted—that however certain may appear the truths which human subtlety has disclosed, however false may appear the doctrines to which she owes her being, it still remains that the former are human and the latter divine of origin. Between the two she proudly holds that there is no disputing; that error possible to man is impossible to divinity; that man's perception of error in the divine tenets of the Church is no more than the manifestation of his own liability to err.

The Church of Rome realized that either she must be entirely, or entirely cease to be. And it is matter for unprejudiced consideration whether the spectacle of her immobility is not more dignified than would have been that of her yielding up her divinities one by one to the expanding humanities, and thus gradually undergoing a course of dismemberment which must in the end remove her last claim to existence. In the attitude she assumed she remained the absolute mistress of her votaries; had she departed from it she must have become their abject servant.

Dr. Rule invites his readers to notice attentively that "no Church but that of Rome ever had an Inquisition."[8] But he neglects to carry the consideration to its logical conclusion, and to add that in no Christian Church but that of Rome could an Inquisition be possible. For it would be impossible to offend heretically against any Church that accommodates itself to new habits of thought in a measure as these occur, and gives way step by step before the onslaught of learning.[9]

The Church of Rome presented her immutable formularies, her unchangeable doctrines to the world. "This," she announced, "is my teaching. By this I hold. This you must accept without reservations, in its entirety, or you are no child of mine."

With that there could be no cavil. Had she but added the admission of man's liberty to accept or reject her teaching, had she but left man free to confess or not her doctrines as his conscience and intelligence directed, all would have been well. Unfortunately she accounted it her duty to go further; she used coercion and compulsion to such an extent that she imbued her children with the spirit of the eighteenth-century Jacobin, exclaiming, "Be my brother, or I kill you!"

Unable by intellectual means to stem the intellectual secession from her ranks, she had recourse to physical measures, and revived the fiercely coercive methods of the first centuries.

A serious heretical outbreak had been occurring in Southern France. There, it would seem, all the schisms that had disturbed the Church since her foundation were gathered together—Arians, Manichæans, and Gnostics—to which were added certain more recent sects, such as the Cathars, the Waldenses, and the Boni Homines, or Good People.

These new-comers deserve a word of explanation.

The Cathars, like the Gnostics, were dualists; indeed, their creed was little more than a development of Gnosticism. They believed that the earth was the only hell or purgatory, that it was given over to the power of the devil, and that human bodies were no more than the prisons of the angel spirits that fell with Lucifer. In heaven their celestial bodies still awaited them, but they could not resume these until they had worked out their expiation. To accomplish this a man must die reconciled with God; failing that, another earthly existence awaited him in the body of man or beast, according to his deserts. It will be seen that, saving for abundant Christian elements introduced into this faith, it was little more than a revival of metempsychosis, the oldest and most fascinating of intelligent beliefs.

The Waldenses, or Vaudois, with whom were allied the Good People, were the earliest Protestants, as we understand the term. They claimed for every man the right to interpret the Bible and to celebrate the sacraments of the Church without the need of being in holy orders. Further, they denied that the Roman Church was the Church of Christ.

These sects were known collectively as the Albigenses, so called because the Council of Lombers, convoked to pronounce their condemnation, had been held in the Diocese of Albi in 1165.

ST. PETER THE MARTYR PREACHING.
From the Painting by Berruguete.

Pope Innocent III made an attempt to convert them; with this aim in view he sent two monks, Peter de Castelnau and one Rodolfe, to restore order amongst them and induce them to return to submission. But when they murdered one of his legates the Holy Father had recourse to those other less legitimate measures of combating liberty of conscience. He ordered the King of France, the nobles and clergy of the kingdom, to assume the crusader's cross, and to proceed to the extirpation of the Albigensian heretics, whom he described as a worse danger to Christendom than the Saracens; and he armed them for the fray with the same spiritual weapons that John VIII had bestowed upon those who went to war in Palestine in the ninth century. Upon all who might die in the service of the Church he pronounced a plenary indulgence.

It is not the present aim to follow the history of the horrible strife that ensued—the massacres, pillages, burnings that took place in the course of the war between the Albigenses under Raymond of Toulouse and the

Crusaders under Simon de Montfort. For over twenty years did that war drag on, and in the course of it the original grounds of the quarrel were forgotten; it passed into a struggle for supremacy between North and South, and thus, properly speaking, out of the history of the Inquisition.[10]

Now, for all that the title "Inquisitor of the Faith" was first bestowed by the Theodosian Code, and for all that persecutions against heretics and others had been afoot since an even earlier date than that of Theodosius, Innocent III is to be considered the founder of the Holy Inquisition as an integral part of the Church. For it is under his jurisdiction that the faculty of persecuting heretics, which hitherto had belonged entirely to the secular arm, is now conferred upon the clergy. He dispatched two Cistercian monks as inquisitors into France and Spain, to engage in the work of extirpating heretics; and he strictly enjoined all princes, nobles and prelates to afford every assistance to these emissaries, and to further them in every way in the work they were sent to do.[11]

Himself, personally, Pope Innocent directed his attention to the Paterini—a sect which rebelled against the celibacy imposed upon the clergy—who were gaining ground in Italy. He invoked the secular arm to assist him in their apprehension, imprisonment, and banishment, in seizing their possessions, which were confiscated, and in razing their houses to the ground.

In 1209 he assembled a council at Avignon, under the presidency of his legates, wherein by his directions it was ordained that every bishop should select such of his subjects, counts, castellans, and knights as might seem to him proper, and swear them to undertake the extermination of all excommunicated heretics.

"And to the end that the bishop may be the better enabled to purge his diocese of heretical pravity, let him swear one priest and two, three or more laymen of good repute in every parish to report to the bishop himself, and to the governors of cities or to the lords and bailiffs of places, the existence of any heretics or abettors of heresy wherever found, to the end that these may be punished according to the canonical and legal dispensations, in all cases suffering forfeiture of property. And should the said governors and others be negligent or reluctant in the execution of this divine service, let their persons be severally excommunicated, and their territories placed under the interdict of the Church."[12]

In the year 1215 Pope Innocent held a further council at the Lateran in which he extended the field of ecclesiastical activity in persecution. He issued an injunction to all rulers, "as they desired to be esteemed faithful, to swear a public oath that they would labour zealously to exterminate from their dominions all those who were denounced as heretics by the Church."[13]

This injunction was backed by a bull which menaced with excommunication and forfeiture of jurisdiction any prince who should fail to extirpate heretics from his dominions—so that at one stroke the Pope asserted his power to an extent that denied liberty of conscience to people and independence to princes.

And meanwhile every heretic against the Holy Catholic and Orthodox Faith, as accepted by the fathers assembled in the Church of St. John, was excommunicated, and there followed these provisions:

"When condemned, the secular powers, or their representatives, being present, they shall be delivered to these for punishment, the clerics being previously degraded from their orders. The property of laymen shall be confiscated; that of clerics bestowed upon their churches. Persons marked with suspicion only shall, unless they can clear themselves, be smitten with the sword of anathema, and shunned by all. If they persist for a year in excommunication, they shall be condemned as heretics.

"Secular powers must be moved or led, or at need compelled by ecclesiastical censure, to make public oath for the defence of the faith, as they themselves desire to be esteemed faithful, undertaking to labour with all their power to extirpate from their dominions those whom the Church shall denounce as heretics."[14]

The excommunication that was to wait upon disobedience was no empty threat, nor yet was it concerned alone with the spiritual part of man. The Pope's anathema imposed the same penalties upon those against whom it was launched as the Druid's curse had imposed of old.[15]

Persons under the ban of the Church might hold no office, nor claim any of the ordinary rights of citizenship, or, indeed, of existence. In sickness or distress none might show them charity under pain of incurring the same curse, nor after death should their bodies be given Christian burial.

By these provisions and injunctions the Inquisition may be said to have entered upon the second stage of its evolution, and to have assumed a strictly ecclesiastical character—in short, to be canonically established.

It was Pope Innocent III who placed in the hands of the Church this terrible weapon of persecution, and who, by the awful severity of his own attitude towards liberty of conscience, of thought, and of expression, afforded to fanaticism and religious intolerance an example that was to be their merciless guide through centuries to come.

CHAPTER III
THE ORDER OF ST. DOMINIC

"If thou wilt be perfect, go and sell that thou hast, and give to the poor, and thou shall have treasure in heaven; and come and follow Me!"

The contrast between the condition thus enjoined by the Founder of Christianity and the worldly position occupied by His Vicar on earth was now fast approaching the climax which was to become absolute with the era of the Renaissance.

From the simple folk foregathering in Rome in the middle of the first century to discuss and to guide one another in the practice of the new doctrine of love and humility, conveyed by word of mouth from the East, in all its pristine simplicity, unburdened as yet by theological complexities, unfettered by formularies, it is a far cry indeed to the proud curial Christians of the Rome of Pope Innocent III.

The successor of Peter, the poor fisherman of Galilee, was enthroned with a splendour outrivalling that of any other earthly potentate. Temporally he was lord of considerable dominions; spiritually he claimed empire over the entire Christian world, and maintained his supremacy with the thunderbolts of anathema which he had forged himself. His glittering court was thronged with rustling, scarlet prelates, with patricians in cloth of gold and silver, captains in steel, mincing fops and stately senators. He was arrayed in garments woven of the very finest fleece, crowned with the triple diadem of white peacock feathers within three flaming circlets of precious stones. On his coronation kings served him upon the knee at table; throughout his reign princes and patricians were his lackeys.

From the steps of the Lateran on the day of his accession he would fling a handful of money to the Roman crowd, exclaiming: "Gold and silver are not for me. What I have I give to thee."

Yet his riches were vast, their sources almost inexhaustible. The luxury in which he lived and moved was the most sumptuous that wealth could command and art and artifice produce.

Nor was this ecclesiastical magnificence confined to Rome and the Papal Court. Gradually it had come to permeate the entire body clerical until it had affected even the monastic orders. From the simplicity of their beginnings these orders had developed into baronial institutions. The fathers presided in noble abbeys over wide tracts of arable and vineyard which they owned and cultivated, and over rural districts and parishes, which they governed and taxed as feudal lords rather than served as priests.

So arrogant and aristocratic was become the spirit of a clergy whose mission was to preach the sublimest and most ideal of democratic doctrines, that the Church seemed no longer within the reach of plebeian and peasant-folk. It was fast becoming an institution of patricians for patricians.

How long this state of things might have endured, what results might have attended its endurance, it were perhaps idle to speculate. That a change was wrought, that provision was made for the lowly and the poor, is due to the advent of two men as similar in much as in much else they were dissimilar. They met in Rome at the foot of the pontifical throne.

Either might have been the founder of a religion had he not found already in the world an ideal religion which he could serve. Both were men born into easy circumstances of life; one, Francesco Bernardone, was the son of a wealthy merchant of Assisi; the other, Domingo de Guzman, of Calahorra, was a nobleman of Spain.

To-day the Church includes them in her Calendar as St. Francis of Assisi and St. Dominic. They are the resplendent twain whom Dante beheld together in his "Paradise":

"L'un fu tutto serafico in ardore,
L'altro per sapienza in terra fue
Di cherubica luce un splendore."[16]

St. Francis—through the sweetness and tenderness that emanated from his poetic, mystic nature, the most lovable of all the saints—came from his native Assisi to implore the Father of Fathers to permit him to band together into an order the barefoot companions he had already gained, to the end that they should practise Christ's injunction of poverty and self-abnegation, and minister to the afflicted.

St. Dominic—and our concern is more with him—had been chosen for his eloquence and learning to accompany the Bishop of Osma upon an inquisitorial journey into Southern France. There he had witnessed the fierce carnage that was toward. He had preached to the heretics at Toulouse, and the burning, passionate eloquence of his oratory had made converts of many of those who were prepared to resist the cruel arguments of fire and steel.

In the ardour of his zeal he had flung aside his rank and the ease and dignity it afforded him. Like St. Francis he went barefoot, embracing poverty and self-denial; yet, less mystical, less tender, entirely practical where the propagation of the Faith was concerned, he had exulted in the bloody victories that Simon de Montfort had won over the heretical Albigenses.

Yet, if he gloried in the end achieved—conceiving it the supremest of all human ends—he must have been touched with regret for the means employed.

He has been termed a fierce and cruel zealot. But ferocity and cruelty do not go hand in hand with such lowly humility as undoubtedly was his. And the very object of his mission to Rome permits, if it does not point to, a very different conclusion. He went deploring the bloodshed he had witnessed, however greatly he may have prized the fruits of it. Inspired by the success that had attended his oratory, he aimed at providing other and gentler means by which in the first instance to seek the attainment of the same ends. He went to implore Pope Innocent's leave to found an order of preachers who in poverty and lowliness should go abroad to win back to the Roman fold the sheep that had strayed into heretical pastures.

Pope Innocent considered the simultaneous requests of both these men—requests which, springing from the same passionate fervour in both, yet came by different, if similar, channels to a sort of unity in the end.

He perceived the services which such men as these might render to the Church, endowed as they were with the magnetic power of creating followings, of inflaming hearts, and replenishing the flickering lamp of public zeal.

He detected no heresy, no irony, in the cult of pauperdom which they would go forth to preach under the sanction and charter of the luxurious, aristocratic, curial court.

But there existed another obstacle to his granting them their prayers. So numerous already were the monastic orders that a Council of the Lateran had decreed that no more should be created. Favouring these petitioners, however, he was applying himself to the surmounting of the difficulty when death took him.

Thus the burden of solving this problem was thrust upon his successor, Honorius III. And it is said that the new pope was spurred to discover a solution by a dream—which has been made the subject of a fresco by Bennozzo Gozzoli—in which he beheld this saintly pair supporting with their hands the tottering Lateran.

Since he could not establish them and their followers as monastic fathers, he had recourse to creating brotherhoods for them. These brotherhoods, he affiliated to the order of St. Augustine, the Dominicans as friars-preachers (*fratres predicatores*) and the Franciscans as friars-minors (*fratres minores*).

Thus were launched these two mendicant orders, which by the enormous following they were so soon to win, were destined to become one of the greatest means of power of the Roman Church.

In the lifetime of their founders the fundamental laws of poverty were observed in all their intended purity. But soon thereafter, being men under their rough habits, and susceptible to the ambition that is man's, upon the acquisition of power followed the acquisition of wealth. Their founders had accomplished a renascence of the original spirit of Christianity. But soon this began to undergo modification, and to respond to worldly influences, until the history of the friars-mendicant repeats and mirrors the history of Christianity itself. In a measure as they spread through Christendom, so they acquired convents, lands, and property as they went. The personal poverty of each brother remained, it is true; they still went abroad barefoot and coarsely garbed, "without staff, or bag, or bread, or money," as their rule decreed. Individually they kept the vow of privation; but considered collectively their poverty "remained outside the convent gate," as Gregorovius says, echoing what Dante had said before him.[17]

For the service of the Church the friars-mendicant became a splendid army, and an army, moreover, whose maintenance made no draught upon the pontifical treasury, since, by virtue of their mendicancy, the orders were entirely self-supporting. And whilst both orders, magnificently organized, grew extremely powerful, the Dominicans became formidable through their control of that Inquisition whose early stirrings had inspired St. Dominic to his task.

His aim had been to found a preaching order whose special mission should be the overthrow of heresy wherever found. The brethren were to combat it, employing their eloquence on the one hand to induce the heretic to abjure his error, on the other to inflame the faithful against him, so that terror should accomplish what might not be possible to persuasion.

It may be that this mission which they had made specially their own, as their founder ordained, peculiarly fitted the Dominicans to assume the government of an ecclesiastical establishment whose aim was identical. It was this order of St. Dominic that was to erect the grim edifice of the Holy Office, and to develop and assume entire control of the terrible machinery of the Inquisition. Their persuasion was to be the ghastly persuasion of the rack; their eloquence was to be the burning eloquence of the tongues of material flame that should lick their agonizing victims out of existence. And all for the love of Christ!

Although it might be difficult to show—as has been attempted—that Domingo de Guzman himself was actually the first ordained Inquisitor, nevertheless as early as 1224, within three years of his death, the Inquisition in Italy and elsewhere was already entirely in the hands of the Dominicans. This is shown by a constitution promulgated at Padua in February of that year by the Emperor Frederic II. It contains the following announcement:

"Be it known to all that we have received under our special protection the preaching friars of the order of preachers, sent into our Empire on business of the Faith against heretics, and likewise all who may lend them assistance—as much in going as in abiding and returning—save such as are already prescribed; and it is our wish that all should give them favour and assistance; wherefore we order our subjects to receive benignly any of the said friars whenever and wherever they may arrive, keeping them secure from the enmity of heretics, assisting them in every way to accomplish their ministry regarding the business of the Faith.... And we do not doubt that you will render homage to God and our Empire by collaborating with the said friars to deliver our Empire from the new and unusual infamy of heretical pravity."[18]

The constitution decreed that heretics when so condemned by the Church and delivered over to the secular arm should be condignly punished; that if any, through the fear of death, should desire to return to the faith, he should receive the penance that might be imposed canonically and be imprisoned for life; that if in any part of the Empire heretics should be discovered by the inquisitors or by other zealous Catholics, the civil powers should be under the obligation of effecting their arrest at the request of the said inquisitors or other Catholics, and of holding them in safe custody until excommunicated by the Church, when they should be burnt; that the same punishment should be suffered by *fautores*—i.e. those guilty of concealing or defending heretics; that fugitives be sought for, and that converts from the same heresy be employed to discover them.

Odious as was this last enactment, there was yet worse contained in the Emperor's constitution. It was decreed that "the sin of *lèse-Majesté divine* being, as it is, greater than that of *lèse-Majesté humaine*, and God being the avenger of the sins of the fathers on the children, to the end that these may not imitate the sins of those, the descendants of heretics to the second generation shall be deemed incapable of honours or of holding any public office—*excepting the innocent children who shall denounce the iniquity of their fathers.*"[19]

The barbarous provision here given in italics calls for no comment.

Within four years of issuing that harsh proclamation against all rebels from the sway of Rome, Frederic himself, in rebellion against the pontiff's temporal sway, was to feel the lash of excommunication. But with that we have no concern. After his reconciliation with the Pope he renewed the constitution of 1224, adding a provision concerning blasphemers, who, in common with heretics of whatever sect, should suffer death by fire; yet if the bishops should desire to save any such, this could only be done subject to the offender's being deprived of his tongue, so that never again should he blaspheme God.

In the year 1227 Ugolino Conti, who had been a friend of Dominic and of Francis, ascended the papal throne under the style of Gregory IX.

It was this pontiff who, carrying forward the work that had been undertaken in that direction by Innocent III, gave the Inquisition a stable form. He definitely placed the control of it in the hands of the Dominican friars, giving them, where necessary, the assistance of the Franciscans. But the participation of the latter in the business of that terrible tribunal is so slight as to be insignificant.

Gregory's bull, given in "Raynaldus,"[20] is one of excommunication against all heretics.

Further, it ordains that all condemned by the Church shall be delivered to the secular arm for punishment, all clerics so delivered being first degraded from their orders; that should any wish to abjure his heresy and return to the Church, penance shall be imposed upon him, and he shall suffer perpetual imprisonment. Abettors, concealers, and defenders of heretics are similarly excommunicated; and if any such shall neglect to procure absolution within one year, he shall be accounted *infamous*, and shall be neither eligible for any public office nor the elector of any other, nor act as witness, testator, inheritor, nor have power to seek justice when wronged. If a judge, no proceedings shall be laid before him, and his sentences, where passed, shall be null and void; if an advocate, he shall not have faculty to plead; if a notary, his deeds shall be void; if a cleric, he shall be deposed from his office and benefices.

Similarly, the ban of excommunication shall fall upon those who hold traffic with any who are excommunicated, and they shall further be punished with other penalties.

Those who are under suspicion of heresy, unless they see to it that they overcome the suspicion either by canonical purgation or otherwise according to the quality of the person and the motives for the suspicion, shall be excommunicated, and if they do not give condign satisfaction within one year, they shall be deemed heretics. Their claims or appeals shall not then be admitted, nor shall judges, advocates, or notaries exercise their functions in favour of them; priests shall refuse to administer the sacraments to them and to admit their alms or oblations, and so shall the Templars and Hospitallers and other regular orders, under pain of loss of office, from which naught can save them but a mandate from the Holy See.

Should any give Christian burial to one who has died under excommunication, he shall himself incur excommunication, from which he shall not be delivered until with his own hands he shall have exhumed the corpse, and so disposed that the place may never again be used for sepulture.

Should any know of the existence of heretics or of any who practise secret conventicles or whose ways of living are uncommon, they are bound under pain of excommunication to divulge the same to their confessor or other by whom they believe it will come to the knowledge of their prelate.

Children of heretics and of the abettors or concealers of heretics shall be deprived until the second generation of holding any public office or benefice.

To the provisions of this bull, additions were made by the civil governor of Rome, as representing the secular arm whose concern it would be to inflict the punishments regarding which the Church refrained from being explicit—confining herself to the promise that they should be "condign."

He provided that: those arrested should be detained in prison until condemned by the Church, when, after eight days, they should be punished.

Their property should be confiscated, one-third going to the delator, one-third to the judge who should pronounce sentence, and one-third to repair the walls of Rome, or otherwise as might be considered.

The dwellings of heretics or of any who should consciously have entertained heretics should be razed to the ground.

If any man should have knowledge of the existence of heretics and fail to denounce them he should be fined the sum of 20 livres. Should he lack the means to pay, he was to be banished until he could find them.

Abettors and concealers of heretics should for the first offence suffer confiscation of one-third of their property, to be applied to keeping the walls of Rome in repair. If the offence were repeated, then they should be banished for ever.

All who were elected senators must swear before taking office that they would observe all laws against heretics; and were any to refuse this oath his acts as senator would be null and void and none should be obliged to follow or obey him, whilst those who might have sworn obedience to him were absolved of their oath. Should a senator accept this oath but afterwards refuse or neglect to respect its terms, he must incur the penalties of perjury, suffer a fine of 200 silver marks, to be applied to the repairing of the walls, and become ineligible for any public office.

Two years later—in 1233—at a Council held at Béziers, the papal legate, Gaultier of Tournai, elaborated these canons by the following provisions:

"All magistrates, nobles, vassals, and others shall diligently seek to discover, apprehend, and punish heretics wherever found. Every parish in which a heretic is discovered shall pay as a penalty for having harboured him one silver mark to the person who shall have discovered him. All houses in which heretics may have preached shall be demolished and the property confiscated, and fire shall be set to all caves and other hiding-places where heretics are alleged to be concealed. All the property of heretics shall be confiscated, and their children shall inherit nothing. Their abettors, concealers, or defenders shall be dealt with in the same manner. Any persons suspected of heresy must make public profession of faith upon oath, under pain of suffering as heretics; they shall be compelled to attend divine service on every feast-day, and all who are *reconciled* to the Church shall wear as a distinguishing badge two crosses externally on their garments—one on the breast, the other on the back—both of yellow cloth, three fingers in width, the vertical limb measuring 2½ hands, the horizontal one 2 hands.[21] If a hood is worn, this must bear a third cross—all under pain of being deemed heretics and suffering confiscation of property."[22]

These enactments by their uncompromising harshness abundantly reveal the extent to which heretics were execrated by the Church in her intolerance and her firm determination to extirpate them. They also reveal something of the far-reaching, pitiless, priestly subtlety and craft which were to render so terrible this tribunal.

The provisions for the punishment of those who should be moved by Christian charity to succour any of the persecuted were devised to the end that terror should stifle all such compassion; whilst the decree that the children of convicted heretics should suffer disinheritance and become ineligible for any honourable appointment was calculatedly introduced to forge a further weapon out of parental love. Where a man might readily, himself, have endured martyrdom for his convictions, he would be made to pause before including his children in the same sacrifice, before suffering them to go destitute and branded.

In the eyes of the Church the end in view could not fail to justify any means that might be employed. The extirpation of heresy was a consummation so very fervently to be desired that any steps—almost any sin—would be condonable if conducive to that end.

It has been argued that this crusade against heresy was political, a campaign waged by the Church to protect herself from the onslaught of liberty of thought, which was threatening her overthrow. Such no doubt had been the case in earlier centuries; but it was so no longer. Roman Catholicism had grown and spread like a mighty tree, until her shadow lay across the face of Europe and her roots were thrust far and wide into the soil. These had taken too firm a hold, they were too full of vigour, to permit that the withering of an occasional branch should give her concern for the vitality of the growth itself. She had no such concern. However abominable, however feral, however unchristian even, may have been the institution of the Holy Office, it is difficult to think that the spirit in which it was founded was other than pure and disinterested.

Photo by Lacoste.

ST. DOMINIC.
From the Painting in the Prado Gallery, attributed to Miguel Zittoz.

It may seem bitterly ironical that men should have been found who in the name of the meek and compassionate Christ relentlessly racked and burnt their fellow-creatures. It was—bitterly, deplorably, tragically ironical. But they were not conscious of the irony. In what they did they were sincere—

as sincere as St. Augustine when he urged the extermination of heretics; and none can call in question his sincerity or the purity of his motives.

To understand their attitude it is but necessary to consider the absolute belief that was the Catholics' in what Lecky calls "the doctrine of exclusive salvation." Starting from the premise that the Church of Rome is the true and only Church of Christ, they held that no salvation was possible for any man who was not a member of it. Nor could ignorance—however absolute—of the true faith be urged as an excuse for error, any more than may ignorance of the law be pleaded in the worldly courts to-day. Thus, not only did they account irrevocably damned those who schismatically deserted from the Church, and those who like Jew and Moslem remained deliberately outside its walls, but similarly—such was man's indifferently flattering conception of divine justice and divine intelligence—the savages who had never so much as heard the name of Christ, and the very babe who died before his heritage of Original Sin could be washed away by the baptismal waters. Indeed, fathers of the Church had waged heated wars of controversy concerning the precise moment at which pre-natal life sets in, and, consequently, damnation is incurred by the soul of the fœtus should it perish in the womb.

When it is considered that such doctrines were held dogmatically, it will be realized that in the sight of the Church—whose business was the salvation of souls—there could be no sin so intolerable, so execrable, as heresy. It will be realized how it happened that the Church could consider those of her children who were guilty of such crimes as murder, rape, adultery, and the sin of the Cities of the Plain, with the tolerance of an indulgent parent, whilst rising up in intolerant wrath to smite the heretic whose life might be a model of pure conduct. The former were guilty of only the sins of weak humanity; and sinners who have the faith may seek forgiveness, and find it in contrition. But heresy was not merely the worst of sins, as some have held. In the eyes of the Church it transcended the realm of sin—it was infinitely worse than sin, because it represented a state that was entirely hopeless, a state not to be redeemed or mitigated by good actions or purity of life.

Taking this view of heresy, the Church accounted it her duty to stamp out this awful soul-pestilence so as to prevent its spreading; and she had St. Augustine's word for it that it was merciful to be merciless in the attainment of that object. When viewed, as it were, from within, there is nothing illogical in the attitude of the Church towards heresy. What is illogical is the conception of God that is involved in the doctrine of exclusive salvation.

Even if we survey the case of Galileo—one of the most illustrious prisoners ever arraigned before the tribunal of the Holy Office—we have no just cause to suppose that, in demanding his retraction of the theory of the earth's movement round the sun, the inquisitors were inspired by any motives beyond the fear lest the spread of a notion—honestly deemed by them to be an illusion—should disturb man's faith in the Biblical teaching with which it was in conflict.

CHAPTER IV
ISABELLA THE CATHOLIC

Llorente agrees with the earlier writers on the subject in considering the Spanish Inquisition as an institution distinct from that which had been established to deal with the Albigenses and their coevals in heresy. It is distinct only in that it represents a further development of the organization launched by Innocent III and perfected by Gregory IX.

Before entering upon the consideration of this Modern Inquisition—as it is called—it will perhaps be well to take a survey of the Spain of the Catholic Sovereigns—Ferdinand and Isabella—in whose reign that tribunal was set up in Castile.

For seven hundred years, with varying fortune and in varying degree, the Saracen had lorded it in the Peninsula.

First had come Berber Tarik, in 711, to overthrow the Visigothic Kingdom of Roderic, to spread the Moslem dominion as far as the mountains in the north and east and west from sea to sea. When the Berber tribe, the Syrians, and the Arabs had fallen to wrangling among themselves, Abdurrahman the Omayyad crossed from Africa to found the independent amirate, which in the tenth century became the Caliphate of Cordova.

Meanwhile the Christians had been consolidating their forces in the mountain fastnesses of the north to which they had been driven, and under Alfonso I they founded the Kingdom of Galicia. Thence, gradually but irresistibly, presenting a bold front to the Moorish conqueror, they forced their way down into the plains of Leon and Castile, so that by the following century they had driven the Saracens south of the Tagus. Following up their advantage, they continued to press them, intent upon driving them into the sea, and they might have succeeded but for the coming of Yusuf ben Techufin, who checked the Christian conquest, hurled them back across the Tagus, and, master of the country to the south of it, founded there the Empire of the Almoravides.

After these came the Almohades—the followers of the Mahdi—and the land rang for half a century with the clash of battle between Cross and Crescent, Castile, Leon, Aragon, and the new-born Kingdom of Portugal striving side by side to crush the common foe at Navas de Tolosa.

In 1236 Leon and Castile—now united into one kingdom—in alliance with Aragon, wrested Cordova from the Moors; in 1248 Seville was conquered, and in 1265 Diego of Aragon drove the Saracen from Murcia, and thereby reduced the Moslem occupation to Granada and a line of Mediterranean seaboard about Cadiz, in which they remained until Ferdinand of Aragon and Isabella of Castile, by virtue of their marriage, had united the two crowns on the death (in 1474) of Henry IV, Isabella's brother.

Ferdinand brought, with Aragon, Sicily, Sardinia, and Naples; Isabella brought, with Castile, Leon and the rest of the Spanish territory, saving Granada and that portion of the coast still in Moorish hands. And thus was founded, by the welding of these several principalities into one single state, that mighty Kingdom of Spain which Columbus was so soon to enrich by a new world.

But though founded by this marriage, this kingdom still required consolidating and subjecting. Generations of misrule in Castile, culminating in the lax reigns of John II and Henry IV, had permitted the spread of a lawlessness so utter that its like was not to be found in any other state at that time. Anarchy was paramount mistress of the land, and Pulgar has left us a striking picture of the impossible conditions that prevailed.

"In those days," he writes, "justice suffered, and was not to be done upon the malefactors who plundered and tyrannized in townships and on the highways. None paid debts who did not want to do so; none was restrained from committing any crime, and none dreamed of obedience or subjection to a superior. What with present and past wars, people were so accustomed to turbulence that he who did not do violence to others was held to be a man of no account.

Citizens, peasants, and men of peace were not masters of their own property, nor could they have recourse to any for redress of the wrongs they suffered at the hands of governors of fortresses and other thieves and robbers. Every man would gladly have engaged to give the half of his property if at that price he might have purchased security and peace for himself and his family. Often there was talk in towns and villages of forming brotherhoods to remedy all these evils. But a leader was wanting who should have at heart the justice and tranquillity of the Kingdom."[23]

The nobility, as may be conceived—and, indeed, as Pulgar clearly indicates— were not only tainted with the general lawlessness, but were themselves the chief offenders, each man a law unto himself, a tyrannical, extortionate ruler of his vassals, lord of life and death, unscrupulously abusing his power, little better than a highway robber, caring nothing for the monarchy so long as the monarchy left him undisturbed, ready to rebel against it should it attempt to curtail his brigandage.

To crush these and other unruly elements in the state, to resolve into order the chaos that had invaded every quarter of the kingdom, was the task which at the outset the young Queen perceived awaiting her—a task that must have daunted any mind less virile, any spirit less vigorous.

And there were other and more pressing matters demanding her instant attention if she were to retain her seat upon this almost bankrupt throne of Castile which she had inherited from her brother.

Alfonso V of Portugal was in arms, invading her frontiers to dispute, on his niece Juana's behalf, Isabella's right.

Henry IV had left no legitimate issue, but his wife Juana of Portugal had brought forth in wedlock a daughter of whom she pretended that he was the father, whilst the King of Portugal, to serve interests of his own, recognized the girl as his legitimate niece. Public opinion, however, hesitated so little to proclaim her bastardy that it had named her La Beltraneja, after Beltran de la Cueva who notoriously had been her mother's lover. And what Beltran de la Cueva, himself, thought about it, may be inferred from the circumstance that in the ensuing struggle he was found fighting for the honour of Castile under the banner of Queen Isabella.

The war demanded all the attention and resources of the Catholic Monarchs, and Isabella's own share in these labours was conspicuous. They resulted in the rout of the Portuguese supporters of the pretender at Toro in 1476. By that victory Isabella was securely seated upon her throne and became joint ruler with Ferdinand of Castile and Aragon.

She was twenty-five years of age at the time, a fair, shapely woman of middle height, with a clear complexion, eyes between green and blue, and a gracious, winsome countenance remarkable for its habitual serenity. Such, indeed, was her self-control, Pulgar tells us, that not only did she carefully conceal her anger when it was aroused, but even in childbirth she could "dissemble her feelings, betraying no sign or expression of the pain to which all women are subject." He adds that she was very ceremonious in dress and equipage, that she was deliberate of gesture, quick-witted, and ready of tongue, and that in the midst of the labour of government—and very arduous labour, as shall be seen—she found time to learn Latin, so that she could understand all that was said in that tongue.

"She was a zealous Catholic and very charitable, yet in her judgments she inclined rather to rigour than to mercy. She listened to counsel, but acted chiefly upon her own opinions. Of a rare fidelity to her word, she never failed to fulfil that to which she had pledged herself, save where compelled by stress of circumstance. She was reproached, together with her husband, of being wanting in generosity, because, seeing the royal patrimony diminished by the alienation of fiefs and castles, she was always very careful of such concessions.

"'Kings,' she was wont to say, 'should preserve with care their dominions, because in alienating them they lose at once the money necessary to make themselves beloved and the power to make themselves feared.'"[24]

Such is the portrait that Pulgar has left us, and considering that he is writing of a sovereign, it would be no more than reasonable to suspect flattery and that curious, undiscriminating enthusiasm which never fails to create panegyrists when it is a question of depicting a prince, however inept, to his contemporaries. But if Pulgar has erred in this instance, it has been on the side of moderation in his portrayal of this gifted, high-spirited woman.

Her actions speak more eloquently of her character than can the pen of any chronicler, and it is in the deeds of princes that we must seek their true natures, not in what may have been written of them in their own day. The deeds of Isabella's life—with one dark exception that is the subject of this history—more than bear out all that Pulgar and others have set down in praise of her.

No sooner had she overthrown those who came from abroad to dispute her right to the crown than she turned her attention to the subjugation of those who disputed her authority at home. In this herculean labour she had the assistance of Alonzo de Quintanilla, her chancellor, and Juan Ortega, the King's sacristan. These men proposed to organize at their own risk one of those brotherhoods which Pulgar mentions as having been so ardently desired by the country for its protection from those who preyed upon it. This *hermandad* was to act under royal sanction and guidance, with the object of procuring peace and protection of property in the kingdom. Isabella readily approved the proposal, and the brotherhood was immediately founded, a tax to support it being levied upon those in whose interest it was established, and very willingly paid by them.

Splendidly organized, this association, half military, half civil, so effectively discharged the functions for which it was created, that twenty years later— in 1498—it was possible to abolish it, and to replace it by a much simpler and less costly system of police which then sufficed to preserve the order that had been restored.

Further to subject the turbulent and insubordinate nobility, Isabella employed methods similar to those adopted in like case by her neighbour, Louis XI of France. She bestowed the offices of state upon men of merit without regard to birth, which hitherto had been accounted the only qualification. The career of the law was thrown open to the burgher classes, and every office under the crown was made accessible to lawyers, who thus became the staunch friends of the sovereign.

If the nobles did not dare to revolt, at least they protested in the strongest terms against these two innovations that so materially affected and weakened their prestige. They represented in particular that the institution of the *hermandad* was the manifestation of a want of confidence in the "faithful nobility," and they implored that four members of their order should be appointed by the Catholic Sovereigns to form a council of supreme direction of the affairs of State, as under the late King Henry IV.

To this the Catholic Sovereigns replied that the *hermandad* was a tutelary institution which was very welcome to the country, and which it was their pleasure to maintain. As for the offices of State, it was for the sovereigns to appoint such men as they considered best qualified to hold them. The nobles, they added, were free to remain at Court or to withdraw to their own domains, as they might see fit; but as for the sovereigns, themselves, as long as it should please God to preserve them in the high position in which He had deigned to place them, it should be their care not to imitate the monarch who was cited to them as an example, and not to become puppets in the hands of their "faithful nobility."

That answer gave the nobles pause. It led them to perceive that a change had taken place, and that the lawless days of Henry IV were at an end. To have made them realize this was something. But there was more to be done before they would understand that they must submit to the altered conditions, and Isabella pursued the policy she had adopted with an unswerving directness, as the following story from Pulgar's Chronicle bears witness:

A quarrel had broken out in the Queen's palace at Valladolid between Don Fadrique Enriquez (son of the Admiral of Castile) and Don Ramiro de Guzman. Knowledge of it reached the Queen, and she ordered both disputants to hold themselves under arrest in their own quarters until she should provide that judgment be given between them by the Courts. Fadrique, however, signified his contempt of the royal mandate by disobeying it and continuing at large. Learning this, Isabella gave the more obedient Guzman his liberty, and the assurance of her word that he should suffer no harm.

A few days later he was riding peacefully through the street, secure in the Queen's safe-conduct, when he was set upon by three masked horsemen of the household of Fadrique and severely beaten. No sooner did the Queen hear of this further affront to her authority than she got to horse, and rode through torrential rain from Valladolid to the Admiral's castle at Simancas. In fact, in such haste did she set out that she rode alone, without waiting for an escort. This, however, followed presently, but did not come up with her save under the very walls of the Admiral's fortress.

She summoned the Admiral, and commanded him to deliver up his rebellious son to her justice, and when Don Alonso Enriquez protested that his son was not there, she bade her followers search the castle from battlements to dungeons. The search, however, proved fruitless, and Isabella returned empty-handed and indignant to Valladolid. Arrived there, she took to her bed, and to those who came to seek news of her health, she replied: "My body aches with the blows delivered yesterday against my safe-conduct by Don Fadrique."

The Admiral, trembling before the royal wrath, resolved to deliver up his son and cast him upon the mercy of the Queen. So the Constable of Castile— Fadrique's uncle—undertook the office of intercessor. He went with Don Fadrique to Valladolid, and imploring Isabella to consider that the young man was but in his twentieth year and that he had sinned through the rashness of youth, begged her to do upon him the justice she might wish or the mercy that was due.

The Queen, however, was not to be moved to mercy for offences that set her royal authority in contempt. She was inexorable. She refused to see the offender, and submitted him to the indignity of being taken to prison through the streets of the city by an alcalde. After a spell of confinement there she banished him to Sicily, prohibiting his return to Spain under pain of severest punishment.

It happened, however, that Don Ramiro de Guzman did not consider his honour sufficiently avenged by his enemy's exile. One night, when the Court was at Medina del Campo, he ambushed himself in his turn with some followers of his own, and attacked the Admiral, to return him the blows received from his son. From this indignity the Admiral was saved by his escort. But when Isabella heard of the affair, she treated Guzman as a rebel, seized his castles in Leon and Castile, as she would have seized his person, but that to escape her anger he fled to Portugal for shelter.[25]

No less determined was her conduct in the matter of the Grand-Mastership of Santiago.

There were in Spain three religio-military orders: the Knights of Alcantara, the celibate Knights of Calatrava—who were the successors of the Knights Templars—and the Knights of Santiago. This last order had been founded for the purpose of affording protection to the pilgrims who came into Spain to visit the shrine at Compostella of St. James the Apostle, who is alleged to have been the first to bear the message of Christianity into the Iberian Peninsula.[26] These pilgrimages, chiefly from France, were a great source of revenue to the country, and it became of importance to ensure their immunity from the predatory hordes that infested the highways. Further, the Knights of Santiago had found employment for their arms in the crusade waged on Spanish soil against the Moors, in token whereof they wore the Crusader's cross in red upon their white cloaks. They acquired great power and wealth, possessing castles and convents in every part of Spain, so that the office of Grand Master of the Order was one of great weight and importance—too great, in the opinion of Isabella, to be in the hands of a subject.

This opinion she boldly manifested in 1476, when the death of Don Rodrigo Manrique left the office vacant. She took horse, as was her custom, and rode to Huete, where the Chapter of the Order was assembled upon the business of the necessary election, and she frankly urged that to an office so exalted it was not fitting that any but the King should be elected.

The proposal was not received with satisfaction. Ferdinand was an Aragonese, and despite the union of the two kingdoms which must be completed when he should succeed to the throne of Aragon, he was still looked upon as a foreigner by the Castilians. Under Isabella's insistence, however, a compromise was effected. The Chapter consented to elect Ferdinand to the office of Grand-Master on condition that he should nominate a gentleman of Castile to act as his deputy for the discharge of the duties of the position. This was done, and Alonso de Cardenas—a loyal servant of the Sovereigns—was chosen as the royal deputy. Thus Isabella established it that the appointment of Grand-Master of the Order of Santiago should be a royal prerogative.

Even more strikingly than in either of the instances cited does the Queen's resolute, spirited nature manifest itself in her manner of dealing with a revolt that took place in Segovia at the commencement of her reign.

During the war with Portugal the Catholic Sovereigns had entrusted their eldest daughter, the Princess Isabella, to the care of Andrés de Cabrera, the Seneschal of the Castle of Segovia, and his wife, Beatriz de Bobadilla.

Cabrera, a man of stern and rigid equity, had occasion to depose his lieutenant, Alonso Maldonado, from his office, conferring this upon his own brother-in-law, Pedro de Bobadilla. Maldonado conspired to avenge himself. He begged Bobadilla's permission to remove some stones that were in the castle, upon the pretext that he required them for his own house, and he sent some men of his own to fetch them. These men, who were secretly armed, having gained admission, stabbed the sentry and seized the person of Bobadilla, whilst Maldonado, with other of his people, took possession of the castle itself. The inmates of the Alcazar, hearing the uproar, fled to the

Homenaje Tower, taking with them the Infanta, who was five years of age at the time. Fortified in this, they defied Maldonado when he attacked it. Finding it impregnable, the rebel ordered Bobadilla to be brought forward, and threatened the besieged that unless they admitted him he would put the prisoner to death.

To this threat Cabrera's dignified reply was that Maldonado must do as he pleased, but the gates would not be opened to him.

By this time a multitude of the townspeople had gathered there, alarmed by the disturbance and armed for any emergency. To these Maldonado cunningly represented that what he was about was being done in their interests against the overbearing tyranny of the Governor, and he invited them to join hands with him in the cause of liberty to complete the work he had so excellently begun. The populace largely took sides with him, so that Segovia was flung into a state of war. There was constant fighting in the streets, and the gates were in the hands of the rebels, with the exception of that of St. John, which was held for Cabrera.

It is believed that it was Maria de Bobadilla herself who, stealing undetected from the Alcazar, escaped from Segovia and bore to the Queen the news of what was taking place, and the consequent peril of the royal child.

Upon learning this, Isabella instantly repaired to Segovia. The leaders of the rebellion had news of her approach, but dared not carry their insubordination to the length of closing the gates against her. They went so far, however, as to ride out to meet her and to attempt to deny admittance to her followers; and her counsellors, seeing the humour of the populace, urged her to be prudent and to accede to their wishes. But her proud spirit flared up under that cautious advice.

"Learn," she cried, "that I am Queen of Castile, that this city is mine, and that no conditions are to be imposed upon me before I enter it. I shall enter, then, and with me all those whom I may judge necessary for my service."

With that she ordered her escort forward, and entered the city by a gate that was held by her partisans, and so won through to the Alcazar.

Thither flocked the infuriated mob, and thundered at the gates, demanding admission.

The Queen, notwithstanding the remonstrances of the Cardinal of Spain and the Count of Benavente, who were with her, ordered the gates to be thrown open and as many admitted as the place would hold. The populace surged into the courtyard, clamouring for the Seneschal. To meet them came the slight, fair young queen, alone and fearless, and when in their astonishment they had fallen silent—

"People of Segovia," she calmly addressed them, "what do you seek?"

Dominated by her serenity, awed by her majesty, their fury fell from them. Humbly now they urged their grievance against Cabrera, accusing him of oppression, and imploring of the Queen's grace his demission.

Instantly she promised them that their request should be granted; whereupon the revulsion was complete, and the mob that but a few moments earlier had been yelling threats and execrations now raised their voices loyally to acclaim her.

She commanded them to return to their homes and their labours, and to leave the administration of justice in her hands, sending her their ambassadors to prefer their complaint against Cabrera, which she would investigate.

As she commanded so it was done, and when she had examined the accusations against the Seneschal and satisfied herself that they were groundless, she announced him free from guilt and reinstated him in his office, the conquered people bowing submissively to her ruling.[27]

In 1477 Isabella moved into Andalusia, in which province, as elsewhere, law and order had ceased to exist. She entered Seville with the proclaimed intention of demanding an account of the guilty. But at the very rumour of her approach and the business upon which she came, some thousands of the inhabitants whose consciences were uneasy made haste to depart the city.

Alarmed by this depopulation, the Sevillans implored the Queen to sheathe the sword of justice, representing that after the bloody affrays that for years had been afflicting the district there was scarcely a family in which some member was not answerable to the law.

Isabella, gentle and merciful by nature—which renders her association with the Inquisition the more deplorable—lent an ear to these representations, and granted an amnesty for all crimes committed since the death of Henry IV. But she was not so lenient with those who had prostituted the justice which they administered in her name. Informed of the judges who were making a trade and extortion of their judgments, she punished them by deposition, and herself fixed the scale of legal costs to be observed in future.

Finding a mass of impending law-suits which the misrule of the past years had put upon the province, she directed her attention to clearing up this Augean stable. Every Friday, attended by her Council, she sat in the great hall of the Alcazar of Seville to hear the plaints of the most humble of her subjects; and so earnestly and vigorously did she go to work that in two months she had disposed of litigations that might have dragged on for years.

Upon her accession she had found the royal treasury exhausted by the inept administration of the last two reigns and the prodigal, reckless grants that Henry IV and Juan II had made to the nobles. This condition of things had seriously embarrassed the Catholic Sovereigns, and they had been driven to various expedients to raise the requisite funds for the war with Portugal. Now that the war was at an end, they found themselves without the means necessary to maintain the royal state.

Isabella made a close investigation of the grants that had been made by her brother and father, and she cancelled all those that were the fruit of caprice and wantonness, restoring to the Crown the revenues that had been recklessly alienated and the taxes that the country had hitherto paid to none but the bandits who oppressed it.

Similarly she found the public credit entirely ruined. Under the late king such had been the laxity, that in three years no less than 150 public mints had been authorized, and this permitted such abuses that a point had been reached where it almost seemed that every Spaniard minted his own money, or that, as Rosseeuw St. Hilaire puts it, "coining was the country's chief industry."

Photo by Alinari.

POPE INNOCENT III. AND ST. DOMINIC.
From a Fresco in the Church of the Sacro Speco, Subiaco.

She reduced the number of mints to five, and exercised the severest control over their output, thereby liberating trade from the fear of fraud that had been stifling it. An increased and steadily increasing prosperity was the almost immediate result of this wise measure.

Having restored order in the country, she turned her attention to the Court, applied herself to the purification of its morals, and set about converting it from the disgusting licence that had prevailed in her brother's time.

Herself of a rigid chastity, she exacted the same purity of conduct in all the women who approached her, and she submitted the noble damsels brought up at her Court to the very strictest surveillance. Loving the King very sincerely, she was notoriously inclined to jealousy: let him but look too assiduously upon any lady of her train, and Isabella found a way to remove her from the Court. She saw to it that the pages who were in waiting upon her should be given a good education, that thus they might avoid the idleness which unfailingly leads to waste of character and to immorality. Finally, according to Bernaldez,[28] she extended her moral reforms to the convents, which were no less in need of them than the Court, and she corrected and punished the great depravity that was permeating all conventual orders.[29]

There is no chronicler of her reign who does not dilate upon her great piety. Bernaldez compares her to St. Helena, the mother of the Emperor Constantine,[30] and describes her as very devoted to the Holy Faith and very obedient to Holy Church. Bernaldez, of course, was writing after the establishment of the Inquisition, of which he, in common with other contemporary and subsequent chroniclers, very warmly approved; and he may have been very largely influenced by consideration of the support which she had unfortunately lent to its introduction into Castile. But that her piety was extreme and sincere we infer from the moment that we see her, after the battle of Toro, which definitely gave her the crown, going barefoot to church to a service of thanksgiving.

Yet, however ardent her piety, it would not carry her the length of recognizing in the Pope the temporal over-lord of Castile.

From the thirteenth century the power of the Church had been increasing in Spain under the dogma of the spiritual sovereignty of Rome over all the Catholic churches of the world. The clergy had amassed enormous wealth with that facility so peculiarly their own when the occasion is afforded them, and to this end they had abused the reckless, foolish liberality of Isabella's predecessors.

Lucius Marinæus informs us that the incomes of the four archbishoprics— Toledo, Santiago, Seville, and Granada—amounted to 134,000 ducats,[31] whilst those of the twenty bishoprics came to some 250,000 ducats.

Surrounded as she was by priestly counsellors whom she respected, she nevertheless manifested plainly her impatience of the clerical usurpation of the rights of the Crown. The chief of these abuses was no doubt that practised by the Pontiff himself, in conferring upon foreigners the highest and richest benefices of the Church of Spain, ignoring that it was the prerogative of the Crown to name the bishops—always subject to papal confirmation. That Isabella, devout and priest-surrounded as she was, should have dared to oppose the Holy See and the terrible Pope Sixtus IV, as fearlessly as she had opposed her predatory nobles, is perhaps the highest proof that history can yield of her strength of character.

Her smouldering indignation flared out when the Pope, ignoring her nomination of her chaplain, Alonzo de Burgos, to the vacant bishopric of Cuenca, appointed his own nephew, Raffaele Riario, Cardinal of San Sisto, to that vacant see.

Twice already had she sought the pontiff's confirmation of nominees of her own for other benefices—the Archbishopric of Saragoza and the Bishopric of Tarragona—and on each occasion her nominee had been set aside in favour of a creature of the Pope's. But this third contemptuous disregard of her prerogative was more than her patience could endure. The Catholic Sovereigns refused to ratify the appointment of Riario, and begged the Pope—submissively at first—to cancel it.

But the harsh, overbearing Sixtus returned an answer characteristic of his arrogant nature. It was his, he announced, to distribute at his pleasure all the benefices of Christendom; and he condescended to explain that the power which it had pleased God to confer upon him on earth could not be limited by any will but his own, and that it was governed only by the interests of the Catholic Faith, of which he was the sole arbiter.

But his stubbornness met a stubbornness as great. The Catholic Sovereigns replied by withdrawing their ambassador from the Papal Court, and issuing an injunction to all Spanish subjects to leave Rome.

Matters were becoming strained; an open rupture impended between Spain and the Vatican. But the Sovereigns had notified the Pope that it was their intention to summon a general council of the Church to settle the matter in dispute, and no Pope of those days could contemplate with equanimity a general council assembled for the purpose of sitting in judgment upon his decrees. Whatever the result, since at these councils the papal authority was questioned, it must follow that thereafter that authority would be impaired. Therefore this was the stock threat employed to bring a recalcitrant pontiff to a reasonable frame of mind.

It made Sixtus realize the strength of purpose that was opposed to him; and, knowing as he did that this resoluteness backed an undeniable right which he had violated, he perceived that he dared carry insistence no further. So, despite his earlier assertion that the power which he held from God could be limited by no will but his own and governed by no consideration but that of the interests of the Faith, he gave way completely.

The three royal nominees were duly confirmed in the vacant sees, and Sixtus gave an undertaking that in future he would make no appointments to the benefices of Spain save of such ecclesiastics as the Catholic Sovereigns should nominate.[32]

It is to be added that in acting upon this signal victory which she had won, Isabella used the faculty it gave her with such pious wisdom, sincerity, and discretion that had the Pope but followed her example in the appointment of dignitaries, it would have contributed to the greater honour and glory of the Church. For she sternly opposed the granting of benefices upon any grounds but those of absolute merit.

Having won her way in this, she was the better able to curb the predatory habits of her clergy by edicts that limited their power to proper clerical confines.

"It is amazing," comments Pulgar, "that a woman should have been able, single-handed and in so little time, by her judgment and perseverance to accomplish what many men and great kings had been unable to do in many years."

"Properly to judge the notable improvements," says Rosseeuw St. Hilaire,[33] "which this reign effected in industry and agriculture, it would be necessary to follow year by year the table of ordinances issued by the Catholic Sovereigns. It would be seen that in many things the genius of the founders of the Castilian Monarchy forestalled the work of centuries. The happy results of these reforms were soon experienced everywhere: the highways were purged of malefactors, new roads of communication were opened up, rivers were bridged, consular tribunals established in commercial centres, consulates created in Flanders, England, France, and Italy; with maritime commerce expanding daily and in a measure with the progress of industry, new buildings sprang up in every city, and the population rapidly increased. All announced a new era of regeneration in Castile. Contemporary writers, struck by these prodigies, exalt with one voice this glorious reign which opens new destinies to Spain."

It is certain that in no other country in Europe at this date were the laws so well maintained and the rights of the individual so well protected. Justice was rigorously done, there were no longer arbitrary imprisonments and sequestrations, whilst the unequal and capricious taxation of the past was abolished for all time.

"Such," says Marinæus, "was the strict justice meted out to each in this happy reign that all men, nobles and knights, traders and husbandmen, rich and poor, masters and servants, were treated alike and received equally their share of it."

Where so much was good, where so much stout service was done to the cause of progress and civilization, it is the more deplorable to find in this reign the one evil thing that is now to be considered—so evil that it must be held to counterbalance and stultify all the excellences of Isabella's sway.

The particular praise which so far we have heard their contemporaries bestowing upon the Catholic Sovereigns, is a praise which every man in every age must echo.

But there was praise as loud upon another score, as universally uttered by every contemporary and many subsequent historians, some no doubt because they were sincere in the deadly bigotry that inspired it, others because they did not dare to express themselves in different terms.

"By her," cries Bernaldez, as a climax to his summing-up of her many virtues and wise provisions, "was burnt and destroyed the most evil and abominable Mosaic, Talmudic, Jewish heresy."

And Mariana, the historian, accounts the introduction of the Inquisition into Spain the most glorious feature of the reign of Ferdinand and Isabella. He is setting it above all the moral splendours of that day when he exclaims:

"Still better and happier fortune for Spain was the establishment in Castile at about this time of a new and holy tribunal of severe and grave judges for the purpose of inquiring into and punishing heretical pravity and apostasy...."[34]

It would be unjust to suppose that there is a man to be found to-day in the Church of Rome, of which the Spanish Inquisition was a deplorable and integral part, who can turn with us in other than regret to consider this black shadow that lies across one of the brightest pages of history.

CHAPTER V
THE JEWS IN SPAIN

You have seen the Catholic Sovereigns instilling order into that distracted land of Spain, enforcing submissiveness to the law, instituting a system of police for the repression of brigandage, curtailing the depredations of the nobles, checking the abuses and usurpations of the clergy, restoring public credit, and generally quelling all the elements of unrest that had afflicted the State.

But one gravely disturbing element still remained in the bitter rancour prevailing between Christian and Jew.

"Some clerics and many laymen," says Pulgar,[35] "informed the Sovereigns that there were in the Kingdom many Christians of Jewish extraction who were Judaizing[36] again and holding Jewish rites in their houses, and who neither believed the Catholic Faith nor performed the Catholic duties. They implored the Sovereigns, as they were Christian princes, to punish that detestable error, because if left unpunished it might so spread that our Holy Catholic Faith must receive great harm."

Exactly to realize the position at the time, and the force behind the arguments employed to induce the Catholic Sovereigns to complete the ordering of the kingdom by the repression of the re-Judaizing, or apostasy, of the New-Christians—as the baptized Jews and their descendants were termed—it is necessary to take at least a brief retrospective survey of the history of the Israelites in Spain.

At what period the Jews first appeared in the peninsula it is not easy to determine with accuracy.

Salazar de Mendoza and other ancient historians, who base their writings upon the work of Tomás Tamayo de Vargas, put forward views upon this subject that are curious rather than important.

They assert that the Kingdom of Spain was founded by Tubal, the son of Japhet, who had Europe for his portion when the division was made among the sons of Noah. Hence it was called Tubalia, and later on Sepharad by the Jews, and Hesperida by the Greeks. They hold that the first Jews in the Iberian Peninsula were probably those who came with Nebuchadnezzar II, King of Chaldea, and that he brought with him, in addition to Chaldeans and Persians, ten tribes of Israel, who peopled Toledo,[37] and built there the most beautiful synagogue that had been theirs since the temple of Solomon. This synagogue, Mendoza states, afterwards became the Convent of Santa Maria la Blanca (a statement which the architecture of Santa Maria la Blanca very flatly contradicts). He further informs us that they built another synagogue at Zamora, and that those who worshipped there always prided themselves— his point of view, of course, is narrowly Christian—that to them had been addressed St. Paul's Epistle to the Hebrews.

They founded a university at Lucena (near Cordova), and schools where the law was taught, so that the holy Jewish religion spread rapidly, and was observed throughout Spain until the coming of Our Lord into the world. Then, in 37 A.D., the Apostle St. James came to preach the new gospel in Iberia, "so that Spain was the first land after Judea to receive the holy law of grace." Following the writings of Vargas, he goes so far as to say: "and although to many it has seemed apocryphal that the Toledo Jews wrote to denounce the Passion of Our Lord, the assertion is not without good foundation."[38]

Amador de los Rios is probably correct in his opinion that the Jews made their first appearance in Spain during the Visigothic dominion, after the fall of Jerusalem; and scarcely had they settled in the peninsula when they began to experience the bitterness of persecution. But after they had been delivered from this by the Saracen invaders, to whom by race and creed they were fairly sympathetic, they enjoyed—alike under Moslem and Christian rule—a season of prosperity in Spain, which endured until the close of the thirteenth century. And this notwithstanding the undercurrent of mutual contempt and hatred, of Christian for Jew and Jew for Christian, that was invincible in an age of strong religious feeling.

To the Christian every Jew he encountered was his natural and hereditary enemy, a descendant of those who had crucified the Saviour; therefore he was an object of execration, a man upon whom it must be meritorious to avenge the world's greatest crime which had been perpetrated by his forbears.

The Jew, on the other hand, held the Christian in a contempt as thorough. From the standpoint of his own pure and unadulterated monotheism, he looked scornfully upon a religion that must appear to him no better than an adaptation of polytheism, developed upon the doctrines of one whom the Jews had rejected as an impostor who had attempted to usurp the place of the promised Messiah. To the truly devout Jew of those days the Christian religion can have been little better than a blasphemy. Nor was that the only source of his contempt. Looking back upon his own splendid ancestry, upon the antiquity of his race and the high order of its culture—the fruit of centuries of intellectual evolution—what but scorn could he entertain for these Spaniards of yesterday's hatching, who were just emerging from the slough of barbarism?

It is clear that mutual esteem between the races was out of all question in an age of strong religious prejudices. Toleration, however, was possible, and the Jew applied himself to win it. To this end he employed at once the vices and the virtues of the unfortunate, which centuries of tribulation had rendered inherent in him.

Armed with a stoicism that was almost pitiful, he donned a mask of indifference to confront expressed hatred and contempt; to violence he opposed cunning and the long-suffering patience that is so peculiarly his own—the patience that is allied with a high order of intelligence; the patience which, interpreted into "an infinite capacity for taking pains," has been urged as the definition of genius, and is the secret of the Jew's success wherever he is established.

In the cohesion in a foreign land of this people that cannot keep together as a nation, and in their extraordinary commercial acuteness, lies the strength of the Jews. They grew wealthy by their industry and thrift, until they were in a position to purchase those privileges which in Christendom are the birth-right of every Christian. Their numbers, too, made it difficult in Spain to treat them with contumely; for upon the reasoned estimate of Amador de los Rios[39] there were close upon a million Jews in Castile at the end of the thirteenth century.

They formed by their solidarity—as they always do—an *imperium in imperio*, a state of their own within the state; they had their own language and customs; they were governed by their own laws, which were enforced by their Rabbis and chiefs, and they pursued their own religion unmolested, for even the observation of the Sabbath was respected by the Castilians. Thus they came to create for themselves in a foreign country a simulacrum of their own native land.

It is true that they were afflicted from time to time by sporadic, local persecutions; but in the main they enjoyed a tolerance and religious liberty which the poor harried Albigenses beyond the Pyrenees might well have envied. For the Church, which had already established the Inquisition, was very far—for reasons that shall be considered in the next chapter—from instigating any persecution of the Children of Israel. Thus, Honorius III, whilst carrying forward the policy of Innocent III, and enjoining the extirpation of heretics in Southern France and elsewhere, confirmed (November 7, 1217) the privileges accorded to the Jews by his predecessors upon the throne of St. Peter. These were that no Jew should be constrained to receive baptism; that should he incline to embrace the Christian Faith he must be received in it with love and benevolence; that his feasts and religious ceremonies must be respected by Christians; that the whipping or stoning of Jews be forbidden and punished; that their burial-places be held sacred.

And when King Ferdinand III—afterwards canonized—wrested Seville from the Moors (1224), he made over one of the best districts of the city to the Jews, and gave them the four mosques contained in it that they might convert them into synagogues.

The only restraint placed upon them by the law was that they must refrain, under pain of death, from attempting to proselytize among Christians, and that they must show respect for the Christian religion.

These were the halcyon days of Hebrew prosperity in Spain. Their distinguished abilities were recognized, and they won to many positions of importance in the government. The finances of the kingdom were in their control, and Castile prospered under their able administration of its commerce. Alfonso VIII, in whose reign it is estimated there were 12,000 Jews in Toledo alone, employed a Jew as his treasurer, and did not disdain to take a Jewess for his mistress—an interesting little fact in view of the law that was so soon to be promulgated on that subject.

Hardly less than their value to the nation's commerce were their services to science, art, and literature. They excelled particularly in medicine and chemistry, and the most skilful doctors and surgeons of the Middle Ages were men of their race.

In the middle of the thirteenth century a change unfortunately set in, and this external harmony so laboriously established was disturbed by an excrescence of the real feelings that had never ceased to underlie it. Largely the Jews were themselves to blame. Deluded by the religious liberty that was conceded them, by the dignities to which men of their faith had climbed, and by the prosperity which they had attained, they failed to perceive that their accumulated wealth was in itself a menace to their safety.

Emboldened by the consideration shown them, they committed the imprudence of giving a free rein to their Oriental taste for splendour; they surrounded themselves with luxury, and permitted themselves an ostentatious magnificence in their raiment and equipages, and thus proclaimed the wealth they had been amassing through generations of comparative obscurity.

Had they confined themselves to this strictly personal display all might yet have been well. But being dressed and housed in princely fashion, they put on princely ways. They grew haughty and arrogant with the horrible arrogance of wealth. They allowed their disdain of the less affluent Christians to transpire in their contemptuous bearing towards them, and being unchecked in this it was but another step to abuse the privileges which they enjoyed.

Their parade of wealth had provoked envy—the most dangerous and maleficent of the passions implanted in the human heart. Their arrogance and cavalier bearing stirred that envy into activity.

Questions arose touching the sources of their wealth. It was propounded against them that their usurious practices had ruined many of the Christians whom they now dared to spurn. And although usury had been sanctioned and it had been proclaimed lawful for them to charge a rate of interest as high as 40 per centum, it was suddenly remembered that usury had in all times been uncompromisingly condemned by the Church—and by the term usury the Church then understood any interest, however slight, paid upon borrowed money.

Fanaticism began to stir uneasily in its slumber, and presently, under the spur of greed, it roused itself and reared its horrid head. Public feeling against the Israelites was increased by the fact that they had practically acquired control of the ever-unpopular offices for the collection of taxes.

The populace grew menacing. Evil tales concerning them were put about, and they were accused, among other ritual abominations, of practising human sacrifices.

Whether there was any real ground for the accusation is one of those historical mysteries that baffle the student. On the one hand it seems impossible to collect sufficient data to establish any single one of the many specific accusations made; whilst on the other hand, in view of the persistence with which the charge crops up in different countries and at different epochs,[40] it would be presumptuous to dismiss it as groundless.

The first official recognition of the accusation is to be found in the code known as the *Partidas*, promulgated by Alfonso XI (1256-1263), which contains the following clause:

"As we hear that in some places the Jews on Good Friday make a mocking commemoration of the Passion of Our Lord Jesus Christ, stealing boys and crucifying them, or making waxen images and crucifying these when boys are not procurable, we order that should it become known that hereafter, in any part of our realm, such a thing is done, all those whom it is ascertained are connected with the deed shall be arrested and brought before the King. And when he shall have satisfied himself of the truth of the charge he shall have them put to death, as many as they may be."[41]

Llorente mentions four specific cases of ritual murder, to which he appears to attach credit:

1250.—A choir-boy of the Metropolitan Church of Zaragoza, named Domingo de Val, crucified by Jews. He was afterwards canonized and worshipped at Zaragoza as a martyr.

1452.—A boy crucified by Jews at Valladolid.

1454.—A boy from the lordship of the Marquess of Almarza, near Zamora, crucified. His heart was afterwards burnt and the ashes were consumed in wine by the Jews who attended the ceremony. The body was afterwards discovered by a dog, and this led to the arrest of the culprits and their conviction.

1468.—At Sepulveda, in the Bishopric of Segovia, a boy was taken on the Thursday of Holy Week, and on Good Friday he was crowned with thorns, whipped, and finally crucified. The Bishop, D. Juan Arias, having received intelligence of this crime, instituted an inquiry which resulted in the arrest of several men, who, being convicted, were put to death.

Llorente gives as his authority for the third and fourth cases the "Fortalicium Fidei" of Espina—by no means an authority to be unquestioningly accepted. For the second he mentions no authority whatever; whilst for fuller information upon the first he refers his readers to the "Historia de Santo Domingo de Val," which is of no more authority than most works of this class.[42] But the canonization of this victim gives rise to thought; for it was never the way of the Church of Rome to proceed recklessly and without due evidence in such matters. Even if it were, however, it would be necessary in this case to show a motive for such recklessness. The only motive possible would be the desire to create justification for a persecution of the Jews. But, as has been said—and as shall presently be made abundantly clear—it never was the aim of the Church of Rome to engage in such persecution or to incite to it.

The famous case of the crucifixion of the "Holy Infant" of La Gardia, whose trial was directed by Torquemada himself, shall be considered in its proper place.

As is well known, the practice of human sacrifice is an extremely old one; and it has been associated in varying forms with many widely different cults. The earliest absolutely historical instance of Jews resorting to it is probably that quoted by Dr. J. G. Frazer (in "The Golden Bough") from the "Historia Ecclesiastica" of Socrates. The scholiast relates how in 416, at Imnestar in Syria, a company of Jews during one of their festivals fell to deriding

Christians and their Christ. At the height of their frenzy they seized a boy, bound him to a cross, and hung him up. A brawl was the result, and the authorities intervened to make the Jews pay dearly for their crime.

Amador de los Rios, in dealing with the spread of this charge against the Spanish Hebrews in the thirteenth century, attributes it to the subject's having been made the theme of an exceedingly dramatic narrative poem in the "Milagros de Nuestra Señora" by Gonzalo de Berceo. At the same time he does not go so far as to urge that the story upon which the ballad was founded may not have had its roots in fact. On the contrary, he suggests that such may have been the case, and having chronicled the persistence of the accusation, he refrains from expressing any definite opinion on the subject, hesitating either to accept, or to dismiss as idle calumnies, these charges of ritual murder.

From the able arguments that have been put forward on this same subject by Frazer and Wendland, it is to be concluded that in any case the Christians were mistaken in assuming that these alleged crucifixions held at the Feast of Purim—whether of human beings or of effigies—were intended as a mockery of the Passion of the Redeemer. Their origin is a far more ancient one, involving a rite of which the Sacrifice of Golgotha may itself have been an individual celebration—the commemoration of the hanging of Haman—which, again, was the continuation of a ritual practised by the Babylonians and acquired from them by the Jews during their captivity.[43]

Photo by Lacoste.

ISABELLA THE CATHOLIC.
From a Painting in the Prado Gallery, attributed to Miguel Zittoz.

Whatever may be the truth of this matter of ritual murder, there is no doubt that these rumours were diligently spread to inflame the popular mind against the Jews.

Fanatical monks—ignoring the papal injunctions of forbearance and toleration towards the Children of Israel—went forth through Castile preaching the iniquity of the Jews and God's wrath to fall upon the land that harboured them. Thus incited, and perceiving profit in the business, the faithful rose to destroy them. Massacres and pillages were the inevitable result, although as a rule the authorities were prompt to intervene and repress the populace's combined fanaticism and quest for plunder.

But when in 1342 the Black Death spread over Europe, the Dominicans and others renewed their denunciations, and led men to believe the Jews responsible for the pestilence that afflicted the land. In Germany they were ruthlessly given to choose between death and baptism, and they suffered horribly until Pope Clement VI stepped in to save them. He besought the Emperor to restrain his murderers; and finding that his pleadings lacked effect, he launched the thunderbolts of excommunication against all who should continue to engage in the persecution of the Jews.

Stricken with terror before that awful menace of the Church, the faithful paused in the carnage, and the voice of denunciation fell silent.

Thus, for a season, they won a little measure of peace. But throughout the fourteenth century spurts of persecution broke out here and there, and massacres took place in Castile, Aragon, and Navarre. The authorities, too, with the precedent of the Partidas before them, whilst not going the length of sanctioning, or even permitting violence where they could repress it, yet practised upon the Jews the most flagrant and cruel injustices. Of these the worst instance is that of the tax of 20,000 gold dobles levied upon the aljamas of Toledo by Henry II on his accession in 1369. To realize this sum he ordered the public sale not only of the property of the Jews, but actually of their persons into slavery, as is to be seen by his decree.[44]

The persecutions with which they were visited were chiefly procured by the monks, who went abroad preaching against them, fomenting the hatred of the Christians against a people who were largely their creditors. Even where the religious incentive was insufficient, the easy way of wiping out debts which this gratification of their piety afforded proved irresistible to a people whose flagrant immorality—in every sense of the term—went hand in hand with their perfervid devoutness.

These persecutions, as we have said, the authorities made haste to quell. But there arose presently a rabid fanatic who proved altogether irrepressible. His name was Hernando Martinez. He was a Dominican friar, and Canon of Ecija. Of his sincerity there can be no doubt; and their sincerity is the most terrible thing about such men, blinding them to the point of utter madness. He was ready to suffer any martyrdom sooner than be silent in a cause in which he considered it his sacred duty to give tongue. About this sacred duty he went forth, screaming his denunciations of the Jews, frenziedly inciting the mob to rise up and destroy this accursed race, these enemies of God, these crucifiers of the Saviour. Indeed, he could not have shown a more fierce and frothing hatred of them had they been the very men who at the throne of Pilate had clamoured for the blood of Christ—and for whose pardon the gentle Redeemer had prayed in His expiring moments: a matter this which escaped the attention of the Archdeacon of Ecija, being—like many another—too full of piety to find room for Christianity in his soul.

Appeals against him were made to the Archbishop of Seville, whose official, or representative, he was. He was ordered by his Archbishop to desist, and when in flagrant disobedience to his superior he continued to preach his gospel of blood and hatred, appeals were made to the King, and even to the Pope; and by King and Pope was he commanded to cease his inflammatory sermons.

But he defied them all alike. In his fanatical fury he carried his contumacy so far as to call in question the papal authority, and to declare illicit the sanction given by the popes for the erection and preservation of synagogues. This was perilously akin to heresy. Men had been sent to the stake for less, and Hernando Martinez must have been utterly mad if he conceived that the Church would permit him to continue the diffusion of such doctrines.

He was brought before the episcopal court to answer for his words. He answered defiantly—told them that the breath of God was in him, and that it was not for men to stop his mouth.

Thereupon Don Pedro Barroso—the archbishop—ordered that he should stand his trial for contumacy and heresy, and meanwhile suspended him from all jurisdiction and all duties as archiepiscopal official.

It happened, however, that Barroso died shortly thereafter, before the trial could take place; and Martinez contrived to get himself elected by the Chapter to the position of one of the provisors of the diocese pending the appointment of a successor to Barroso. Thus he resumed his power and the faculty to preach; and he used it so ruthlessly that in December of 1390 several synagogues in Seville were laid in ruins by the mob acting in obedience to his incitement.

The Jews appealed to the King for protection, and the authorities, now thoroughly roused, ordered that Martinez be deposed from his office and forbidden to preach, and that the demolished synagogues be rebuilt by the Chapter which had made itself responsible by electing him.

But Martinez, ever defiant, disregarded both King and Chapter. He pursued his bloodthirsty mission, stirring up a populace that was but too ready to perceive—through his arguments—a way to perform an act that must be pleasing to God whilst enriching itself at the same time. What populace could have been proof against such reasoning?

Finally, in the summer of 1391, the whole country was ablaze with fanatical persecution. The fierce flames broke out first in Seville, under the assiduous fanning of the deposed archdeacon.

Three years before, in view of the harm that it was urged the Jews were doing to religion by their free intermingling with Christians, King John I had ordered them to live apart in districts appointed for them, which came to be known as Juderias (Jewries or ghettos). It was commanded that the Christians should not enter these, and that for purposes of trade the Jews should come to the public markets and there erect tents, but they must own no house or domicile beyond the precincts of the Juderias, and they must withdraw to these at nightfall.

Into the Juderia of Seville the mob now penetrated, wrought by Martinez to a pitch of frenzy almost equal to his own. They went armed, and they put the place to sack and slaughter, butchering its every tenant without discrimination or pity for age or sex. The number of the slain has been estimated at some four thousand, men, women, and children.[45]

From Seville the conflagration spread to the other cities of Spain, and what had happened there happened in Burgos, Valencia, Toledo, and Cordova, and further in Aragon, Cataluna, and Navarre, whilst the streets of Barcelona are said to have run with the blood of immolated Jews.

Into the Jewry of every town went the infuriated mob to force Christ—as these Christians understood Him—upon the inhabitants; to offer the terror-stricken Jews the choice between steel and water—death and baptism.

So mighty and violent was the outbreak that the authorities were powerless to quell it, and where they attempted to do so with any degree of determination they were themselves caught in the fury of the populace. Nor did the slaughter cease until the Christians were glutted, and some fifty thousand Jews had perished.

The churches were now filled with Jews who came clamouring for baptism, having perceived that through its waters lay the way to temporal as well as to spiritual life, and having in most cases—in the abject state of terror to which they had been reduced—more concern for the former than for the latter.

Llorente estimates the number of baptized at over a million, and this number was considerably swelled by the conversions effected by St. Vincent Ferrer, who came forth upon his mission to the Jews in the early years of the fifteenth century, and who induced thousands to enter the fold of Christianity by his eloquence and by the marvels which it is said he wrought.

The fury of the mob having spent itself, peace was gradually restored, and little by little those Jews who had remained faithful to their religion and yet survived began to come forth from their hiding-places, to assemble, and, with the amazing, invincible patience and pertinacity of their race, to build up once more the edifice that had been demolished.

But if the sword of persecution was sheathed, the spirit that had guided it was still abroad, and the Jews were made to experience further repressive measures. Under decrees of 1412-13 they lost most of the few privileges that the late king had left them.

It was ordained by these that henceforth no Jew should occupy the position of a judge even in a Hebrew court, nor should any Jew be permitted to bear witness. All synagogues were to be closed or converted into Christian temples, with the exception of one in every town in which Jews should be established. They were forbidden to continue the practice of the professions of medicine, surgery, and chemistry, in which they had specialised with such good results to the community. They were no longer to occupy the offices of tax-collectors, and all commerce with Christians was forbidden them. They must neither buy nor sell in trade with Christians, nor eat with them, nor use their baths, nor send their children to the same schools. The ghetto was ordered to be walled round, so as to be enclosed and cut off from the rest of the city, and they were forbidden to issue from it. Intercourse between a Jew and a Christian woman was forbidden under pain of death by burning, even though the woman were a prostitute. They were forbidden to shave, and compelled to allow their beards and hair to grow, in addition to which they were ordered to wear as a distinguishing mark a circle of red cloth upon the shoulder of their gabardines. They were further compelled to hear three sermons annually from a Christian preacher, whose aim it was to pour abuse and contumely upon them, to inveigh against their accursed race and creed, to assure them of the certainty of the damnation that awaited them, and to exalt before them the excellences of the Catholic religion (based, be it remembered, that we may fully savour the irony, upon Faith, Hope, and Charity).[46]

When King John I had established the Juderias in 1388, curtailing at the same time the privileges which until then the Jews had enjoyed—at least by paying for them—there had been many who, finding the restraint imposed upon them altogether intolerable, had abandoned the faith of their fathers and embraced Christianity. Those who held the affairs of this world in esteem had sought baptism, and whilst many in doing so had entirely broken with the past—and often, as is the way of converts, become zealots in their observance of the faith embraced—many others, whilst outwardly complying with the obligations of the Christian religion, continued in secret to observe the law of Moses and their Jewish rites. Similarly these further decrees against their liberty had the effect of causing still more numerous conversions to Christianity.

These converts were termed "New-Christians" by the Spaniards. By those of their own race who had remained faithful they were called "marranos"—a contemptuous epithet derived from *Maran-atha*, ("The Lord is coming"), but supposed by the Christians to signify "accursed." It came into general use before very long.

These New-Christians, as a consequence of their conversion, gained not merely the privileges recently lost to them as Jews, but found themselves upon a footing of absolute equality with the Old-Christians; every profession was open to them, and by applying themselves to these with all their energy and intelligence, they found themselves before very long in possession of some of the highest offices in the land.

But in the meanwhile the rigour of the decrees of 1412 came to be considerably relaxed; a degree of liberty and of intermingling with Christians was permitted to the Jews, and many of the offices which they had occupied of old came once more under their control, chiefly those concerned with commerce and finance and the farming of the taxes. Under the deplorable rule of Henry IV the nobles, whose slave he was, demanded that he should "expel from his service and States the Jews who, exploiting public misery, have contrived to return to the appointments of tax-gatherers."

The weak King agreed, but neglected to execute his promise; it was presently forgotten, and the Jewish section of the community was allowed to continue under the conditions of ease we have described. Under these conditions was it found by Ferdinand and Isabella upon their accession, nor does it appear that they paid any particular attention to it until invited to do so by the "clerics and laymen" who, as Pulgar[47] tells us, represented to them that in the re-Judaizings that were taking place was matter for their jurisdiction.

CHAPTER VI
THE NEW-CHRISTIANS

It must clearly be understood that so far the Inquisition, which for some three centuries already had been very active in Italy and Southern France, had not reached Castile.

Even as recently as 1474, when Pope Sixtus IV had ordered the Dominicans to set up the Inquisition in Spain, and whilst in obedience to that command inquisitors were appointed in Aragon, Valencia, Cataluña, and Navarre, it was not held necessary to make any appointment in Castile, where no heresy of any account could be perceived. Trials of such offences against the Faith as might occur were conducted by the bishops, who were fully empowered to deal with them; and such offences being rare, the necessity for a special tribunal did not suggest itself, nor did the Pope press the matter, desirous though he might be to see the Inquisition universally established.

There was, of course, a large Hebrew population, and also a considerable number of Moslems, in the peninsula. But these did not come within the jurisdiction of any ecclesiastical court. The Inquisition itself could take no cognizance of them, as they did not offend against the Faith.

Explanation is perhaps necessary. We touch here upon a point on which the religious persecution known as the Inquisition compares favourably with any other religious persecution in history, and in common justice this point should not—as but too frequently has been the case—be obscured. There is too little to be urged in favour of this tribunal so terribly inequitable in its practices that we can afford to slur over the one feature of its constitution that is invested with a degree of equity.

Whatever may have been the case in the course of civil and popular persecutions, whatever may have been done by a frenzied populace at the instigation of odd fanatical preachers acting without the authority of their superiors in giving rein to the fierce bigotry they had nurtured in their souls, the Church herself, it must be clearly understood, neither urged nor sanctioned the persecution of those born into any religion that was not in itself a heresy of the Roman Faith. The tribunal of the Inquisition was established solely—and moved solely—to deal with those who apostatized or seceded from the ranks of the Roman Church, precisely as an army deals with deserting soldiers. Fanatical, horribly narrow, cruelly bigoted as was the spirit of the Inquisition, yet the inquisitors confined their prosecutions to apostates, to the adulterers of a faith whose purity and incorruptibility they had made it their mission to maintain.

If the Church repressed liberty of conscience, if she stifled rationalism and crushed independence of thought, she did so only where her own children were concerned—those who had been born into the Catholic Faith or who had embraced it in conversion. With those born into any other independent religion she had no concern. To Jew, Moslem, Buddhist, and Pagan, and to the savages of the New World, when it came presently to be discovered, she accorded the fullest religious freedom.

To appreciate this, it is but necessary to consider such enactments as those of Honorius III for the protection of the Jews, of Clement VI, who threatened their persecutors with excommunication, and the action of Pope and Archbishop in the case of the inflammatory sermons of Hernando Martinez. It is sufficient to consider that when the Jews were driven out of Spain—as shall presently be seen—they actually found a refuge in Rome itself, and were received with kindliness by Pope Alexander VI (Roderigo Borgia), which in itself is one of the oddest ironies that ecclesiastical history can offer.

And if this is not sufficient, let us for a moment consider the immunity and comparative peace enjoyed by the Jews who dwelt in Rome itself, in their district of Trastevere.

They were a recognized section of the community in the Papal City. On his coronation procession each Pope would pause near the Campo de'Fiori to receive the company of Jews that came, headed by the Rabbi, to pay homage to their sovereign—precisely as their ancestors had come to pay homage to the emperor.

To the Vicar of Christ the Rabbi would now proffer the rolls of the Pentateuch, swathed in a cloth. The Pope would take them into his hands, to show that he respected the law contained in them, and would then put them behind him, to signify that this law now belonged to the past. From behind the Pontiff the Rabbi would receive back his sacred scriptures, and depart with his escort, usually accompanied by the jeers, insults, and vituperations of the Roman populace.[48]

It will be understood, then, that the Inquisition's establishment in Spain was not urged for the purpose of persecuting the Jews. It had no concern with Jews, if we confine the term purely to its religious meaning, signifying the observers of the law of Moses. Its concern was entirely with the apostasy of those who, although of the Jewish race, had become Christians by conversion. By the subsequent secret re-Judaizings, or return of these New-Christians to the religion of their fathers (which they had abandoned out of material considerations), they came within the jurisdiction of the Inquisition, and rendered themselves liable to prosecution as heretics, a prosecution which could never have overtaken them had they but continued in their original faith.

There is no denying that many of those who had been baptized against their will, as the only means of saving their lives when the fury of the Christian mob was unleashed against them, had remained Jews at heart, had continued in secret to practise the Jewish rites, and were exerting themselves to bring back to the fold of Israel their apostate brethren. Others, however, upon receiving baptism may have determined to keep the law to which they now pledged themselves and to persevere honestly in Christianity. Yet many of the old Jewish observances were become habitual with them: the trained—almost the hereditary—repugnance to certain meats, the observance of certain feast days, and several minor domestic laws that are part of the Jewish code, were too deeply implanted in them to be plucked up by the roots at the first attempt. Time was required in which they could settle into Christian habits; two or three generations might be necessary in some families before these habits came to be perfectly acquired and the old ones to be entirely obliterated. Had those who urged the Sovereigns to introduce the Inquisition into Castile, or had the Sovereigns themselves but perceived this and exercised the necessary and reasonable patience in the matter, Spain might have been spared the horrors that took root in her soil and sapped the vigour and intellectual energy of her children, so that in her case decadence pressed swift and close upon the very heels of supreme achievement.

Execrable as is the memory of the Inquisition to all the world, to none should be it so execrable as to Spain, since the evil that it wrought recoiled entirely upon herself.

It was on the occasion of Isabella's first visit to Seville—that punitive visit already mentioned—that the establishment of the Holy Office in Spain was first proposed to her. The King was at the time in Estremadura upon the business of fortifying his frontiers against Portugal.

The proposal came from Alonso de Ojeda, the Prior of the Dominicans of Seville, a man who enjoyed great credit and was reputed saintly ("vir pius ac sanctus," Paramo calls him).

Seeing her zeal to put down lawlessness and to purify and restore order to the country, Ojeda urged upon her notice the spread of the detestable Judaizing movement that was toward. He laid stress upon the hypocrisy that had underlain so many of the conversions of the Jews. He pointed out—with some degree of justice—that these men had made a mock of the Holy Church, had defiled her sacraments, and had perpetrated the most abominable sacrilege by their pretended acceptance of the Christian faith. He urged that not only must this be punished, but that the havoc which these Judaizers were working among the more faithful New-Christians, and the proselytizing which they went so far as to attempt among Old-Christians, must be checked.

To carry out this urgently-required purification, he implored the Queen to establish the Inquisition.[49]

There was a speciousness, and even a justice, in his arguments which must have impressed that pious lady. But her piety, intense as it was, did not carry her to the lengths required of her by her priestly counsellor. The balance of her splendid mind was singularly true. She perceived that here was matter that called for a remedy; but she perceived also the fanaticism inspiring the friar who stood before her, and realized how his fanaticism must exaggerate the evil.

She was aware also of the extreme malevolence of which the New-Christians were the object. By their conversion they might have deflected the religious hostility of the Castilians; but the more deeply-rooted racial antagonism remained. It not only remained, but it was quickened by the envy which these New-Christians were exciting. The energy and intelligence inherent in men of their race were serving them now, as they had served them before, to their undoing. There were no offices of eminence in which New-Christians were not to be found; there were none in which they did not outnumber the Old-Christians—the pure-blooded Castilians.

This the Queen knew, for she was herself surrounded by converts and the descendants of converts. Several of her counsellors, her three secretaries—one of whom was that chronicler, Pulgar, whose record of the situation has been quoted—and her very treasurer were all New-Christians.[50]

These men Isabella knew intimately, and esteemed. Judging the New-Christians generally by those in her immediate service, she was naturally led to discount Ojeda's imputations against them. She perceived the source of these imputations, and she must have taken into consideration the ineradicable bitterness of the popular feeling against Jews and the intensity of a prejudice which extended—as we have said—to the New-Christians to such an extent that they continued to be known as "Judios," notwithstanding their conversion, so that often in contemporary chronicles it is difficult to determine to which class the writer is referring.

We have said that, in spite of conversions, the racial hostility remained. The Christian attitude towards the Hebrew had not changed in the hundred years that were sped since, under the incitings of the Archdeacon of Ecija, the mob had risen up and massacred them. They were the descendants of the crucifiers always.

A vestige of this feeling lingers to this day in the peninsula. In the vocabulary of the Portuguese lower orders, and even of the indifferently educated, there is no such word as "cruel." "Jew" is the term that has entirely usurped its functions, and as an injunction against cruelty to man or beast, "Don't be a Jew!" (*Não seja judeu!*) is still the only phrase.

No conception of what was the popular feeling at the time can be conveyed more adequately than by a translation of the passage from Bernaldez concerning the manners and customs of the Jews. Bernaldez was a priest, and therefore, to some extent, an educated man—as in the main his history bears witness—yet a piece of writing so ludicrously stupid and detestably malicious as this passage can only have emanated from a mind in which bigotry had destroyed all sense of proportion.

The only historical value of the passage lies in the deplorable fact that undoubtedly it may be accepted as a faithful mirror of the prejudice that existed in Isabella's day.

It runs:

"Just as heretics and Jews have always fled from Christian doctrines, so they have always fled from Christian customs. They are great drinkers and gluttons, who never lose the Jewish habit of eating garbage of onions and garlic fried in oil, and of meat stewed in oil, which they use instead of lard; and oil with meat is a thing that smells very badly, so that their houses and doorways stink vilely of that garbage; and they have the peculiar smell of Jews in consequence of their food and of the fact that they are not baptized. And although some have been baptized, yet the virtue of the baptism having been annulled by their credulity [*i.e.* their adherence to their own faith] and by their Judaizing, they stink like Jews. They will not eat pork save under compulsion. They eat meat in Lent and on the eve of feast days.... They keep the Passover and the Sabbath as best they can. They send oil to the synagogues for the lamps. Jews come to preach to them in their houses secretly—especially to the women, very secretly. They have Rabbis to slaughter their beasts and poultry. They eat unleavened bread in the Jewish season. They perform all their Jewish rites as much in secret as possible, and women as well as men seek whenever possible to avoid the sacraments of Holy Church.... They never confess truthfully, and it happened that a priest, once confessing one of these, cut a fragment of cloth from his garment, saying: 'As you have never sinned, let me have this as a relic to heal the sick.'... Not without reason did Our Lord call them *generatio prava et adultera*. They do not believe that God rewards virginity and chastity, and all their endeavour is to multiply. And in the days of the strength of this heresy many monasteries were violated by their merchants and wealthy men, and many professed nuns were ravished and derided, they not believing in or fearing excommunication, but rather doing this to vituperate Jesus Christ and the Church. Commonly swindling people by many wiles and cheats, as in buying and selling, they have no conscience where Christians are concerned. Never would they undertake agriculture, ploughing or tilling or raising cattle, nor have they ever taught their children any office but that of sitting down to earn enough to eat by as little labour as possible. Many of them have raised up great estates in a few years, not being sparing of their thieving and usury, maintaining that they earn it from their enemies...."[51]

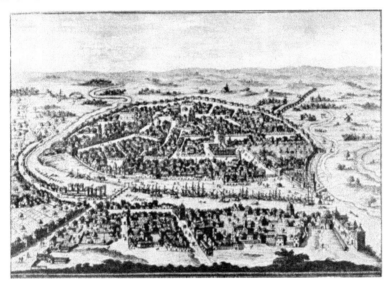

Photo by Donald Macbeth.

SEVILLE.
From Colmenar's "Délices d'Espagne."

This atrocious tissue of misrepresentation would be utterly negligible and contemptible were it not for the fact—as has been said—that it was written in good faith (the good faith of a bigot) and reflects what was currently believed, fostered by the envy which is plainly revealed when Bernaldez alludes to the occupations of the Jews and the New-Christians—all of whom he assumes to be false to the faith they have embraced.

Isabella must have been conscious of this feeling, and she must have rated it at its proper value. She had received in 1474 a very pitiful narrative poem of the New-Christian Anton Montoro, which painted with terrible vividness a slaughter of the *conversos* and implored justice upon the assassins, protesting the innocence of the New-Christians and the sincerity of their conversions. Her gentle nature must have been moved to compassion by that lament, and

- 59 -

her acute mind must have perceived the evil passions and the envy that were stirring under the fair cloak of saintly zeal.

All these considerations being weighed, she resisted the representations of Ojeda.

But weightier than any may have been the reflection of the power which the tribunal of the Inquisition must place in the hands of the clergy. Already and very bravely she had expressed her resentment of clerical usurpation of royal rights in Spain, and to repress it she had not hesitated to front the Pope himself. If she acceded now to Ojeda's request, she would be permitting the priesthood to set up a court which, not being subject to any temporal law, must alienate from her some portion of that sovereignty which so jealously she guarded.

Thus she came to dismiss the petition of the Dominican, and there can be little doubt when all the circumstances are considered—as presently they shall be—that in this she had the entire support of the Cardinal of Spain, Don Pedro Gonzalez de Mendoza, Archbishop of Seville, who was with her at the time.

Ojeda withdrew, baffled, but by no means resigned. He awaited a more favourable season, what time he kept the popular feeling in a state of ferment. And no sooner had Ferdinand come to rejoin his Queen in Seville than the Dominican renewed his importunities.

He hoped to find an ally in the King. Moreover he was now supported by Fr. Filippo de' Barberi, the Sicilian Inquisitor. The latter had newly arrived in Spain, where he came to seek at the hands of the Catholic Sovereigns—who were rulers of Sicily—the confirmation of an ancient decree promulgated in 1223 by the Emperor Frederic II. By virtue of this decree one-third of the confiscated property of heretics became the perquisite of the Inquisition; and it also ordained that the governors of all districts should afford protection to the inquisitors and assistance in their work of prosecuting heretics and any Jew who might have contracted marriage with a Christian.

These privileges the Sovereigns duly confirmed, accounting it their duty to do so since they related to the Inquisition as established by Honorius III. But not on that account did Isabella yet lean towards the introduction of the tribunal into Castile.

It happened, however, that to the arguments of Ojeda and Barberi were added the persuasions of the papal legate *a latere* at the court of Castile— Nicolao Franco, Bishop of Trevisa—who conceived, no doubt, that the institution of the Inquisition here would be pleasing to Pope Sixtus IV, since it must increase the authority of the Church in Spain.

To Ferdinand it is probable that the suggestion was not without allurement, since it must have offered him a way at once to gratify the piety that was his, and—out of the confiscations that must ensue from the prosecution of so very wealthy a section of the community—to replenish the almost exhausted coffers of the treasury. When the way of conscience is also the way of profit, there is little difficulty in following it. But, after all, though joint sovereign of Spain and paramount in Aragon, Ferdinand had not in Castile the power of Isabella. It was her kingdom when all was said, and although his position there was by no means that of a simple prince-consort, yet he was bound by law and by policy to remain submissive to her will. In view of her attitude, he could do little more than add his own to the persuasions of the three priestly advocates, and amongst them they so pressed Isabella that she gave way to the extent of a compromise.

She consented that steps should be taken not only to check the Judaizing of the New-Christians, but also to effect conversions among the Jews themselves; and she entrusted the difficult task of enforcing the observance of the Christian faith and the Catholic dogmas to the Cardinal of Spain—than whom, from a Christian and humanitarian point of view, no man of his day could have been more desirable, which is as much as to say that from the point of view of his Catholic contemporaries no man could have been less so.

Isabella's announcement of her determination in the matter must have come as something of a shock to Ojeda, who conceived himself on the way to prevail with her. This concession to his wishes was far from being the concession that he sought, since it passed over the heads of the preaching friars, who had made such work—by their own methods—their special mission.

The Queen, however, had decided, and there was no more to be said. The Cardinal of Spain went about his task in that sincere Christian spirit and with that zeal for truth and justice that is associated with his name. He compiled for the purpose of his mission an *instrucción*, which has not survived, but which Ortiz de Zuñiga[52] and Pulgar[53] inform us was in the form of a catechism.

In this "he indicates," says Pulgar, "the duties of the true Christian from the day of his birth, in the sacrament of baptism as in all other sacraments which it is his obligation to receive, as well as what he should be taught, what believe and what perform as a faithful Christian at all times and on all days until the day of his death."

Mariana, Zurita, and other historians, upon the word of Paramo[54] and of Salazar de Mendoza, have ventured to ascribe the establishment of the Inquisition in Castile to the Cardinal of Spain. Their object in so doing has been to heap honour and glory upon his name and memory; for in their opinion he could have had no greater claim than this to the gratitude and reverence of humanity. But the justice of a less bigoted age demands that truth shall prevail in this respect, and that his memory be deprived of that very questionable honour. The Cardinal's contemporaries do not justify what Paramo claims for him. And, to reduce the argument to its lowest plane, it would have been extremely unlikely that Cardinal Mendoza should advocate the establishment of a court that must deprive him and the other Spanish bishops of the jurisdiction in *causas de Fé* hitherto vested in themselves.

The Primate pursued, then, the task imposed upon him, causing his "catechism" to be expounded and taught by all parish priests in all pulpits and schools.

But however zealous his methods, they were not the methods desired by Ojeda and the papal legate. The Dominican, vexed by the turn of events, and determined to return to the assault as soon as ever occasion offered, cast about him for fresh arguments that should prevail with the Sovereigns.

And then there befell an incident in Seville to supply his fanatical needs and place in his hands the very weapon that he sought.

A young nobleman of the famous house of Guzman had engaged in an amorous intrigue with the daughter of a New-Christian. In the pursuit of this amour he repaired secretly to her father's house on the night of Thursday in Holy Week of that year 1478, and was admitted by the girl. But the lovers being disturbed by voices in the house, Guzman was driven to conceal himself. From his concealment he overheard the conversation of several Judaizers who were being entertained by the father of his mistress. He heard them vehemently denying the divinity of Christ and as vehemently blaspheming His name and the Holy Faith.

Having quitted the house, he went straight to the Prior of the Dominicans to relate what he had overheard and to denounce the blasphemers.

This young Castilian is so very interesting a type that a slight digression to consider him more closely may be permitted. It is of assistance to understand the mental attitude, the crass complacency of the bigot. He knew that the highest virtue that a Christian could practise was the virtue of chastity, and, conversely, that the worst offence against God into which he could fall was that of unchastity. Or at least he had been taught these things, and he accepted them in a sub-conscious, automatic sort of way. Yet since the sin was his own, it gave his consciousness no uneasiness that he should perpetrate it, that he should slink like a thief into the house of this New-Christian to debauch his daughter. But let him hear this New-Christian or his friends express opinions of disbelief in this God whom he believed in and—by his own lights—insulted, and behold him outraged in all his feelings against those unspeakable fellows. Behold him running hot-foot to Prior Ojeda to relate with horror the tale of this vileness that he had overheard, so little concerned about the vileness through which he himself had acquired his knowledge that he makes no effort to conceal it. And, apparently, the Dominican, in a like horror at the New-Christians' offence against a God in whom they do not believe, accounts of little moment the Castilian's offence against the God in whom he does believe.

It is a nice illumination of the contrast between the theory and the practice of Christianity.

Upon the young man's information Ojeda instituted an inquiry, and six Judaizers were arrested. They confessed their guilt, and begged to be reconciled to the Church. As the Inquisition had not yet been established, with its terrible decree against "relapsos,"[55] their prayer was granted, after the fulfilment of the penance imposed.[56]

With the tale of this "execrable wickedness" Ojeda repaired at once to Cordova, whither the Sovereigns had by now withdrawn. The story would lose nothing in its repetition by this pious and saintly man, and he was in a position to add to it that the good folk of Seville were almost in revolt from indignation at that happening in their midst.

Having shown thus how urgently it was required, he once more implored the Sovereigns to establish the Inquisition. And it is not to be doubted that his petition would be backed by that of the legate Franco, who was at the Court.

Yet Isabella still showed repugnance, still hesitated to consent to the extreme course advocated.

But at this moment, according to Llorente,[57] another advocate appears upon the scene to plead the cause of the Faith—a figure in the white habit and black cloak of the Dominican Brotherhood, a man in his fifty-eighth year, tall and gaunt and stooping slightly at the shoulders, mild-eyed, of a cast of countenance that is gentle, noble, and benign.

This is Frey Tomás de Torquemada, Prior of the Dominican Convent of Holy Cross of Segovia, the nephew of the late illustrious Juan de Torquemada, Cardinal of San Sisto.

His influence with the Queen is vast; his eloquence fiery; his mental energy compelling. Ojeda looks on, and his hopes grow confident at last.

CHAPTER VII
THE PRIOR OF HOLY CROSS

If ever a name held the omen of a man's life, that name is Torquemada. To such an extraordinary degree is it instinct with the suggestion of the machinery of fire and torture over which he was destined to preside, that it almost seems a fictitious name, a *nom de guerre*, a grim invention, compounded of the Latin *torque* and the Spanish *quemada*, to fit the man who was to hold the office of Grand Inquisitor.

It was derived from the northern town of Torquemada (the Turre Cremata of the Romans), where the illustrious family had its beginnings. This family first sprang into historical distinction with the knighting by Alfonso XI of Lope Alonso de Torquemada (*Hijodalgo a los Fueros de Castilla*), and thereafter was maintained in prominence by several members who held more or less distinguished offices. But the most illustrious bearer of the name was the cultured Dominican Juan de Torquemada (Lope Alonso's great-grandson), who was raised to the purple with the title of Cardinal of San Sisto. He was one of the most learned, eminent, and respected theologians of his age, an upholder of the dogma of the Immaculate Conception, and the most ardent champion since Thomas Aquinas of the doctrine of papal infallibility. He enriched theological literature by several works, the best known of which is his "Meditations."

Fr. Tomás de Torquemada was the son of the Cardinal's only brother, Pero Fernandez de Torquemada. He was born at Valladolid in 1420, and after a scholastic career of some distinction—if Garcia Rodrigo is to be believed in this particular[58]—he followed in his uncle's footsteps, soliciting the habit of the Order of St. Dominic, which he assumed in the Convent of St. Paul of Valladolid upon completing his studies of philosophy and divinity, and receiving a doctor's degree.

He filled with distinction the chair of canon law and theology, and in the fullness of time was elected Prior of the Convent of Santa Cruz of Segovia. He so distinguished himself in the discharge of the duties of this office by his piety, his learning, and his zeal, that he was repeatedly re-elected, there being at the time no rule of the order to inhibit it. Such was the austerity of his character that he never ate meat, or used linen either in his clothing or on his bed.[59] He observed the rule of poverty imposed by his order so rigorously that he was unable to provide his only sister with an endowment suitable to her station, and could allow her no more than would permit her to live as a nun under the rule of the tertiary order of St. Dominic.

At what epoch the Prior of Holy Cross first became the confessor of the Infanta Isabella it is not now possible to ascertain. Jaime Bleda tells us that in the fulfilment of this office he had extracted from her, during her youth at the Court of her brother King Henry IV, a promise that should she ever come to the throne she would devote her life to the extirpation of heresy from her realm.[60]

This may be dismissed as one of those popular fictions that arise concerning the intimate affairs of princes, for it cannot be said that it is borne out by the circumstances under consideration.

Isabella's reluctance to proceed to extreme—or even vigorous—measures against those of her subjects accused of Judaizing is admitted by every serious student of her reign, however opinions may vary as to the motives that swayed her in this course.

There remains, however, out of Bleda's anecdote, the fact that Torquemada had been Isabella's confessor in early years—which in itself bears out the statement that the Dominican had achieved distinction. It follows by virtue of his having occupied this office that he must have acquired over the mind of a woman so devout a considerable ascendancy where matters connected with the Faith were concerned.

This influence he came now to exert.

To support it he brought an indubitable sincerity and disinterestedness of motives; he brought a reputation for sanctity derived from the rigid purity of his life and the stern asceticism which he practised—a reputation which could not fail to act upon the imagination of a woman of Isabella's pious temperament; and, finally, he brought the dominant, masterful personality and the burning eloquence that were his own.

When all this is taken into account it is not surprising that the Queen's resistance, weakened already by the onslaughts of Ojeda and his associates, the King and the papal legate, should at last have broken down; and that under the compelling persuasion of the Prior of Holy Cross she should reluctantly have consented to the establishment of the Holy Office in her dominions.

Thus it befell that by order of the Catholic Sovereigns their Orator at the Pontifical Court, D. Francisco de Santillana, applied to Sixtus IV for a bull that should empower Ferdinand and Isabella to set up the tribunal of the Inquisition in Castile, to enable them—as Bernaldez puts it—to proceed to the extirpation of heresy "by the way of fire"—*por via del fuego*.

This bull was duly granted under date of November 7, 1478.

It gave the Sovereigns the faculty of electing three bishops or archbishops or other God-fearing and upright priests, regular or secular, of over forty years of age, who must be masters or bachelors of divinity and doctors or licentiates of canon law, to make inquisition throughout the kingdom against heretics, apostates, and their abettors.

His Holiness accorded to the men so elected the requisite jurisdiction to proceed according to law and custom, and he further empowered the Sovereigns to annul such nominations as they might make and to replace their nominees as they saw fit.[61]

The Sovereigns were in Cordova when the bull reached them in the following month of December. But they did not at once proceed to act upon it. Before doing so, Isabella made one last effort to repress the Judaizing and apostatizing movement by the gentler measures concerted with the Cardinal of Spain in 1477.

To the task of continuing with increased vigour the teachings of the "catechism" drawn up by Mendoza she now appointed Diego Alonso de Solis, Bishop of Cadiz, D. Diego de Merlo, Coadjutor of Seville, and Alonso de Ojeda, to whom these royal orders must have been a fresh source of disappointment and chagrin.

Torquemada, we must assume, had withdrawn once more to his convent of Segovia, and perhaps the removal of his stern influence enabled the Queen to make this last effort to avoid the course to which he had all but constrained her.

Having concluded these arrangements, the Sovereigns repaired to Toledo. There, in the spring of the year 1480, the Cortes assembled to make oath of fealty to the infant Prince of Asturias to whom Isabella had given birth in June of 1478. Whilst this oath was the chief motive of the assembly, it was by no means the only business with which it had to deal. Many other matters received attention; amongst them the necessity for remedying the evils arising out of the commerce between Christians and Jews was seriously considered.

It was decreed that the old laws concerning the Jews, which lately had been falling into partial desuetude, should be re-enforced, particularly those which prescribed that all Jews should wear the distinguishing badge of the circlet of red cloth on the shoulders of their gabardines; that they should keep strictly to their Juderias, always retiring to these at nightfall; that walls to enclose these Juderias should be erected wherever they might still be wanting, and that no Jew should practise as a doctor, surgeon, apothecary, or innkeeper.

Beyond that, however, the Cortes did not go; and the institution of the Inquisition to deal with Judaizers was not so much as mentioned, which circumstance Llorente accepts as a further proof of the Queen's antipathy to the Holy Office.

Coming at a time when the Jews were once more beginning to taste the sweets of freedom, there can be little doubt that these provisions, which thrust them back into bondage and ignominy, must have been extremely galling to them. It is possible that these measures against the men of his race spurred a New-Christian to the rash step of publishing a pamphlet in which he criticized and censured the royal action in the matter. Carried away by his feelings, the writer—intentionally or not—fell into heresy in the course of his writings, to which the Jeronymite monk, Hernando de Talavera, published a reply.

Rodrigo[62] assumes that this heretical pamphlet put an end to the Queen's patience. It may very well have been the case, or at least it may have afforded Ferdinand and the others who desired the Inquisition a final argument whereby to overcome what reluctance still lingered with her.

Be that as it may, it was very soon after this—September 27, 1480—that the Sovereigns, who at the time were at Medina del Campo, acted at last upon the papal bull which had now been in their hands for nearly two years, and delegated their faculty of giving inquisitors to Castile to the Cardinal of Spain and Fr. Tomás de Torquemada.

Mendoza and Torquemada proceeded at once to carry out the task entrusted to them, and appointed as inquisitors of the faith for Seville—where Judaizing was represented to be most flagrant—the Dominican friars Juan de San Martino and Miguel Morillo. The latter was the Provincial of the Dominicans of Aragon, and was already a person of experience in such matters, having acted as inquisitor in Rousillon. To assist them in the discharge of their office, the secular priest Juan Ruiz de Medina, a doctor of canon law, and Juan Lopez de Barco, one of the Queen's chaplains, were appointed, the former to the position of assessor, the latter to that of fiscal.

It is necessary, in view of the much that has been written, and although the danger be incurred of labouring the point, to examine more closely the attitude of the Sovereigns towards the tribunal which they now sanctioned.

Isabella's zeal, both pious and political, urged her, as has been said, to proceed in such a way as should set a term to the unrest arising out of the public feeling against Judaizers and apostatizing Moriscoes (baptized Moors). Ferdinand not only shared her feelings, but pious zeal in him went to the lengths of bigotry, and he aimed essentially at a political unity that should be inseparably allied and interwoven with religious unity.

Isabella would have laboured slowly, preferring, even at the sacrifice of time, to achieve her ends by gentle means and the exercise of that patience which was so very necessary if good results were to be obtained. Ferdinand, perhaps less pitiful, perhaps—to do him full justice—less hopeful of the power of argument and indoctrination, lending an ear to the priestly assertion "contra negantes veritatis nulla est disputatio," would have proceeded at once to the introduction into Castile of the stern repressive measures already being exerted in his native Aragon.

On the score of their different attitudes the Sovereigns might have found themselves in conflict, but that in this matter they had a ground of common interest. Both were agreed that in no case should Spain be brought under the ecclesiastical sway which the establishment of the usual form of Inquisition must set up. If this were to be—as usual hitherto—under pontifical control, its officers would be appointed by the Pope, or, vicariously, by the Dominican provincials, and a proportion of the confiscations consequent upon conviction would be gathered into the pontifical coffers.

For all his bigotry and his desire to see the Holy Office instituted in Castile, Ferdinand was as averse as Isabella to its introduction in a form that must restore the clerical usurpations they had been at such pains to repress.

If Isabella admitted the Inquisition as a last means of quelling the disturbing elements in her kingdom, it must be an Inquisition on lines entirely different from those which hitherto had obtained elsewhere. The appointment of its officers must no more rest with the Pope than the bestowal of Spanish benefices. It must be the prerogative of the Sovereigns themselves, and it must carry with it the power to depose and replace, where necessary, such inquisitors as they might appoint. Further, Rome must have no share in the property confiscated from Spanish subjects, the disposal of this being entirely controlled by the Sovereigns.

It has been argued that here was the cause of all Isabella's hesitancy: that greed and statecraft were the mainsprings of her conduct in the matter, and that humanitarian considerations had no part in it; that the bull had been applied for earlier than has been generally supposed, and that the delay had resulted from the Pope's disinclination to grant any such terms as were demanded.

The latter statement may not be without foundation. But to say deliberately that no humanitarian considerations governed the Queen's conduct is to say a great deal more than the circumstances warrant. To establish this hypothesis it would be necessary to advance some adequate reason for her reluctance to act upon the bull when once it was in her hands. For the bull of November 1478 conceded all that the Sovereigns demanded, all that they desired. Yet Isabella allowed nearly two years to pass before proceeding to exercise the faculties conferred by it, and during that time Cardinal Mendoza and his co-operators diligently pursued the work of effecting conversions by means of his "catechism."

The conclusion that this was dictated by humane considerations on the part of the Queen is the only one that appears reasonable, nor is any alternative put forward to account for the delay of nearly two years.

When the Cardinal of Spain and the Prior of Holy Cross, acting jointly on behalf of the Sovereigns, appointed the first inquisitors for Castile, they instructed these to set up a tribunal in Seville, which of all the cities of Spain was the one where Judaizing was alleged to be most flagrantly conducted.[63]

The Sovereigns issued on October 9 a command to all loyal subjects to afford the two inquisitors every assistance they might require on their journey to Seville and all facilities there for carrying out their mission.

The subjects, however, were so little loyal on this occasion that upon the arrival of the inquisitors at Seville, these found a reception of all solemnity awaiting them and every respect accorded to them, but no assistance. To such an extent was this withheld that they found it quite impossible to set about the business upon which they came. They complained of this state of things to the King, and as a result he sent special orders on December 27 to the Coadjutor of Seville and the civil authorities of the district, commanding them to lend the inquisitors every support.

In consequence of this they were at last enabled to establish their court and proceed to the business upon which they came.[64]

The very rumour of their approach had filled the New-Christians with anxiety, and a glimpse of the gloomy funereal pageant—the white-robed, black-hooded inquisitors, with their attendant familiars and barefoot friars, the procession headed by a Dominican carrying the white cross—on its way to the Convent of St. Paul, where they took up their quarters, was enough to put to flight some thousands of those who had cause to fear that they might become the objects of the attention of that fearful court.

These fugitives sought refuge in the feudal lordships of the Duke of Medina Sidonia, of the formidable Rodrigo Ponce de Leon, Marquis of Cadiz, and of the Count of Arcos.

But in all ages it had been the way of the Inquisition not only to suspect readily, but to allow suspicion to usurp the place that elsewhere is reserved for proof. And so they proceeded to construe into evidence of guilt this flight of the timorous, as is shown by the edict they published on January 2 of 1481.

In this—having set forth their appointment by the Sovereigns, and the terms of the bull under which such appointment had been made—they announced that, inasmuch as it had come to their knowledge that many persons had departed out of Seville in fear of prosecution upon grounds of heretical pravity, they commanded the Marquess of Cadiz, the Count of Arcos, and the other nobles of the Kingdom of Castile, that within fifteen days of the publication of this edict they should make an exact account of the persons of both sexes that had sought refuge in their lordships or jurisdictions; that they should arrest all these and bring them safely to the prison of the Inquisition in Seville, confiscating their property and placing this together with an inventory in the hands of some person of trust, to be held by them at the disposal of the inquisitors; that none should dare to shelter any fugitive, but comply exactly with the terms of this edict under pain of greater excommunication and the other penalties by law established against abettors of heretics, amongst which penalties was that of the annulment of their dignities and offices, their subjects and vassals being absolved of all vassalage and subjection; and the inquisitors reserved to themselves and their superiors the power of absolution from the ecclesiastical censure incurred by all who might fail to obey the terms of this edict.

CHAPTER VIII
THE HOLY OFFICE IN SEVILLE

The stern purpose of the inquisitors and the severity with which they intended to proceed were plainly revealed by that edict of January 2, 1481. The harsh injustice that lay in its call upon the authorities to arrest men and women merely because they had departed from Seville before departure was in any way forbidden is typical of the flagrantly arbitrary methods of the Inquisition. That it should have struck terror into the New-Christians who had remained in Seville, and that it should have moved them to take measures to protect themselves against a court in which justice seemed little likely to be observed, and to whose cruel mercies the most innocent might find himself exposed at any moment, is not surprising—particularly when it is considered how great was the number of New-Christians who occupied positions of eminence in Seville.

A group of these prominent citizens assembled at the invitation of Diego de Susan, one of the wealthiest and most influential men of Seville, whose fortune was estimated at ten million maravedis. They came together to consider what measures should be taken for the defence of themselves, their persons and property, from the unscrupulous activities of this tribunal, and they determined that if necessary they would resort to force.

Among those who entered into this conspiracy were some ecclesiastics, and several who held office under the Crown, such as the Governor of Triana, Juan Fernandez Abolafio, the Captain of Justice and farmer of the royal customs, his brother Fernandez the licentiate, Bartolomé Torralba, and the wealthy and well-connected Manuel Sauli.

Susan addressed them. He reminded them that they were the principal citizens of Seville, that they were wealthy not only in property but in the good-will of the people, and that it but required resolution and solidarity on their part to enable them to prevail against the inquisitors in the event of these friars making any attempt upon them.

All concurring, it was concerted that each of the conspirators should engage himself to provide a proportion of the men, arms, and money and what else might be necessary for their purpose.

But Susan to his undoing had a daughter. This girl, whose beauty was so extraordinary that she was surnamed *la hermosa fembra*, had taken a Castilian lover. What motives may have actuated her, what part the lover may have played in these, does not transpire. All that is known is that she betrayed the conspiracy to the inquisitors—"impiously violating the natural laws engraved by God's finger upon the human heart."

Susan and his unfortunate confederates were seized as a consequence of that infamous delation; they were lodged in the cells of the Convent of St. Paul, which meanwhile did duty as a prison, and brought to trial before the Court of the Holy Office sitting in the convent.[65]

They were tried for heresy and apostasy, of course; since upon no other grounds was it possible for the Holy Office to deal with them. It is unfortunate that Llorente should have unearthed no record of this trial—one of the first held by the Inquisition in Castile—and that nothing should be known of what took place beyond the fact that Susan, Sauli, Bartolomé Torralba, and the brothers Fernandez were found guilty of the alleged offence of apostasy and were delivered up to the secular arm for punishment.

Garcia Rodrigo has devoted a couple of pages of his "Historia Verdadera" to an elaborate piece of fiction in which he asserts that these men were persistent in their error in spite of the strenuous efforts made to save them. He invests the fanatical Ojeda with the character of an angel of mercy, and represents him hovering round the condemned, exhorting them, almost with tears, to abjure their error, and he assures us that although the Dominican persevered in his charitable efforts up to the last moment, all was vain.

There is not a grain of evidence to support the statement, nor does Garcia Rodrigo pretend to advance any. As a matter of fact, Bernaldez, the only available authority who mentions Susan's end, tells us specifically that he died a Christian. And when it is considered that Bernaldez is an ardent admirer and champion of the Inquisition, such a pronouncement from his pen is sufficient to convict the inquisitors Morillo and San Martin of having proceeded in a manner that was vindictive and *ultra vires*. For at this epoch it was not yet decreed that those who had relapsed (*relapsos*) should suffer capital punishment unless they persisted in their apostasy—as Rodrigo, obviously for the purpose of justifying the inquisitors, unwarrantably asserts did Susan and his confederates.

Llorente considers the blood-lust of the inquisitors established by these merciless convictions, urging that it is incredible that all the prisoners should have refused to recant and to submit themselves to penance—even assuming that they were actually guilty of apostasy as alleged. For when all is considered it must remain extremely doubtful whether they had Judaized at all, and it is not improbable—from what we see of the spirit that actuated the inquisitors—that Morillo and San Martin may have construed the action of those men into an offence against the Faith for the purpose of bringing them within the jurisdiction of the Holy Office.

They were condemned to be the chief actors in the first Auto de Fé that was held in Seville. This took place on February 6.[66]

There was about this Auto comparatively little of that pomp and ceremonial, that ghastly theatricality that was presently to distinguish these proceedings. But the essentials were already present.

Susan and his fellows were led forth barefoot, in the ignominious, yellow penitential sack, a candle in the hand of each. Hemmed about by halberdiers, they were paraded through the streets of a city in which they had won the goodwill and respect of all, to be gazed upon by a people whose eyes must have been filled with horror and dismay. To head the procession went a black-robed Dominican holding aloft the green cross of the Inquisition, now swathed in a veil of crape; behind him, walking two by two, came the familiars of the Holy Office, members of the Confraternity of St. Peter the Martyr; next followed the doomed men amid their guards; and last came the inquisitors with their attendants and a considerable body of Dominicans from the Convent of St. Paul, headed by their prior, the fanatical Ojeda.

The procession headed for the Cathedral, where the sufferers were taken to hear Mass and forced to listen to a sermon framed for the occasion which was preached by Ojeda, and must have increased the exquisite torment of their protracted agony. Thence they were conducted—once more processionally—out of the city to the meadows of Tablada. There they were attached to the stakes that had been erected, fire was set to the faggots, and thus they perished miserably, to the greater honour and glory of the Catholic Apostolic Church.[67]

Ojeda may have looked with satisfaction upon that holocaust, upon those cruel flames which more than any man in Spain he had been instrumental in kindling, and which being kindled would continue to cast their lurid glow over that fair land for close upon four centuries. It was the first burning that Ojeda witnessed, and it was the last. His own hour was at hand. His mission, whatever ends it had to serve in the eternal scheme of things, was completed there on the meadows of Tablada, and he might now depart. A few days later he lay dead, stricken down by the plague that was ravaging the south of Spain, and sought him out for one of its first victims.

And from the pulpits of Seville the Dominicans thundered forth declarations that this pestilence was a visitation of God upon an unfaithful city. They never paused to consider that if that were indeed the case either God's aim must be singularly untrue since the shafts of His wrath overtook such faithful servants as Ojeda, or else....

But an incapacity to conduct its reasonings to a logical conclusion, and an utter want of any sense of proportion, are the main factors in all fanaticism.

Lest they should themselves be stricken by these bolts of pestilence launched against the unfaithful, behold next the inquisitors scuttling out of Seville!

They go in quest of more salubrious districts, and, presumably upon the assumption that these—since they remain healthy—are escaping divine attention, the Dominicans zealously proceed to light their fires that they may repair this heavenly oversight.[68]

But that *villegiatura* of theirs did not take place until they had transacted a deal more of their horrible business in Seville. Great had been the results of the edict of January 2. The nobles, not daring to run the risk of the threatened ecclesiastical censure, proceeded to effect the arrests demanded, and gangs of pinioned captives were brought daily into the city from the surrounding country districts where they had sought shelter. And in the city itself the familiars of the Holy Office were busily effecting the capture of suspects and of those against whom, either out of bigotry or malice, delations had been made.

So numerous were the arrests that by the middle of the month of January already the capacity of the Convent of St. Paul was strained to its utmost, and the inquisitors were compelled to remove themselves, their tribunal and their prison to the ampler quarters of the Castle of Triana, accorded to them by the Sovereigns in response to their request for it.[69]

The edict of January 2 was soon succeeded by a second one, known as the "Edict of Grace." This exhorted all who were guilty of apostasy to come forward voluntarily within a term appointed, to confess their sins and be reconciled to the Church. It assured them that if they did this with real contrition and a firm purpose of amendment, they should receive absolution and suffer no confiscation of property. And it concluded with a warning that if they allowed the term of grace to expire without taking advantage of it, and they should afterwards be accused by others, they would be prosecuted with the utmost rigour of the law.

Amador de los Rios is of opinion that Cardinal Mendoza was "instrumental" in having this edict published, in which case it would hardly be too much to assume that he was the instrument of Isabella in the matter. Nor is it too much to assume that the inspiration was purely merciful, and that there was no thought in the mind of either Queen or Cardinal of the edict's being turned, as it was, to treacherous account.

The response was immediate. It is estimated that not less than 20,000 *conversos* who had been guilty of Judaizing came forward to avail themselves of its promise of amnesty and to secure absolution for their infidelity to the religion they had embraced. They discovered to their horror that they had walked into a trap as cruel as any that smooth-faced, benign-voiced priestcraft had ever devised.

The inquisitors had thought well to saddle the promised absolution and immunity from punishment with a condition which they had not published, a condition which they had secretly reserved to spring it now upon these self-convicted apostates at their mercy. They pointed out with infernal subtlety that the edict provided that the contrition of the self-accused must be sincere, and that of this sincerity the penitents must give the only proof possible by disclosing the names of all Judaizers known to them.

The demand was an infamy; for not even under the seal of private confession is a priest authorized to impose upon a penitent as a condition of absolution that he shall divulge the name even of an accomplice or a partner in guilt. Yet here it was demanded of these that they should go much further, and denounce such sinners as they knew; and the demand was framed in such specious terms—as the only proof they could offer of the sincerity of their own contrition—that none dared have taxed the inquisitors with malpractice or with subverting the ends and purpose of this edict they had been forced to publish.

The wretched apostates found themselves between the sword and the wall. Either they must perpetrate the infamy of betraying those of their race whom they knew to be Judaizers, or they must submit not only to the cruel death by fire, but to the destitution of their children as a consequence of the confiscation of their property. Most of them gave way, and purchased their reconciliation at the price of betrayal. And there were men like Bernaldez, the parish priest of Palacios, who applauded this procedure of the Holy Office. "A very glorious thing" (*muy hazañosa cosa*), he exclaims, "was the reconciliation of these people, as thus by their confessions were discovered all that were Judaizers, and in Seville knowledge was obtained of Judaizers in Toledo, Cordova, and Burgos."[70]

Upon the expiry of the term of grace a further edict was published by Morillo and San Martin, in which they now commanded, under pain of mortal sin and greater excommunication, with its attendant penalties, the discovery of all persons known to be engaged in Judaizing practices.

And that there should be no excuse offered by any on the score of ignorance of such practices, these were published in thirty-seven articles appended to the edict, articles whose malign comprehensiveness left no man secure.

They set forth the following signs by which New-Christians guilty of Judaizing might be recognized:

> I. Any who await the Messiah, or say that he has not yet come, and that he will come to lead them out of captivity into the promised land.

II. Any who after baptism have returned expressly to the Mosaic faith.

III. Any who declare that the law of Moses is as good as that of Jesus Christ and as efficient for salvation.

IV. Any who keep the Sabbath in honour of the law of Moses—of which the proof is afforded by their assuming clean shirts and more decent garments than on other days, and clean covers on the table, as well as by their refraining from lighting fires and from engaging in all work from Friday evening.

V. Any who strip the tallow or fat from meats that they are to eat and purify it by washing in water, bleeding it, or extracting the glandule from the leg of lambs or other animals slaughtered for food.

VI. Any who cut the throats of animals or poultry that are intended for food, first testing the knife on their finger-nail, covering the blood with earth, and uttering certain words that are customary among Jews.

VII. Any who eat meat in Lent and on other days on which it is forbidden by Holy Church.

VIII. Any who keep the great fast of the Jews known by different names, or the fast of *Chiphurim* or *Quipur* in the tenth Hebrew month—whereof the proof shall be their having gone barefoot during the period of the said fast, as is the custom of the Jews, their having said Jewish prayers, or asked pardon one of another, or fathers having laid hands upon the heads of their children without making the sign of the Cross or saying anything but "By God and by me be thou blessed."

IX and X. Any who keep the fast of Queen Esther, which is observed by the Jews in memory and imitation of what they did in captivity in the reign of Ahasuerus, or the fast of *Rebeaso.*

XI. Any who shall keep other fasts peculiar to the Jews, such as those of Monday and Thursday, of which the proof shall be: their not eating on such days until after the appearance of the first evening star; their having abstained from meat; their having washed on the previous day or cut their nails or the points of their hair, keeping or burning these; their reciting certain Jewish prayers, raising or lowering their heads with their faces to the wall, after washing their hands in water or in earth; their dressing themselves in sackcloth and girding themselves with cords or strips of leather.

XII, XIII, and XIV concern any who keep the Paschal seasons; which is to be discovered by their setting up green boughs, inviting to table and sending presents of comestibles, and the keeping of the feast of candles.

XV to XIX concern any who observe Hebrew table-customs: whether they bless their viands according to the Jewish custom, whether they drink "lawful" wine—*i.e.* wine that has been pressed by Jews—and eat meat that has been slaughtered by Jews.

XX. Any who recite the Psalms of David without concluding with the versicle "Gloria Patri et Filio et Spiritu Sancto."

XXI. Any woman who abstains from going to church for forty days after delivery of child, out of reverence for the law of Moses.

XXII to XXVI concern any who circumcise their children, give them Hebrew names, or after baptism cause their heads to be shaven where anointed with the sacred oil, or any who cause their children to be washed on the seventh day after birth in a basin in which, in addition to the water, they have placed gold and silver, pearls, wheat, barley, and other things.

XXVII. Any who are married in the Jewish manner.

XXVIII. Any who hold the *Ruaya*—which is a valedictory supper before setting out upon a long journey.

XXIX and XXX. Any who carry Hebrew relics or make burnt-offerings of bread.

XXXI. Any who *in articulo mortis* have turned or been turned with their faces to the wall to die in this attitude.

XXXII. Any who wash a corpse in warm water or shave it according to the Jewish custom, and otherwise dress it for the grave as is prescribed by the Mosaic law.

XXXIII to XXXVI concern Jewish expressions of mourning, such as the abstaining from meat, the spilling of water from the jars in the dwelling of the deceased, etc.

XXXVII. Any who bury their dead in virgin soil or in a Jewish cemetery.[71]

Reference has already been made to the inherent character of many Jewish customs, which even the most sincere of New-Christians retained despite themselves; these customs, being racial rather than religious, were very far from signifying Judaic apostasy, since they contained nothing that was directly opposed to the Christian teaching. In the list published by the Seville inquisitors it will be seen that such customs were deliberately included as evidences of apostasy.

Consider Articles IV, V, and VII, concerning the assumption of clean linen on Saturdays and the stripping of fat from beef and mutton, which nowise offend against the Christian faith, and might well be the perpetuation of customs acquired before baptism was received.

Even more flagrant is Article XXXI, which lays it down as evidence of Judaizing that a man shall turn his face to the wall when at the point of death; but most flagrant of all is Article XXVIII, concerning the valedictory meal partaken of before setting out upon a journey, for it is a custom that at all times has been as much in vogue among Christians as among men of any other religion.

Clearly not a New-Christian in Seville was safe from the delations of the malevolent, since such ridiculously slight grounds of suspicion were set forth by the tribunal. So extravagant and absurd are some of these articles that one is forced to agree with Llorente, that in formulating them the inquisitors proceeded with deliberate malice. He contends that deliberately they cast a wide net that by their heavy draught they should satisfy the Queen that she had heard no more than the truth as to the extent to which Judaizing was rampant in Castile, and the urgent need there was for the introduction of the Inquisition.

Whether in this they proceeded according to instructions received from Torquemada or Ojeda does not transpire, but there can be little doubt that the results obtained must have been in accordance with the wishes of both, since they justified to the Queen the representations these friars had so insistently made to her.

And the system of espionage which the inquisitors set up to increase their haul of victims was as sly and cunning as anything in the history of spying. Conceive the astuteness of the friar who climbed to the roof of the Convent of St. Paul on Saturday mornings to observe and note the houses of New-

Christians from whose chimneys no smoke was to be seen issuing, that he might lay the information thus obtained before the tribunal, which would proceed to arrest the inhabitants upon a strong suspicion that they were Judaizers who would not desecrate the Sabbath by lighting fires.[72]

"What," asks Llorente, "could be expected of a tribunal that began in this way?" And he at once supplies the answer: "That which happened—neither more nor less."

With the methods of procedure that obtained in the trials conducted by these inquisitors we need not just now concern ourselves. For the moment it is enough to say that to the vices inherent in such a judicial system must be added, in the case of the first inquisitors of Seville, a zeal—not only to convict, but actually to be burning heretics—so ferociously excessive as to proclaim that they were gratifying their hatred of these Jews.

This upon the word of that sober chronicler Pulgar, who, whilst in general terms approving the introduction of the Inquisition, as has been seen, denounces in the following particular terms the practices of Morillo and San Martin: "In the manner in which they conducted their proceedings they showed that they held those people in hatred."[73]

The Auto of February 6 was followed by another on March 26, at which seventeen victims were burnt on the fields of Tablada. And now that the fires were lighted, the inquisitors saw to it that they were well supplied with human fuel. Burnings followed one another at such a rate that by the month of November—upon the word of Llorente—298 condemned had been sent to the flames in the town of Seville alone, whilst 79 others by reconciling themselves to the Church secured the commutation of their sentence to one of perpetual imprisonment.

Mariana, the historian who gave thanks to God for the introduction of the Inquisition into Castile, informs us with flagrant calm that the number of Judaizers burnt in the Archbishopric during that year 1481 amounted to 8,000, whilst some 17,000 were submitted to penance.

In addition to those burnt alive, many who had fled the country were burnt in effigy, having been tried and found guilty during an absence described as contumacious. And similarly the court went through the horrible farce of sitting in judgment upon many who were dead, and, having convicted them, it dug up their bones and flung these to the flames.

Such was the prodigious activity of the Holy Office, and to such an extent did its holocausts promise to continue, that the Governor of Seville ordered the erection on the fields of Tablada of a permanent platform of stone of vast proportions known as the Quemadero, or Burning-place. It was adorned by figures of the four Prophets. At each of its four corners towered one of these colossal statues of plaster, and Llorente tells us that they were not merely for ornament. He says that they were hollow and so contrived that a condemned person might be placed in each and so die by slow fire.[74]

This Quemadero remained standing, a monument to religious intolerance and fanatical cruelty, until the soldiers of Napoleon demolished it in the nineteenth century.[75]

So ruthless were Morillo and San Martin, and so negligent of equity or even the observance of the ordinary rules of judicial procedure, that in the end we find the Pope himself—in January of 1482—addressing a letter of protest to the Sovereigns.

The first edict commanding the nobles to arrest all those who had fled from Seville had had the effect of driving many of these fugitive New-Christians farther afield in their quest for safety. Some had escaped into Portugal, others had crossed the Mediterranean and sought shelter in Morocco, whilst others still had taken their courage in both hands and sought sanctuary in Rome itself, at the very feet of the Pontiff. Other fugitives followed presently, when the tribunal had already inaugurated its terrible work; and these came clamouring their grievances and protesting that in spite of their innocence they dared no longer remain in a State where no New-Christian was safe from the hatred and injustice shown by the inquisitors to men of their race. Therefore they were driven to seek from Christ's Vicar the protection to which all Christians and true Catholics were entitled at his hands.

Photo by Lacoste.

FERDINAND OF ARAGON AND THE INFANTE DON JUAN.
From the Painting in the Prado Gallery attributed to Miguel Zittoz.

They informed the Pontiff of the methods that were being pursued; they set forth how the inquisitors in their eagerness to secure convictions proceeded entirely upon their own initiative and without the concurrence of the assessor and diocesan ordinary, as had been prescribed; how they were departing from all legal form, imprisoning unjustly, torturing cruelly and unduly, and falsely stigmatizing innocent men as formal heretics, thereafter delivering them to the secular arm for punishment, in addition to confiscating their property so that their children were left in want and under the brand of infamy.

The Pope gave ear to these plaints, convinced himself of their truth, and made his protest to Ferdinand and Isabella. He announced in his brief that he would have deprived the inquisitors of their office but that he was restrained by consideration for the Sovereigns who had appointed them; nevertheless, he was sending them a brief of admonition, and should they again give cause for complaint he would be constrained to depose them. In the meantime he revoked the faculty given the Sovereigns of appointing inquisitors, protesting that when conceding this he had not sufficiently considered that already there were inquisitors in the Sovereigns' dominions and that the General of the Dominicans and the Spanish provincials of that order had the right to make such appointments. The bull that he had granted was therefore in opposition to that right, and would never have been granted had the matter been sufficiently considered.[76]

CHAPTER IX
THE SUPREME COUNCIL

The Sovereigns appear to have submitted without protest to this papal interference and to the revocation of the faculty bestowed upon them of nominating the inquisitors in their kingdom. This submission was hardly to have been expected from their earlier attitude, but there are two reasons, either or both of which may possibly account for it.

It will be remembered that there was a considerable number of New-Christians about the Court and in immediate attendance upon the Queen, one of whom was her secretary Pulgar. What view Pulgar took of the Seville proceedings we know, and it is not too much to assume that his view was the view of all Christians of Jewish extraction. These New-Christians and others may very well have urged upon the notice of the Sovereigns the cruelties and injustices that were being practised, drawing their attention to the decree that made innocent children suffer for the offences of which their parents had been convicted—a decree which, hideous enough when the parents were actually guilty, became unspeakably hideous when that guilt was no more than presumed.

In view of such representations the Sovereigns may have found the papal rebuke unanswerable and the Pope's action justified.

Then, again, they may have taken into consideration the projected war upon Granada, the last province of the peninsula remaining in Moorish hands. Funds were urgently required for this campaign, and the confiscations that were daily being effected by the Holy Office were rapidly supplying these—for the early victims of the Inquisition, as we know, were persons of great wealth and distinction.[77]

Now the papal brief, whilst it cancelled the royal prerogative of appointing inquisitors, did not attempt to divert the course of this stream of confiscated property, nor, indeed, made any mention of the matter. So that they may have hesitated to oppose themselves to measures which they recognized as just and which continued to supply them with the means for what they looked upon as a righteous crusade.

Bigotry and acquisitiveness were again joining forces, and, united, they must prove, as ever, irresistible.

But on February 11, 1482, the Roman Curia issued another brief addressed to the Sovereigns, wherein—entirely ignoring what already had been written—it was announced that the General of the Dominicans, Fr. Alonso de Cebrian, having represented to the Pope the need to multiply the number of inquisitors in Spain, his Holiness had resolved to appoint the said Fr.

Alonso and seven other Dominicans to conduct the affairs of the Holy Office in that kingdom, commanding them to exercise their ministry in conjunction with the diocesan ordinary and in accordance with the terms set forth in the briefs that were being addressed to them.[78]

One of the eight Dominicans mentioned by the Pope was Fr. Tomás de Torquemada, who by now was become confessor to the King and to the Cardinal of Spain.

This brief, following so rapidly upon that which revoked the Sovereigns' power, may have caused Ferdinand and Isabella to look upon it as the second move in an intrigue whose aim was to strengthen the ecclesiastical arm in Spain to the detriment of the royal authority.

On April 17 Sixtus sent the promised instructions to the inquisitors of Aragon, Cataluña, Valencia, and Mallorca. These indicated a procedure in matters of faith so contrary to common law, that no sooner did the inquisitors attempt to carry them into execution than there was an uproar which afforded Ferdinand grounds upon which to indite a protest to the Holy Father.

A reply came in the following October. Sixtus wrote that the briefs of last April had been drawn up after conference with several members of the Sacred College; that these cardinals were now absent from Rome, but that on their return the matter should be further considered. Meanwhile, however, in view of the results that had attended those briefs, he was informing the inquisitors that they were exempt from acting upon the terms set forth in them and instructing them to proceed, as formerly, in co-operation with the diocesan ordinaries.

But in the meantime, for all the Pope's protest against the excessive severity of the Seville tribunal, this severity continued so undiminished, not only in Seville but also in the districts under the jurisdiction of other inquisitors, that there was a continuous emigration from Spain of the wealthy New-Christian families. Many of these repaired to Rome to appeal to the Pontifical Courts and to procure there an absolution which should accord them immunity from the Spanish tribunals of the Holy Office.

But even when this absolution was procured a large number of these emigrants never thought of returning to Spain, considering it wiser to settle in a country in which they were in less danger of persecution.

Although it is certain that the Sovereigns can have had no prevision of what actually was to happen as a consequence—though not in their own day, nor for some time afterwards—although they may have been very far from foreseeing that by driving out these energetic, industrious, intelligent men they were depriving the country of the financially able, wealth-producing element of the community—still they did undoubtedly perceive what was immediately before them; and they began to fear the possibility of their country's being drained of its present wealth if these emigrations were to continue.

So Isabella wrote to the Pope entreating him to establish a court of appeal in Spain, and thus dispose that proceedings started within the kingdom could there be carried to their conclusion without the need for these appeals to Rome. To this the Pope replied in affectionate terms on February 23, 1483, promising to give the matter every consideration.[79]

Shortly thereafter he held a conference of the Spanish Cardinals, the principal of whom in wealth, importance, and distinction was Roderigo Borgia, Cardinal of Valencia. At this conference several provisions were agreed upon, and these were embodied in the briefs dispatched from the Vatican on May 25 following.

The first of these was to the Sovereigns. It contained a gracious assent to their petition, and exhorted them to be zealous in this matter of the Faith, reminding them that Jehu had consolidated his kingdom by the destruction of idolatry, and that the Sovereigns would meet with the same good fortune, as already God was giving them many victories over the Moors to reward their piety and the purity of their faith.

The second was to Iñigo Manrique, Archbishop of Seville (having succeeded in this see to the Cardinal of Spain, who was now Archbishop of Toledo), appointing him judge of appeal in *Causas de Fé*.

The remaining briefs were addressed to the Archbishop of Toledo and the other Spanish archbishops, commanding them, to the end that the functions of the Inquisition should be discharged with integrity, that in the event of there being in their ecclesiastical provinces any bishops who were of Jewish descent, they should suavely admonish these not to intervene in person in the proceedings of the Holy Office, but to allow themselves to be represented by their principal officials, provisors, and diocesan vicars-general—always provided that none of these was of Jewish blood.

This decree was natural enough, and there was some occasion for it, considering the number of Spanish families of Jewish consanguinity as a consequence of marriages between Christians and *conversos*—many of these marriages having been contracted between Castilians of good birth and the daughters of wealthy baptized Jews. It is a decree that entirely contradicts Pulgar's assertion that Torquemada was of Jewish extraction.

The appointment of Manrique as judge of appeal was a very brief one, nor did it work satisfactorily and accomplish what the Queen desired. In the following August came another papal brief, stating that, notwithstanding that appointment, fugitive New-Christians from the Archbishopric of Seville continued to arrive in Rome and to make their appeals to the Apostolic Courts, protesting that they dared not address these to the appointed tribunal in Seville, for fear of being treated with excessive rigour.

Many stated that, by virtue of the ban against them for having left the city, they were fearful of being flung into prison unheard. Many, again, had already been tried during their absence and burnt in effigy, and they were apprehensive that if they returned their appeals would be refused a hearing, and they would be sent at once to the flames in execution of the sentence already pronounced against them.

Therefore the Pope now ordered Manrique to admit to reconciliation all who might seek it, in despite of any judgment or sentence already passed upon them.

Had these commands prevailed, the destruction wrought by the Inquisition would have been considerably reduced, since none could have suffered but the persistent apostate. The brief, however, does not appear to have been even dispatched. No sooner was its merciful decree indited than it was regretted and retracted. Eleven days later Sixtus wrote to Ferdinand acquainting him with the terms of that brief which had been intended for Manrique, but explaining that these had not been sufficiently considered, and that, therefore, he was retaining it whilst fresh measures were deliberated.

The position must have been growing intolerable to the Sovereigns, for the Holy Office in Spain, directed in this fashion from Rome, was governed by unstable and ever-shifting elements that were eminently disturbing to the State—particularly now that the Inquisition was growing rapidly in importance. Therefore Isabella wrote again, imploring the Holy Father to give that institution a settled form. To this the Pope acceded, perhaps himself aware of the necessity for the thing requested. A head was necessary for the consolidated institution it was now proposed to form, and Frey Tomás de Torquemada, from what was known of his life, his character, and his ability, was judged to be the man to fill this important office. Accordingly he was recommended to Sixtus by the Sovereigns, and he received his appointment from the Pope, first as Grand Inquisitor for Castile, and soon after (by the bull of October 17, 1483) his jurisdiction was extended to include Aragon; so that he found himself at the head of the Holy Office in Spain, and invested with the fullest powers. It was his to elect, depose, and replace subaltern inquisitors at his will, and the jurisdiction of all those he appointed was subject to and dependent upon himself.[80]

Llorente says of him: "The result accredited the election. It seemed almost impossible that there should be another man so capable of executing the intentions of King Ferdinand to multiply confiscations, the intentions of the

Roman Curia to propagate its jurisdiction and pecuniary maxims, and the intentions of the projectors of the Inquisition and its Autos de Fé to inspire terror."[81]

With his elevation to that important position—a position whose importance his own energy and determination were to increase until his power in the land should almost rival that of the Sovereigns themselves—the Spanish Inquisition enters now upon a new phase. Under the jurisdiction and control of that stern-souled, mild-eyed ascetic, the entire character of the Holy Office is transformed.

Immediately upon his appointment he set about reconstituting it so that it should be in harmony with the wishes of the Sovereigns. To assist him he appointed as his assessors the jurisconsults Juan Gutierrez de Lachaves and Tristan de Medina, and he proceeded to establish four permanent tribunals: one in Seville, under Morillo and San Martin, whom he left undisturbed in their office, but subject to the new rules which he laid down for the transaction of affairs; one in Cordova, under Pedro Martinez de Barrio and Anton Ruiz Morales, with Fr. Martin de Caso as assessor; one in Jaen, under Juan Garcia de Cañas and Fr. Juan de Yarza; and one in Villa Real,[82] which shortly afterwards was transferred to Toledo, under Francisco Sanchez de la Fuente and Pedro Dias de Costana.

In addition to these he appointed other inquisitors who, without being attached to any permanent tribunal, were to proceed wherever he should direct them as occasion arose to set up temporary courts.

In Toledo, Valladolid, Avila, Segovia, and other cities there were inquisitors already of the Pope's appointing. Some of these failed to show the complete submission to his orders which Torquemada demanded, with the result that they were promptly deposed and their places filled by others whom he nominated. Those who manifested obedience to his rule he confirmed in their appointments, but usually he sent a nominee of his own to act in conjunction with them.

Torquemada himself remained at Court; for now that the Inquisition was established upon its new footing it became necessary that he should be in constant communication with the Sovereigns for whom he acted. Consultations were necessary on the score of the measures to be taken for the administration of what was rapidly become a corporation of great importance in the realm. From this it presently resulted that to the four royal councils already in existence for the conduct of the affairs of the kingdom, a fifth was added especially to deal with inquisitorial matters. Whether the suggestion emanated from the Sovereigns or from Torquemada, there are no means of ascertaining, nor does it greatly signify.

This Supreme Council of the Inquisition was established in 1484. It consisted of three royal councillors: Alonso Carillo, Bishop of Mazzara, Sancho Velasquez de Cuellar, and Poncio de Valencia, all doctors of laws, and of Torquemada's two assessors. To preside over this "Suprema"—as the council came to be called—Torquemada was appointed, thus enormously increasing the power and influence which already he wielded.

The three royal councillors had a definite vote in all matters that appertained to the jurisdiction of the Sovereigns; but in all matters of spiritual jurisdiction, which was vested entirely in the Grand Inquisitor by the papal bull, their votes were merely consultative—amounting to no more than an expression of opinion.

It was Torquemada's desire that his subordinates should act with absolute uniformity in the discharge of the duties entrusted to them, and that the courts of the Holy Office throughout Spain should one and all be identical in their methods of procedure, the instruments of his will and the expression of his conceptions. With this end in view he summoned the inquisitors by him appointed to the Tribunals of Seville, Cordova, Jaen, and Villa Real to confer with him and his assessors and the royal councillors.

The assembly took place in Seville on October 29, and its business was the formulation of the first instructions of Torquemada for the guidance of all inquisitors.

In the library of the British Museum there is a vellum-bound copy of the edition of this code, which was subsequently published at Madrid in 1576.[83] It contains, in addition to Torquemada's articles of 1484 and subsequent years, others added by his successors, and there are marginal notes giving the authorship of each. The work is partly printed, partly in manuscript, and a considerable number of pages remain in blank, that further instructions may be filled in as the need occurs. The printed matter is frequently underscored by the pen of one or another of the inquisitors through whose hands this copy passed during its active existence.

The twenty-eight articles compiled by Torquemada at the assembly of 1484, and constituting his first "Instructions for the Governance of the Holy Office," demand a chapter to themselves.

CHAPTER X
THE JURISPRUDENCE OF THE HOLY OFFICE—THE FIRST "INSTRUCTIONS" OF TORQUEMADA

The first manual for the use of inquisitors was probably written somewhere about 1320. It was the work of the Dominican friar Bernard Gui—"Practica Inquisitionis Heretice Pravitatis—Bernardo Guidonis, Ordinis Fratrum Predicatorum"—and it summarised the experience gathered during a hundred years by the inquisitors of Southern France.

It is divided into five parts. The first three are directly concerned with procedure, and the formulæ are given for every occasion—citation, arrest, pardon, commutation, and sentence—with the fullest particulars for the guidance of inquisitors. The fourth part treats of the powers vested in the tribunal of the Inquisition, and cites the authorities—*i.e.* the decrees of pontiffs and of councils. The fifth part surveys and defines the various heretical sects of Gui's day, gives particulars of the doctrines, rites, and ceremonies by which each one may be known, and lays down methods by which heretical guile may be circumvented in examination.

The work was used by French inquisitors in general and those of Toulouse in particular, and it is more than probable that it inspired Nicolaus Eymeric to compile his voluminous "Directorium Inquisitorum" towards the middle of the fourteenth century.

Nicolaus Eymeric was Grand Inquisitor of Aragon, and he prepared his directory, or manual of procedure, as a guide for his confrères in the business of prosecuting those guilty of heretical pravity.

The work circulated freely in its manuscript form, and it was one of the first to be printed in Barcelona upon the introduction of the printing-press, so that in Torquemada's day copies were widely diffused, and were in the hands of all inquisitors in the world.

The bulk of the "Directorium" is little more than a compilation. It is divided into three parts. The first lays down the chief Articles of the Christian Faith; the second is a collection of the decretals, bulls, and briefs of the popes upon the subject of heretics and heresies, and the decision of the various councils held to determine matters connected with heretics and their abettors, sorcerers, excommunicates, Jews and infidels; the third part, which is Eymeric's own contribution to the subject, deals with the manner in which trials should be conducted, and gives a detailed list of the offences that come under the jurisdiction of the Holy Office.

It may be well before proceeding further to give a résumé of the grounds upon which the Inquisition instituted proceedings, as set forth in the "Directorium."

All heretics in general are subject to the animadversions of the Holy Office; but there are, in addition, certain offenders who, whilst not exactly guilty of heresy, nevertheless render themselves justiciable by the Inquisition. These are:

BLASPHEMERS who in blaspheming say that which is contrary to the Christian Faith. Thus, he who says, "The season is so bad that God Himself could not give us good weather," sins upon a matter of faith.

SORCERERS AND DIVINERS, when in their sorceries they perform that which is in the nature of heresy—such as re-baptizing infants, burning incense to a skull, etc. But if they confine their sorceries to foretelling the future by chiromancy or palmistry, by drawing the short straw, or consulting the astrolabe, they are guilty of simple sorcery, and it is for the secular courts to prosecute them.

Amongst the latter are to be placed those who administer love-philtres to women.

DEVIL-WORSHIPPERS: Those who invoke devils. These are to be divided into three classes:

> (*a*) Those who worship the devil, sacrificing to him, prostrating themselves, singing prayers and fasting, burning incense or lighting candles in his honour.

> (*b*) Those who confine themselves to offering a *Dulie* or *Hyperdulie* cult to Satan, introducing the names of devils into the litanies.

> (*c*) Those who invoke the devil by tracing magic figures, placing an infant in a circle, using a sword, a bed, or a mirror, etc.

In general it is easy to recognize those who have dealings with devils on account of their ferocious aspect and terrible air.

The invocation in any of the three manners cited is always a heresy. But if the devil should only be asked to do things that are of his office—such as to tempt a woman to the sin of luxury—provided that this is done without adoration or prayer, but in terms of command, there are authors who hold that in such cases the person so proceeding is not guilty of heresy.

Amongst those who invoke devils are astrologers and alchymists, who when they do not succeed in making the discoveries they seek never fail to have recourse to the devil, sacrificing to him and invoking him expressly or tacitly.

JEWS AND INFIDELS: The first when they sin against their religion in any of the articles of faith that are the same with them as with us—*i.e.* that are common alike to Jew and to Christian—or when they attack dogmas that are, similarly, common to both creeds.

As for infidels, the Church and the Pope, and consequently the Inquisition, may punish them when they sin against the laws of nature—the only laws they know.

Jews and infidels who attempt to pervert Christians are also regarded as abettors or *fautores*.

In spite of the prohibition to succour a heretic, a man would not be regarded as an abettor who gave food to a heretic dying of hunger, since it is possible that if spared the latter might yet come to be converted.

EXCOMMUNICATES who remain in excommunication during a whole year, by which are to be understood not merely those who are excommunicate as heretics, or abettors of heretics, but excommunicate upon any grounds whatsoever. In fact, the indifference to excommunication renders them suspect of heresy.

APOSTATES.—Apostate Christians who become Jews or Mohammedans (these religions not being heresies), even though they should have apostatized through fear of death. The fear of torture or death not being one that can touch a person who is firm in the Faith, no apostasy is to be excused upon such grounds.[84]

With the "Directorium" of Eymeric before him, Torquemada set to work to draw up the first articles of his famous code. Additions were to be made to it later, as the need for such additions came to be shown by experience; but no subsequent addition was of the importance of these original twenty-eight articles. They may be said to have given the jurisprudence of the Spanish Inquisition a settled form, which continued practically unchanged for over three hundred years after Torquemada's death.

A survey of these articles and of the passages from Eymeric that have a bearing upon them, together with some of the annotations of the scholiast Francesco Pegna,[85] should serve to convey some notion of the jurisprudence of the Holy Office and of the extraordinary spirit that inspired and governed it—a spirit at once crafty and stupid, subtle and obvious, saintly and diabolical, consistent in nothing—not even in cruelty, for in its warped and dreadful way it accounted itself merciful, and not only represented but believed that its aims were charitable. It practised its abominations of cruelty out of love for the human race, to save the human race from eternal damnation; and whilst it wept on the one hand over the wretched heretic it flung to the flames, it exulted on the other in the thought that by burning one who was smitten with the pestilence of heresy it saved perhaps a hundred from infection and from purging that infection in an eternity of hell-fire.

They are rash who see hypocrisy in the priestly code that is to follow. Hypocrites there may have been, there must have been, and many; such a system was a very hotbed of hypocrisy. Yet the system itself was not hypocritical. It was sincere, dreadfully, tragically, ardently sincere, with the most hopeless, intolerable, and stupid of all sincerity—the sincerity of fanaticism, which destroys all sense of proportion, and distorts man's intellectual vision until with an easy conscience he makes of guile and craft and falsehood the principles that shall enable him to do what he conceives to be his duty by his fellow-man.

The doctrine of exclusive salvation was the source of all this evil. But that doctrine was firmly and sincerely held. Torquemada or any other inquisitor might have uttered the words which an inspired poet has caused to fall from the lips of Philip II.:

"The blood and sweat of heretics at the stake
Is God's best dew upon the barren field."[86]

And he would have uttered them with a calm and firm conviction, assured that he did no more than proclaim an obvious truth which might serve him as a guide to do his duty by man and God. For all that he did he could find a commandment in the Scriptures. Was burning the proper death for heretics? He answered the question out of the very mouth of Christ, as you shall see. Should a heretic's property be confiscated? Eymeric and Paramo point to the expulsion of Adam and Eve from Eden as a consequence of their disobedience—the first of all heresies—and ask you what was that but confiscation. Is it proper to impose a garment of shame upon those convicted of lesser heresies, or upon penitents who are reconciled? Paramo will answer you that Adam and Eve wore skins after their fall, and implies that this is a proper precedent for the infamous *sanbenito*.

And so on: Moses, David, John the Baptist, and the gentle Saviour Himself are made to afford reason for this course and for that, as the need arises, and each reason is more grotesque than the other, until you are stunned by the blows of these clumsy arguments. You cease to wonder that the translation of the Bible was forbidden, that its study was inhibited. If those who were learned in theology could interpret it so extravagantly, what might not the unlearned achieve?

But let us pass on to the consideration of Torquemada's code.

ARTICLE I

Whenever inquisitors are appointed to a diocese, city, village, or other place which hitherto has had no inquisitors, they shall—after having presented the warrants by which they are empowered to the prelate of the principal church and to the governor of the district—summon by proclamation all the people and convoke the clergy. They shall appoint a Sunday or holiday upon which all are to assemble in the cathedral or principal church to hear a sermon of the Faith.

They shall contrive that this sermon is delivered by a good preacher or by one of the actual inquisitors, as they deem best. Its aim shall be to expound the capacity in which they are there, their powers, and their intentions.

COPILACION
DE LAS INSTRVCIONES DEL
Officio de la sancta Inquisicion, hechas por
el muy Reuerendo Señor Fray Thomas de Torquemada, Príor del
Monasterio de sancta Cruz de Segouia, primero Inquisidor
general de los Reynos y Señorios de España.

E POR LOS OTROS REVERENDISSIMOS SENO-
res Inquisidores generales que despues succedieron, cerca de la orden que se ha de tener en el
exercicio del Sancto Officio. Donde van puestas successiuamente por su parte todas las
Instructiones que tocan a los Inquisidores. E a otra parte, las que tocan a cada
vno delos Officiales y Ministros del sancto Officio: las quales se copilaron
en la manera que dicha es, por mandado del Illustrissimo y Reuerendissimo
señor don Alonso Manrrique, Cardenal de los
doze Apostoles, Arçobispo de Seuilla Inquisidor
General de España.:.

EN MADRID,
En casa de Alonso Gomez, Impressor de su
Magestad. Año. 1576.

TITLE-PAGE OF THE FIRST PRINTED EDITION OF THE
"INSTRUCTIONS" OF TORQUEMADA.

Photo by Donald Macbeth

Upon the conclusion of this sermon the inquisitors shall order all faithful Christians to come forward and make oath upon the Cross and the Gospels to favour the Holy Inquisition and its ministers, and to offer them no impediment directly or indirectly in the prosecution of their mission.

This oath shall be specially imposed upon the governors or other justiciaries of the place, and it shall be witnessed by the notaries of the inquisitors.

Article II

After the conclusion of the said sermon the inquisitors shall order to be read and published an admonition with censures against those who are rebellious or who contest the power of the Holy Office.

Article III

After the conclusion of the said sermon the inquisitors shall publish an edict granting a term of grace, of thirty or forty days—as they may deem proper—so that all persons who have fallen into the sin of heresy or apostasy, who have observed Jewish rites or any other that are contrary to the Christian Religion, may come forward to confess their sins, assured that if they do so with a sincere penitence, divulging all that is known to them or that they remember, not only of their own sins but also of the sins of others, they shall be received with charity.

They shall be subjected to a salutary penance, but they shall not suffer death, imprisonment, or confiscation of their property, nor shall they in any way be mulcted unless the inquisitors, in consideration of the quality of the penitents and of the sins they confess, should think well to impose some pecuniary penance upon them.

Concerning this grace and mercy that their Highnesses consider well to accord to those who are reconciled, the Sovereigns order the delivery of letters-patent, bearing the royal seal, whose tenor shall be included in the published edict.

It is sufficiently plain, from the terms of this article, that the edict of grace was published by royal command, and that it was not, as Garcia Rodrigo represents it, a merciful dispensation spontaneously emanating from the Holy Office.

ARTICLE IV

Self-delators shall present their confessions in writing to the inquisitors and their notaries with two or three witnesses who shall be officers of the Inquisition or other upright persons.

Upon receipt of this confession by the inquisitors, let the oath be administered to the penitents in legal form, not only concerning the matters confessed but concerning others that may be known to them and upon which they may be questioned. Let them be asked how long it is since they Judaized or otherwise sinned against the Faith, and how long it is since they abandoned their false beliefs, repented, and ceased to observe those ceremonies. Next let them be examined upon the circumstances of the matters confessed, that the inquisitors may satisfy themselves that these confessions are true. Especially let them be questioned as to what prayers they recite, where they recite them, and with whom they have been in the habit of assembling to hear the law of Moses preached.

Self-delators who seek reconciliation to Holy Mother Church shall be required publicly to abjure their errors, and penance shall publicly be imposed upon them at the discretion of the inquisitors, using mercy and kindness as far as it is possible for them to do so with an easy conscience.

The inquisitors shall admit none to secret penance and recantation unless his sin shall have been so secret that none else knows or could know of it save his confessor; such a one all inquisitors may reconcile and absolve in secret.

Llorente says that the admission to secret penance was a source of much gold to the Roman Curia, as thousands appealed to the Pope offering a secret confession and firm purpose of amendment if secretly absolved, for which a papal brief was necessary.

A word must here be said on the score of ABJURATION. It was the amende provided by Eymeric[87] for those who by their speech or conduct should have fallen into suspicion of heresy; those, for instance, who abstained from the sacraments imposed by Mother Church being liable to this suspicion.

There were three degrees of suspicion into which a man might fall: light, vehement, and violent. The abjuration required was practically the same in all three cases, but the punishment imposed upon the abjurer varied according to the degree. This abjuration must be publicly made in church before the assembled people, the suspects being placed—like all penitents or convicts of heresy—upon a raised platform in full view of the assembled faithful. The inquisitor would read out the Articles of the Christian Faith, and a list of the principal errors against it, laying particular stress upon those errors of which the penitents were suspected, and which they were required to abjure with both hands upon the Gospels, and according to the formula laid down by Eymeric.

Those who are suspected lightly (*leviter*) are admonished that should they again fall into error they will be abandoned to the secular arm for punishment. With that admonition, and the imposition of a penance which may take the form of fasts, prayers, or pilgrimages, they are dismissed.

Those suspected vehemently (*vehementer*) are similarly admonished, but in addition they may be sent to prison for a time, whereafter they must undergo a heavy penance, such as standing on certain days at the door of the principal church or near the altar during the celebration of Mass holding a candle— but not wearing a *sanbenito*, as, properly speaking, they are not heretics—or they may be sent upon a pilgrimage.

He who is violently suspected (*violenter*) shall be absolved of the excommunication incurred, but as his crime may not go unpunished, and to the end that he may suffer less severely in the next world, he is sentenced to a term of imprisonment, whereafter he shall be condemned to stand at the church door during the great feasts of the year wearing the penitential scapulary known as the *sanbenito*, that all may be made aware of his infamy.

After passing sentence, the inquisitor shall admonish the penitent in these terms:

"My dear Son, be patient and do not despair; if we observe in you the signs of contrition we shall soften your penance; but beware of departing from what we have prescribed for you; should you do so you shall be punished as an impenitent heretic."

The punishment for the impenitent was, of course, the fire.

The inquisitor shall conclude the ceremony by granting an indulgence of forty days to all who have attended it and an indulgence of three years to those who shall have taken part in it.

The sentence of prison, with its bread-and-water diet, might be relaxed; but never that of the *sanbenito*, which is considered by Eymeric—and inquisitors generally—as the most salutary of penances for him that undergoes it and the most edifying to the public generally.

The self-delators admitted by Torquemada to abjuration were treated as suspects of the first degree—*leviter*.

ARTICLE VI

> Inasmuch as heretics and apostates (although they return to the Catholic Faith and become reconciled) are infamous at law, and inasmuch as they must perform their penances with humility and sorrow for having lapsed into error, the inquisitors shall order them not to hold any public office or ecclesiastical benefice, and they shall not be lawyers or brokers, apothecaries, surgeons or physicians, nor shall they wear gold or silver, coral, pearls, precious stones or other ornaments, nor dress in silk or camlett, nor go on horseback nor carry weapons all their lives, under pain of being deemed relapsed (*relapsos*) into heresy, as must all be considered who after reconciliation do not carry out the penances imposed upon them.

This decree was no more than the revival of the enactment made a century and a half earlier by Alfonso XI in the code known as the Partidas, which had mercifully been allowed to fall into desuetude. It was, Llorente tells us, a considerable source of wealth to the Roman Curia. Frequent appeals for "rehabilitation" were made in consequence, and accorded under an apostolic brief whose heavy charges the appellants were required to defray.

Torquemada mercifully stops short of ordering the self-delators to wear the *sanbenito*. Even so, however, by decreeing that they must wear no garments of silk or wool, and therefore none but the very plainest raiment, unadorned by any precious metal or jewel—not to mention the prohibition to use weapons or go on horseback—he imposed upon them a garb that was only some degrees removed from the penitential sack and served the same purpose of marking them out for infamy.

The wearing of the *sanbenito*, too, was a custom that had fallen somewhat into desuetude. But the ascetic Torquemada was not the man to allow a form of penance accounted so very salutary to continue neglected. He revived and extended the use of it, adding innovations of his own, so that it came to be imposed not only upon condemned heretics, but upon the reconciled—other than self-delators—and upon suspects, who were required to wear it during the abjuration ceremony.

This odious garment, its origin and history, shall presently be more fully considered.

ARTICLE VII

As the crime of heresy is a very heinous one, it is desired that the reconciled may realize by the penances imposed upon them how gravely they have offended and sinned against Our Lord Jesus Christ. Yet, as it is our aim to treat them very mercifully and kindly, pardoning them from the pain of fire and perpetual imprisonment, and leaving them all their property should they, as has been said, come to confess their errors within the appointed time of grace, the inquisitors shall, in addition to the penances imposed upon the said reconciled, order them to bestow as alms a certain portion of their property, according to the position of the penitent and the gravity of the crimes confessed. These pecuniary penances shall be applied for the Holy War which the most serene Sovereigns are making upon the Moors of Granada, enemies of our Holy Catholic Faith, and to other pious works that may be undertaken. For just as the said heretics and apostates have offended against Our Lord and His Holy Faith, so, after re-incorporation in the Church, it is just that they should bear pecuniary penances for the defence of the Holy Faith.

> These pecuniary penances shall be at the discretion of the inquisitors; but they shall be guided by the tariff given them by the Reverend Father Prior of Holy Cross (*i.e.* by Torquemada).

It was no inconsiderable proportion of their property that was required of them, as may be seen from the penance of "alms" for the war against Granada imposed upon those who were reconciled in Toledo two years later; one-fifth of their property being demanded.[88]

ARTICLE VIII

> Should any person guilty of the said crime of heresy fail to present himself within the appointed period of grace, but come forward voluntarily after its expiry and make his confession in due form before having been arrested or cited by the inquisitors, or before the inquisitors shall have received testimony against him, such person shall be received to abjuration and reconciliation in the same manner as those who presented themselves during the term of the said edict, and he shall be submitted to penances at the discretion of the inquisitors. But such penances shall not be pecuniary because his property is confiscate [*so that his admission to abjuration is not quite upon the same terms*].

> But if at the time of his coming to confess and seek reconciliation, the inquisitors should already be informed by witnesses of his heresy or apostasy, or should already have cited him to appear before the Court to answer the charge, in such a case the inquisitor shall receive the penitent to reconciliation—if he entirely confesses his own errors and what he knows of the errors of others—and shall impose upon him heavier penances than upon the former, even up to perpetual imprisonment should the case demand it.

This is merely one of those quibbles that permeate this jurisprudence. The article in this last respect is so framed as to make it appear that under such circumstances the inquisitors would be acting more mercifully than against an accused heretic; but the latitude of punishment is such that they need display no such mercy—perpetual imprisonment being the punishment prescribed for any heretic (who is not "relapsed") seeking reconciliation.

> But no persons who shall come to confess after expiry of the period of grace shall be subjected to pecuniary penances—unless their Highnesses should mercifully

condescend to remit all or portion of the confiscation incurred by those so reconciled.

This last clause seems rather in the nature of a provision against any merciful weakness on the Sovereigns' part.

ARTICLE IX

If any children of heretics having fallen into the sin of heresy by indoctrination of their parents, and being under twenty years of age, should come to seek reconciliation and to confess the errors they know of themselves, their parents and any other persons, even though they should come after the expiry of the term of grace, the inquisitors shall receive them kindly, imposing penances lighter than upon others in like case, and they shall contrive that these children be tutored in the Faith and the Sacraments of Holy Mother Church, as they are to be excused upon the grounds of age and education.

They are not, however, to be excused to the extent of enjoying any of their parents' property. That is confiscate by virtue of the parents' heresy; and by virtue of that same heresy on the part of their parents these children and their own children must remain under the ban of infamy, inhibited from wearing gold or silver, etc., and from holding any office under the crown or any ecclesiastical benefice. It seems almost ironical to talk of imposing light penances upon wretches who are automatically subject to such penalties as these. But by that "light penance" Llorente conceives would be meant their wearing a *sanbenito* for a couple of years, appearing in it at Mass and being paraded in it in processions.

ARTICLE X

Persons guilty of heresy and apostasy, by the fact of their having fallen into these sins, incur the loss of all their property and the administration of it, counting from the day when first they offended, and their said property is confiscate to their Highnesses' treasury. But in the matter of ecclesiastical pains in the case of those reconciled, the inquisitors in pronouncing upon them shall declare them to be heretics, apostates, or observers of the rites and ceremonies of the Jews; but that since they seek conversion with a pure heart and true faith, and they are ready to bear the penances that may be imposed, they shall be absolved and reconciled to Holy Mother Church.

The object of this article is really to make the act of confiscation retrospective where necessary, so as to circumvent any who should attempt, by alienation of his property, to avoid its confiscation. Since the confiscation was incurred upon the date of the first offence against the Faith, the inquisitors were to trace any property that might subsequently have been disposed of by the delinquent, and even should it have gone to the paying of debts or the endowment of a daughter married to one who was an old and "clean" Christian, the Holy Office must seize and confiscate it to the Royal Treasury.

ARTICLE XI

If any heretic or apostate who shall have been arrested upon information laid against him should say that he desires reconciliation and confess all his faults, what Jewish ceremonies he may have observed, and what is known to him of the faults of others, entirely and without reservations, the inquisitors shall admit him to reconciliation subject to perpetual imprisonment as by law prescribed. But should the inquisitors, in conjunction with the diocesan ordinary, in view of the contrition of the offender and the quality of his confession, think well to commute this penance to another lighter one, they shall have faculty so to do.

It seems that this should take place chiefly if the heretic at the first sitting of the court, or upon his first appearance before it, without awaiting the declaration of his offences, should announce his desire to confess and abjure; and such confession should be made before there is any publication of witnesses or of the matters urged by them against him.

ARTICLE XII

Should the prosecution of an accused have been conducted to the point of the publication of witnesses and their depositions, but should he then confess his faults and beg to be admitted to reconciliation, desiring formally to abjure his errors, the inquisitors shall receive him to the said reconciliation subject to perpetual imprisonment, to which they shall sentence him—save if in view of his contrition and other attendant circumstances the inquisitors should have cause to consider that the reconciliation of such a heretic is simulated; in such case they must declare him an impenitent heretic and abandon him to the secular arm: all of which is left to the conscience of the inquisitors.

"Abandonment to the secular arm" is, as shall presently be considered, the ecclesiastical equivalent to a sentence of death by fire.

The term "publication of witnesses" must not be accepted literally. What it really meant will become clear upon reading Article XVI, which was specially framed by Torquemada to modify and limit this time-honoured custom of civil and ecclesiastical courts.

ARTICLE XIII

If any of those who are reconciled during the period of grace or after its expiry should fail to confess all their own sins and all that they know of the sins of others, especially in grave cases, and should such omission arise not from forgetfulness but from malice, as may afterwards be proved by witnesses, since it is clear that the said reconciled have perjured themselves, and it must be presumed that their reconciliation was simulated, although they may have been absolved let them be proceeded against as impenitent heretics as soon as the said fiction and perjury are discovered.

Similarly if any person reconciled at the time of the edict of grace or afterwards, shall boast himself in public in such a manner that this can be proved, saying that he did not commit the sins to which he confessed, he must be deemed impenitent and a simulated convert, and the inquisitors shall proceed against him as if he were not reconciled.

ARTICLE XIV

If any, upon being denounced and convicted of the sin of heresy, shall deny and persist in his denial until sentence is passed, and the said crime shall have been proved against him, although the accused should confess the Catholic Faith and assert that he has always been and is a Christian, the inquisitors must declare him a heretic and so sentence him, for juridically the crime is proved, and by refusing to confess his error the convict does not permit the Church to absolve him and use him mercifully.

But in such cases the inquisitors should proceed with great care in their examination of the witnesses, closely cross-questioning them, gathering information on the score of their characters, and ascertaining whether there exist motives why they should depone out of hatred or ill-will towards the prisoner.

ARTICLE XV

> If the said crime of heresy or apostasy is half-proven
> (*semiplenamente provado*) the inquisitors may deliberate upon
> putting the accused to the torture, and if under torture he
> should confess his sin, he must ratify his confession on one
> of the following three days. If he does so ratify he shall be
> punished as convicted of heresy; if he does not ratify, but
> revokes his confession as the crime is neither fully proved
> nor yet disproved, the inquisitors must order, on account of
> the infamy and presumption of guilt of the accused, that he
> should publicly abjure his error; or the inquisitors may
> repeat the torture.

There is nothing in this article that may be considered as a departure from or an enlargement upon any of the rules laid down by Eymeric in his "Directorium," as we shall see when we come to deal with this gruesome subject of torture.

It is urged by apologists that, when all is said, the torture to which the inquisitors had recourse, and, similarly, the punishment of death by fire, were not peculiarly ecclesiastical institutions; that they were the ordinary civil methods of dealing with offenders, and that in adopting them the Church had simply conformed, as was her custom, with that which was by law prescribed.

It is quite true that originally these were the methods by which the secular tribunals proceeded against those who sinned against the Faith. But it must also be borne in mind that if the civil authorities so proceeded they implicitly obeyed the bull "ad extirpanda" of Sixtus IV, which imposed this duty upon them under pain of excommunication.

Owing to the inconvenience that attended this procedure in so far as torture and questions upon matters of Faith were concerned, it was later accounted desirable that the inquisitors themselves should take charge of it. They were enjoined, however, to see to it that there should be no shedding of blood or loss of life, since it was against the Christian maxims that a priest should be guilty of such things. So that when by misadventure it happened that blood was shed or a patient died under the hands of the torturers, the inquisitor conducting the examination became guilty of an irregularity. For this he must seek absolution at the hands of a brother cleric; and the inquisitors were informed—to make matters easier for them and to spare them anxieties in this matter—that they had the right to absolve one another under such circumstances.

But even if we fully admit that the use of torture—and similarly of fire—had been secular institutions of which the Church had simply availed herself as the only methods that commended themselves in such an age, it must still be held against the inquisitors that these methods were by no means tempered or softened in their priestly hands.

ARTICLE XVI

It being held that the publication of the names of witnesses who depone upon the crime of heresy might result in great harm and danger to the persons and property of the said witnesses—since it is known that many have been wounded and killed by heretics—it is resolved that the accused shall not be supplied with a copy of the depositions against him, but that he shall be informed of what is declared in them, whilst such circumstances as might lead to the identification of the deponents shall be withheld.

But the inquisitors must, when proof has been obtained from the examination of the witnesses, publish these depositions, withholding always the names and such circumstances as might enable the accused to learn the identity of the witnesses; and the inquisitors may give the accused a copy of the publication in such form [*i.e.* truncated] if he requires it.

If the accused should demand the services of an advocate, he shall be supplied. The advocate must make formal oath that he will faithfully assist the accused, but that if at any stage of the pleadings he shall realize that justice is not on his side, he shall at once cease to assist the delinquent and shall inform the inquisitors of the circumstance.

The accused shall pay out of his own property, if he have any, the services of the advocate; if he have no property, then the advocate shall be paid out of other confiscations, such being the pleasure of their Highnesses.

It is extremely doubtful if a more flagrant departure from all the laws of equity would be possible than that which is embodied in Torquemada's enactment on the subject of witnesses.

The notion of an accused hearing nothing of what is deposed against him, of his not even being informed of the full extent of such depositions nor yet confronted with his accusers, is beyond a doubt one of the most monstrously unjust features of this tribunal. And by taking the fullest advantage of that enactment and reducing the proceedings to a secrecy such as was never known in any court, the inquisitors were able to inspire a terror which was even greater than that occasioned by the fires they fed with human fuel at their frequent Autos.

Torquemada based this enactment upon the caution laid down by Eymeric on the score of divulging the names of witnesses. But Eymeric went no further than to say that these names should be suppressed where a possibility of danger to the delators lay in their being divulged. The accused, however, might have the full record of the proceedings read to him, and he might infer for himself who were his accusers. There was no question in Eymeric of any truncations.

Torquemada's aim is perfectly clear. It was not based, as is said in the article, upon concern for any danger that the delators might incur. For, after all, it shall be made plain before we conclude the survey of inquisitorial jurisprudence, that the wounding or even the death of those witnesses would be regarded (professedly, at least) as an enviable thing; they would be suffering for the Faith, and thus qualifying for the immortal crown of martyrdom. Rather was Torquemada's object to remove all fear that might trammel delators and stifle delations. The delator must be protected solely to the end that other delators might come forward with confidence to inform against secret heretics and apostates, so that the activities of the Holy Office should suffer no curtailment.

Trasmiera, a later inquisitor, in the course of an eulogium of secrecy, speaks of it as "the pole upon which the government of the Inquisition is balanced, calling for the veneration of the faithful; it facilitates the delations of witnesses, and it is the support and foundation of this tribunal; once deprived of it, the architecture of the edifice must undoubtedly give way."[89]

The clause relating to advocates is founded upon the ancient ecclesiastical law which forbade an advocate to plead for heretics. His being enlisted under the present clause would clearly serve to increase the peril of the accused.

ARTICLE XVII

> The inquisitors shall, themselves, examine the witnesses, and not leave such examinations to their notaries or others, unless a witness should be ill or unable to come before the inquisitor and the inquisitor similarly unable to go to the witness, in which case he may send the ordinary ecclesiastical judge of the district with another upright person and a notary to take the depositions.

ARTICLE XVIII

When any person is put to the torture the inquisitors and the ordinary should be present—or, at least, some of them. But when this is for any reason impossible, then the person entrusted to question should be a learned and faithful man (*hombre entendido y fiel*).

ARTICLE XIX

to the door of the church of the district to which he belongs, and after thirty days' grace the inquisitors may proceed to try him as contumaciously absent. If there is sufficient evidence of his guilt, sentence may be passed upon him. Or, if evidence is insufficient, he may be branded a suspect and commanded—as is due of suspects—to present himself for canonical purgation. Should he fail to do so within the time appointed, his guilt must be presumed.

Proceedings against the absent may be taken in any of the following three ways:

(1) In accordance with the chapter "Cum contumatia de hereticis," citing the accused to appear and defend himself upon certain matters concerning the Faith and certain sins of heresy, under pain of excommunication; if he does not respond, he shall be denounced as a rebel, and if he persists in this rebellion for one year he shall be declared a formal heretic. This is the safest and least rigorous course to adopt.

(2) Should it seem to the inquisitors that a crime against any absent can be established, let him be cited by edict to come and prove his innocence within thirty days—or a longer period may be conceded if such is necessary to permit him to return from wherever he may be known to be. And he shall be cited at every stage of the proceedings until the passing of sentence, when, should he still be absent, let him be accused of rebellion, and should the crime be proved he may be condemned in his absence without further delay.

(3) If in the course of inquisitorial proceedings there is presumption of heresy against an absent person (although the crime is not clearly proved) the inquisitors may summon him by edict commanding him to appear within a given time to clear himself canonically of the said error, on the understanding that should he fail to appear, or, appearing,

should fail to clear himself, he shall be deemed convicted and the inquisitors shall proceed to act as by law prescribed.

The inquisitors, being learned and discriminating, will select the course that seems most certain and is most practical under the particular circumstances of the case.

Any person condemned as contumacious became an outlaw, whom it was lawful for any man to kill.

CANONICAL PURGATION, which is mentioned in this article, differs considerably from ABJURATION, and the difference must be indicated.

It is applicable only to those who are accused by the public voice—*i.e.* who have acquired the "reputation" of heresy—without yet having been detected in any act or speech that might cause them to be suspected of heresy in any of the defined degrees of such suspicion.

It almost amounts to a distinction without a difference, and is an excellent instance of the almost laboured equity in which this tribunal indulged in matters of detail whilst flagrantly outraging equity in the main issues.

For Canonical Purgation, says Eymeric,[90] the accused must find a certain number of sureties or *compurgatores*, the number required being governed by the gravity of the (alleged) offence. They must be persons of integrity and of the same station in life as the accused, with whom they must have been acquainted for some years. The accused shall make oath upon the Gospels that he has never held or taught the heresies stated, and the *compurgatores* shall swear to their belief that this is the truth. This Purgation must be made in all cities where the accused has been defamed.

The accused shall be given a certain time in which to find his *compurgatores*, and should he fail to find the number required he shall at once be convicted and condemned as a heretic.

And Pegna adds, in his commentary upon this, that any who shall be found guilty of heresy after having once been in this position is to be regarded as a "relapso" and delivered to the secular arm. For this reason he enjoins that Canonical Purgation should not lightly be ordered, as it is so largely dependent upon the will of third parties.

Eymeric adds, further, that sometimes Canonical Purgation may be ordered to those who are defamed by the public voice but who are not in the hands of the inquisitors. Should they refuse to surrender, the inquisitors shall proceed to excommunicate them, and if they persist in their excommunication for one year they shall be deemed heretics, and subject to the penalties entailed by such a sentence.

ARTICLE XX

> If any writings or trials should bring to light the heresy of a person deceased, let proceedings be taken against him— even though forty years shall have elapsed since the offence—let the fiscal accuse him before the tribunal, and if he should be found guilty the body must be exhumed.
>
> His children or heirs may appear to defend him; but should they fail to appear, or, appearing, fail to establish his innocence, sentence shall be passed upon him and his property confiscated.

It will, of course, be obvious that since no good or useful purpose could be served by instituting proceedings against the dead, nothing but cupidity can have inspired so barbarous a decree as this. The avowed object of the Inquisition—and very loudly and insistently avowed—was the uprooting of heresies to prevent their spread, and the inquisitors maintained that it was a painful necessity thrust upon them by their duty to God to destroy those who persisted in heresy, lest these, by their teaching and example, should contaminate and imperil the souls of others. Thus the Inquisition justified itself, and removed all doubt as to the purity of its motives.

But how should this justification apply to the trial of the dead—even though they should have been dead for over forty years?

The provision, however, was not Torquemada's own. He followed in the footsteps of earlier inquisitors. He found his precedent in the 120th question propounded by Eymeric—"Confiscatio bonorum hæretici fieri potest post ejus mortem." In this the author of the "Directorium" lays it down that although in civil law legal action against a criminal ceases with his death, such is not to be the case where heresy is concerned, on account of the enormity of the crime. (It may seem that, had he been quite honest, he would have said, "on account of the profits that may accrue from the prosecution.")

Heretics, he pursues, may be proceeded against after their death, and, if convicted, their property may be confiscated—and this within forty years of their decease—depriving the heirs of all enjoyment of it, even though the third generation should be in possession.

All that Torquemada did was to extend the term of procedure beyond the forty years to which Eymeric had limited it.

And to the foregoing Eymeric adds that, should the heirs at any time have acquired knowledge that the deceased was a heretic, they shall be censured for having acted in bad faith and kept the matter secret! By this he actually puts it upon men to come forward voluntarily and accuse their dead fathers or grandfathers of heretical practices, to the end that they themselves may be rendered destitute and infamous to the extent of being incapacitated from holding any public office or following any honourable profession—and this though they themselves should be the most faithful of Catholics, untouched by the faintest breath of suspicion!

It is beyond words a monstrous and inequitable enactment. Yet, like all else, they can justify it. If there is one thing in which the inquisitors were truly admirable, it is in the deftness with which they could justify and reconcile with their conscience the most inhuman practice. They would answer questions as to the lawfulness of this proceeding by urging that they did it with the greatest reluctance, but that their duty demanded it to the end that the living should beware how they failed in fidelity to the Faith, lest punishment should overtake them in their descendants after they themselves had passed beyond the reach of human justice. Thus would they represent the act as salutary and to the advantage of the Faith. And since there is at least a scintilla of truth in this, who shall say that they did not tranquillize their consciences and delude themselves that the confiscations were a mere incident which nowise swayed their judgment?

That proceedings against persons deceased were by no means rare is shown by the frequent records of corpses burnt—one of the purposes for which they were exhumed; the other being that they must cease to defile consecrated ground.

ARTICLE XXI

The Sovereigns desiring that inquisition be made alike in the domains of the nobles as in the lands under the Crown, inquisitors shall proceed to effect these, and shall require the lords of such domains to make oath to comply with all that the law ordains, and to lend all assistance to the inquisitors. Should they decline to do so, they shall be proceeded against as by law established.

ARTICLE XXII

Should heretics who are delivered to the secular arm leave children who are minors and unmarried, the inquisitors shall provide and ordain that they be cared for and reared by some persons who will instruct them in our Holy Faith. The inquisitors shall prepare a memorial of such orphans and the circumstances of each, to the end that of the royal bounty alms may be provided to the extent necessary, this being the wish of the Sovereigns when the children are good Christians, especially in the case of girls, who should receive a dower sufficient to enable them to marry or enter a convent.

Llorente tells us that although he went through very many records of old proceedings of the Inquisition, in no single instance did he discover a record of any such provision in favour of the child of a condemned heretic.[91]

Harsh as were the decrees of the Inquisition in all things, in nothing were they so harsh as in the enactments concerning the children of heretics. However innocent themselves of the heresy for which their parents or grandparents might have suffered, not only must they go destitute, but further they must be prevented from ever extricating themselves appreciably from that condition, being inhibited—to the second generation—from holding any office under the Crown, or any ecclesiastical benefice, and from following any honourable or lucrative profession. And, as if that were not in itself sufficient, they were further condemned to wear the outward signs of infamy, to go dressed in serge, without weapons or ornaments, and never ride on horseback, under pain of worse befalling them. One of the inevitable results of this barbarous decree was the extinction of many good Spanish families of Jewish blood in the last decade of the fifteenth century.

This the inquisitors understood to be the literal application to practical life of the gentle and merciful precepts of the sweet Christ in Whose name they acted.

Eymeric and his commentator Pegna make clear, between them, the inquisitorial point of view. The author of the "Directorium" tells us that commiseration for the children of heretics who are reduced to mendicity must not be allowed to soften this severity, since by all laws, human and divine, it is prescribed that the children must suffer for the sins of the fathers.[92]

The scholiast expounds at length the justice of this measure. He says that there have been authors, such as Hostiensis, who pretend that it lacks the equity of the ancient laws, which admitted Catholic children to inheritance. But he assures us that they are wrong in holding such views, that there is no injustice in the provision, and that it is salutary, since the fear of it is calculated to influence parents and to turn them—out of love for their offspring—from the great crime of heresy.

To minds less dulled by bigotry it must have been clear that by this, as, for that matter, by many other of their decrees, all that was achieved was to put a premium upon hypocrisy.

Another consideration that escaped their notice—being, as they were, capable of perceiving one thing only at a time—was that if this precious measure was prescribed by all laws, human and divine, it should have been unavoidable. Yet they themselves provided the means of avoiding it—as we know—for the child vile enough to lay information of his parents' heresy. By what laws, human or divine, did they dare to encourage such an infamy? By no law but their own—a law whose chief aim, it is obvious at every turn, was to swell the number of convictions.

What opinion was held of children who informed against their parents to avert the awful fate that awaited them should their parents' heresy be discovered by others, is apparent in the case of the daughter of Diego de Susan—who, very possibly, was actuated by just such motives.

ARTICLE XXIII

Should any heretic or apostate who has been reconciled within the term of grace be relieved by their Highnesses from the punishment of confiscation of his property, it is to be understood that such relief applies only to that property which by their own sin was lost to them. It does not extend to property which the person reconciled shall have the right to inherit from another who shall have suffered confiscation. This to the end that a person so pardoned shall not be in better case than a pure Catholic heir.

ARTICLE XXIV

As the King and Queen in their clemency have ordained that the Christian slaves of heretics shall be freed, and even when the heretic is reconciled and immune from confiscation, this immunity shall not extend to his slaves; these shall be manumitted in any case, to the greater honour and glory of our Holy Faith.

ARTICLE XXV

Inquisitors and assessors and other officers of the Inquisition, such as fiscal advocates, constables, notaries, and ushers, must excuse themselves from receiving gifts from any who may have or may come to have affairs with the Inquisition, or from others on their behalf; and the Father Prior of Holy Cross orders them not to receive any such gifts under pain of excommunication, of being deprived of office under the Inquisition and compelled to make restitution and repay to twice the value of what they may have received.

Eymeric's "Directorium" permitted the reception of gifts by inquisitors, provided that these gifts were not too considerable, but he enjoined inquisitors not to show too much avidity—not, it would seem, on account of the sin that lurks in avidity, but so as not to give scandal to the laity.[93]

ARTICLE XXVI

Inquisitors shall endeavour to work harmoniously together; the honour of the office they hold demands this, and inconveniences might result from discords amongst them. Should any inquisitor be acting in the place of the diocesan ordinary, let him not on that account presume that he enjoys pre-eminence over his colleagues. If any difference should arise between inquisitors and they be unable themselves to adjust it, let them keep the matter secret until they can lay it before the Prior of Holy Cross, who, as their superior, will decide it as he considers best.

ARTICLE XXVII

Inquisitors shall endeavour to contrive that their officers treat one another well and dwell in harmony and honourably. Should any officer commit an excess, let them punish him charitably, and should they be unable to cause an officer to fulfil his duty, let them advise the Prior of Holy Cross thereof, and he will at once deprive such a one of his office and make such an appointment as may seem best for the service of Our Lord and their Highnesses.

ARTICLE XXVIII

Should any matter arise for which provision has not been made by this code, the inquisitors shall proceed as by law prescribed, it being left to them to dispose as their consciences show them to be best for the service of God and their Highnesses.

To these twenty-eight articles Torquemada was to make further additions—in January of the following year, in October of 1488 and in May of 1498. We shall indicate to them, but for the moment it is sufficient to say that—saving some of those of 1498—they are of secondary importance, being mainly in the nature of corollaries upon those we have dealt with, and chiefly concerned with the internal governance of the Inquisition rather than with its relations to the outside world.

CHAPTER XI
THE JURISPRUDENCE OF THE HOLY OFFICE—THE MODE OF PROCEDURE

No complete notion of the jurisprudence of the Holy Office can be formed without taking a glance at this tribunal at work and observing the methods upon which it proceeded in its dealings with those who were arraigned before it.

Its scope has already been considered, and also the offences that came within its pitiless jurisdiction at the time of Torquemada's appointment to the mighty office of Grand Inquisitor and President of the Suprema. It remains to be added that in his endeavours to cast an ever-wider net he sought to increase the jurisdiction of the Inquisition beyond matters immediately concerned with the Faith and to include certain offences whose connection with it was only constructive.

Whether he succeeded to the full extent of his aims we do not know. But we do know that he contrived that bigamy should become the concern of the Holy Office, contending that it was primarily an offence against the laws of God and a defilement of the Sacrament of Marriage. Adultery, which is no less an offence against that sacrament, and which is not punishable by civil law, he passed over; but he contrived that sodomy should be brought for the first time within inquisitorial jurisdiction and that those convicted of it should be burnt alive.

Himself a man of the most rigid chastity, he must have been moved to anger by the unchastity so prevalent among the clergy. It was, however, beyond his power to deal with it without special authority from Rome, and he would have been bold indeed to have sought such authority at the hands of that flagrant paterfamilias Giovanni Battista Cibo, who occupied the Chair of St. Peter with the title of Pope Innocent VIII.

The most scandalous form of this unchastity was that known as "solicitation"—*solicitatio ad turpia*—or the abuse of the confessional for the purpose of seducing female penitents. It was a matter that greatly vexed the Church as a body, since it placed a terrible weapon in the hands of her enemies and detractors. It was admittedly rampant, and it is more than probable that it was directly responsible for the institution of the confessional-box—enforced in the sixteenth century—which effectively separated confessor from penitent, and left them to communicate through a grille.

The matter, like all other offences of the clergy, was entirely within the jurisdiction of the bishops, who would vigorously have resisted any attempts on the part of Torquemada to encroach further upon their province. So the Church was left to combat that evil as best she might; and, with the exception of an odd bishop who assumed a stern attitude and dealt with it as became his own dignity and the honour of the priesthood, the utmost lenience appears to have prevailed,[94] as we may judge by the penances imposed upon convicted offenders.

The perils and temptations to which a priest was exposed in the course of the intimate communications that must pass between him and his penitents were given full recognition and allowed full weight in the balance against the offence itself.

Later on, however, this matter which Torquemada had considered beyond his power was actually thrust within the jurisdiction of the Inquisition by a Church resolved, for the very sake of its existence, that the evil should cease.

Vexatious as this crime of "solicitation" had always been, it became most urgently and perilously so after the Reformation, when it provided those who denounced the confessional with an apparently unanswerable reason for their denunciations. It was wisely thought that the methods of the Holy Office were best calculated to deal with it, and the matter was relegated to the inquisitors. The defilement of the sacrament was the link that connected solicitation with heresy. Moreover, in some cases there might be heresy of a more positive kind; as when, for instance, the priest assured the penitent that her consent was not a sin. And the woman accusing a priest of solicitation before the Holy Office was always questioned closely upon this particular point.

In the later editions of the "Cartilla," or Manual for the guidance of Inquisitors—all of which publications were issued by the private press of the Inquisition—are to be found under the heading "Causas de Solicitacion" instructions for the examination of a woman who denounces a priest upon these grounds.[95]

Even so, however, it could not be in the interests of the Church to parade these offenders, and thus expose the sore places in her own body.

Limborch urges that delinquents be sent to the galleys, or even delivered to the secular arm. But for that—as Llorente points out—it would have been necessary to include them in an Auto de Fé of which there could be no question on account of the scandal which must ensue in view of the character of the offence. This is very true, and none can doubt the desirability of avoiding publicity for such a matter, or suppose that the Church was in the least blame-worthy for so proceeding. At the same time, however justifiable we may account this secrecy, it is almost impossible to justify the lenience of the sentences that were passed. It is above all extraordinary that the usual punishment did not even go so far as to unfrock these offenders. The inquisitors confined themselves to depriving the convicted priest of the faculty of hearing confessions in future, and imposed a penance of some years' residence in the seclusion of a convent.

It is possible, however, that this punishment was heavier than may at first appear. For—to their credit be it said—the regulars into whose convent the penanced cleric was sent undertook that this penance should be anything but easy.

This comes to light in the course of a case of which Llorente cites the full particulars from the records he unearthed.[96]

It is the case of a Capuchin brother tried in the eighteenth century by the Grand Inquisitor Rubin de Cevallos; and as much in the quality and extent of the offence as in the brazenly ingenious defence set up by the friar, the record reads like one of the least translatable stories from Boccaccio's "Decameron." He was sentenced to go into retreat for five years in a convent of his order; and so great a dread did that sentence strike into the Capuchin that he besought of the inquisitors the mercy of being allowed to serve the sentence in one of the dungeons of the Inquisition. Questioned as to his reasons for a request that sounded so extraordinary, he protested that he knew too well the burden his brethren were wont to impose upon a friar penanced as was he.

His petition was dismissed, the Grand Inquisitor refusing to alter the sentence; and Llorente adds that the Capuchin died three years later in the convent to which he was sent.

How far the crime was rampant when the Inquisition was entrusted with its prosecution may be gathered from the statistics given by H. C. Lea.[97] It appears from these that in the city of Toledo alone, during the first thirty-five years that the matter was in the hands of the Holy Office, fifty-two sentences were passed upon priests found guilty of "solicitation," and it is not to be supposed, as Lea very shrewdly observes, that delations were forthcoming in more than a proportion of the cases that occurred, or that more than a proportion of these delations could lead to conviction—since, to avert scandal as much as possible, no action would be taken save where the indications of guilt were very clear.

This view is certainly supported by the injunction of caution and the other instructions in the Manual under the heading "Causas de Solicitaciones," already cited.

Finally on this subject, Llorente's statistics show that the offenders were chiefly friars; the proportion of secular priests convicted being only one in ten. This does not, however, signify greater chastity on the part of secular priests. Llorente offers the obvious explanation—an explanation too obvious to need repeating here.[98]

Another offence that came later to be added to those within the jurisdiction of the Holy Office was that of usury. But in Torquemada's day neither this nor solicitation was allowed to be the concern of the Inquisition.

In its methods of procedure the tribunal of the Holy Office under the zealous rule of the Prior of Holy Cross followed closely upon the lines laid down by Eymeric. Indeed in the "Cartilla" or "Manual" that was issued later for the use of inquisitors—of which several editions are in existence to-day—these rules taken bodily from the "Directorium" were incorporated as a supplement to the code promulgated by Torquemada, consisting of the articles already considered and of others to be added later.

These methods we will now consider.

The accused was brought before the tribunal sitting in the audience-chamber of the Holy Office—or Holy House (*Casa Santa*) as the premises of the Inquisition came to be styled.

The court was composed of at least one of the inquisitors delegated by Torquemada, the diocesan ordinary, the fiscal advocate, and a notary to take down all that might transpire. They were seated about a table upon which stood a tall crucifix, between two candles, and the Gospels upon which the accused was to be sworn.

The oath being administered, the prisoner was asked his name, birthplace, particulars of his family, and the diocese in which he resided. Next he was vaguely questioned as to whether he had heard speak of such matters as those upon which he was accused.[99]

Pegna warns inquisitors against being too precise in their questions, lest they should suggest answers to the accused.[100] Another reason for this vagueness was that being precisely questioned the accused might in his answers confine himself to the matter of those questions, whilst where the inquiry was conducted in vague, general terms, he might in his reply betray matters or persons hitherto unsuspected.

Obviously with the same end in view, the scholiast suggests that the accused be asked whether he knows why he has been arrested, and whom he suspects of having accused him; whilst as a means of instantly testing whether he is an observer of his Catholic duties the inquisitors are instructed to ask him who is his confessor and when he was last at confession. The answer of one who was secretly an apostate, or even who had neglected to comply with his religious duties as prescribed, must necessarily be enormously incriminating. It would justify violent suspicion of heresy against him, which has already been considered, together with its consequences.

Pegna further enjoins inquisitors to be careful that they do not afford the accused any means of evading their questions, and not to be imposed upon by protestations or tears, heretics being, he assures them, of an extreme cunning in dissembling their errors.

Eymeric specifies ten different methods employed by heretics to trick inquisitors. These are not of any real importance, nor do they leave us in the least convinced that any such ruses were actually employed. They are obviously based upon an intimate acquaintance with priestly guile rather than upon any experience of the craftiness of actual heretics. They may, in short, be said to be just such ruses as the inquisitors themselves might employ if they found the tables turned upon themselves and the heretic sitting in the seat of justice.

He urges the inquisitors to meet guile with guile: "ut clavus clavo retundatur." He justifies recourse to hypocrisy and even to falsehood, telling the inquisitors that thus they will be in a position to say: "Cum essem astutus dolo vos cepi," and to the ten evasive methods which he asserts are adopted by heretics, he bids their paternities oppose ten specified rules by which to capture and entrap them.

These rules and Pegna's commentaries upon them are worth attention for the sake of the intimate glimpse they afford us of the mediæval ecclesiastical mind.

The accused is to be compelled by repeated examinations to return clear and precise answers to the questions asked.

If the accused heretic is resolved not to confess his fault, the inquisitor should address him with great sweetness (*blande et mansuete*), giving him to understand that all is already known to the court, speaking as follows:

"Look now, I pity you who are so deluded in your credulity, and whose soul is being lost; you are at fault, but the greater fault lies with him who has instructed you in these things. Do not, then, take the sin of others upon yourself, and do not make yourself out a master in matters in which you have been no more than a pupil. Confess the truth to me, because, as you see, I already know the whole affair. And so that you may not lose your reputation, and that I may shortly liberate and pardon you and you may go your ways home, tell me who has led you—you who knew no evil—into this error."

By similar kind words (*bona verba*), always imperturbable (*sine turbatione*), let the inquisitor proceed, assuming the main fact to be true and confining his questions to the circumstances.

Pegna adds another formula, which he says was employed by Fr. Ivonet. Thus:

"Do not fear to confess all. You will have thought they were good men who taught you so-and-so; you lent ear to them freely in that belief, etc.... You have behaved with credulous simplicity towards people whom you believed good and of whom you knew no evil. It might very well happen to much wiser men than you to be so mistaken."[101]

Thus was the wretch coaxed to self-betrayal, caressed and stroked by the velvet glove that muffled and dissembled the iron hand within.

In the case of a heretic against whom the witnesses have not supplied matter for complete conviction, let him be brought before the inquisitor and let the inquisitor question him at random. When the accused shall have denied something (*quando negat hoc vel illud*) that has been put to him, let the inquisitor take up the minutes of the preceding examinations, turn the leaves and say:

"It is clear that you conceal the truth; cease to employ dissimulation."

Thus the accused may suppose that he is convicted, and that the minutes supply proof against him.

Or let the inquisitor hold a document in his hand, and when the accused denies, let him feign astonishment and exclaim:

"How can you deny such a thing? Is it not clear to me?" He will then peruse his document anew, making changes, and then reading once more, let him say, "I was right! Speak, then, since you perceive that I know."

The inquisitor must be careful not to enter into any details that might betray his ignorance to the accused. Let him keep to generalities.

If the accused persists in his denial, the inquisitor may tell him that he is about to set out upon a journey and that he doesn't know when he will be returning. Thus:

"Look now, I pity you, and I wanted you to tell me the truth, for I am anxious to expedite the affair and yourself. But since you are obstinate in refusing to confess, I must leave you in prison and in irons until I return; and I am sorry, because I do not know when I shall return."

Photo by Donald Macbeth.

TOLEDO.
From Colmenar's "Délices d'Espagne."

If the accused persists in denial, let the inquisitors multiply examinations and questions; then either the accused will confess, or (becoming confused) will contradict himself. If he contradicts himself that will suffice to put him to torture, that thus the truth may be extracted from his mouth. But frequent interrogations should not be employed save with one of extreme stubbornness, because to frequent questions upon the same matter it is easy to obtain variable answers; there is hardly anybody who would not be surprised into a contradiction.

Here we have a glimpse of the extraordinary flexibility of the inquisitorial conscience. The letter of the law must ever be observed in all proceedings; but its spirit must by all means be circumvented where it is expedient to do so. Certain conditions, presently to be examined, must be present before an accused could be put to torture. One of these was that under examination he should contradict himself. This rule they scrupulously observed; but they had no qualms on the score of bringing about the requisite condition by a trick— of compelling the accused to contradict himself by repeated questions upon the same subject. And Eymeric himself admits that hardly anybody could avoid varying in his answers under such a test.

It may be uncharitable to suppose that the last paragraph of this rule is intended as a hint rather than as the warning it pretends to be. But it is a suspicion which the further consideration of the inquisitorial conscience must inspire in every thoughtful mind. It is so much of a piece with the inquisitors' extraordinary attitude towards the letter of the law to proceed in that way.

If the accused still persists in denial, the inquisitor should now soften his conduct; let him contrive that the prisoner has better food, and that worthy people visit him and win his confidence; these shall then advise him to confess, promise that the inquisitor will pardon him (*faciet sibi gratiam*), and that they themselves will act as mediators.

The inquisitor himself may in the end go so far as to join them, and promise to accord grace (*i.e.* pardon) to the accused, and grant him this grace in effect, since all is grace that is done in the conversion of heretics; penances being themselves graces and remedies. When the accused, having confessed his crime, demands the promised "grace," let him be answered in general terms that he shall receive even more than he could ask, so that the whole truth may be discovered and the heretic converted[102]—"and his soul saved, at least," adds Pegna.[103]

Thoroughly to appreciate the deliberate duplicity here practised, it is necessary to take into account the double or even treble meaning of the term grace—"gratia"—employed by Eymeric, and having in Spanish (*i.e.* its equivalent "gracia") precisely the same meanings as in Latin.

Although not so popularly used in these various meanings, the English term "grace" can also signify (*a*) the prerogative of mercy exercised as a complete pardon, (*b*) the same prerogative exercised to relieve part of the penalty incurred, or (*c*) a state of acceptance with God.

The accused was deliberately led to suppose that "gratia" was employed in the sense of a complete pardon. It remained with the inquisitor to quiet his conscience for this *suggestio falsi* by preferring the letter to the spirit of his promise; he would enlighten the accused that by "grace" no more was meant than a remission of part of the penalty incurred (an insignificant remission usually), or even that all that he had in mind was the grace of divine favour into which his soul would enter—so that this might be saved at least, as Pegna explains.

Pegna has a good deal more to say on the same subject, and all of it is extremely interesting.

He propounds the questions: "May an inquisitor employ this ruse to discover the truth? If he enters into such a promise is he not obliged to keep it?" By this latter question he means, of course, the promise to pardon which the prisoner was given to understand was made him.

He proceeds to tell us that Dr. Cuchalon decided the first of these questions by approving the use of dissimulation, justifying it by the instance of Solomon's judgment between the mothers.

It really seems as if there is nothing that theologians cannot justify by inversion, subversion, or perversion of some precedent (more or less apocryphal in itself) to suit their ends.

The scholiast himself agrees with the reverend doctor, and considers that although jurisconsults may disapprove of such methods in civil courts, it is quite fit and proper to use them in the courts of the Holy Office; explaining that the inquisitor has ampler powers than the civil judge [which seems to be an extraordinary reason for justifying his abuse of them].

Thus, Pegna pursues, in this edifying treatise upon the uses of hypocrisy, provided that the inquisitor does not promise the offender absolute impunity, he may always promise him "grace" (which by the offender is taken to signify "absolute impunity") and keep his promise by diminishing somewhat the *canonical* pains that depend upon himself.

In actual practice this would mean that a heretic who has incurred the stake may be promised pardon if he will confess to the sins of which it is necessary to convict him before he can be burnt. And when, having confessed and delivered himself into the hands of the inquisitor, he claims his pardon, he is to be satisfied with the answer that the pardon meant was pardon for his sins—absolution, that his soul may be saved when they burn his body.

On the score of the second question propounded by the scholiast—"If the inquisitor enters into such a promise is he not obliged to keep it?"—he answers it by telling us that many theologians do not consider there is any such obligation on the part of the inquisitor. This attitude they explain by urging that such a fraud is salutary and for the public good; and, further, that if it is licit to extract the truth by torture, it is surely much more so to accomplish it by dissimulation—*verbis fictis*.

This is the general but by no means the universal opinion, we gather. There are some writers who are opposed to it. And now the scholiast becomes more extraordinary still. Hear him:

"These two divergent opinions may be reconciled by considering that whatever promises the inquisitors make, they are not to be understood to apply to anything beyond the penalties whose rigour the Inquisition has the right to lessen—namely, canonical penances, and not those by law prescribed."

He writes this knowing that these promises are understood by the prisoner to mean something very different—that the prisoner is desired so to understand them, made so to understand them.

The honesty of Pegna's reasoning is not to be suspected. He is not an apologist of the Holy Office writing for the world in general, and employing bad arguments perforce because he must make the best of the only ones available, even though he should lapse into suspicion of bad faith. He is writing, as a preceptor, for the private eye of the inquisitor. Therefore we can only conclude that these learned casuists who plunge into such profundities of thought and pursue such labyrinthine courses of reasoning had utterly failed to grasp the elementary moral fact that falsehood does not lie in the word uttered, but in the idea conveyed.

"However little," he continues, in the course of polishing this gem of casuistry, "may be the remission granted by the inquisitor, it will always be sufficient to fulfil his promise."

You see what a stickler he is for the letter of the law. You shall see a good deal more of the same sort of thing before we have gone much further.

But here the scholiast begins to labour. His conscience is stirring; possibly a ray of doubt penetrates his gloomy confidence that right is wrong and wrong is right. And so, we fancy, to quiet these uneasy stirrings comes the last paragraph on this subject:

"However, for greater safety of conscience, inquisitors should make no promises save in very general terms, and never promise more than they can fulfil."[104]

There is one more of Eymeric's ruses for combating the guile of stubborn heretics:

Let the inquisitor obtain an accomplice of the accused, or else a person esteemed by the latter and in the inquisitor's confidence, and engage him to talk often to the accused and extract his secret from him. If necessary, let this person pretend to be of the same heretical sect, to have abjured through fear, and to have declared all to the inquisitor.

Then one evening, when the accused shall have gained confidence in this visitor, let the latter remain until he can say that it is too late to return home and that he will spend the night in the prison. Let persons be suitably placed to hear the conversation of the accused and if possible a notary to take down in writing the confessions of the heretic, who should now be drawn by the spy into relating all that he has done.

Upon this subject Pegna moralizes[105] for the benefit of the spy, pointing out how the latter may go about his very turpid task without involving himself in falsehood or besmirching in the least the delicate, sensitive soul that we naturally suppose must animate him.

"Be it noted that the spy, simulating friendship and seeking to draw from the accused a confession of his crime, may very well pretend to be of the sect of the accused, but" [mark the warning] "he must not say so, because in saying so he would at least commit a venial sin, and we know that such must not be committed upon any grounds whatever."

Thus the scholiast. He makes it perfectly clear that a man may simulate friendship for another for the purpose of betraying that other to his death; that to make that betrayal more certain he may even pretend to hold the same religious convictions; all this may he do and yet commit no sin—not even a venial sin—so long as he does not actually clothe his pretence in words. What a store the casuist sets by words!

It is just such an argument as Caiaphas might have employed with Judas Iscariot one evening in Jerusalem.

It is a cherished thesis with apologists of the Holy Office that in its judicial proceedings it did neither more nor less than what was being done in its day in the civil courts; that if its methods were barbarous—if they shock us now—we are to remember that they were the perfectly ordinary judicial methods of their time.

But there was no secular court in Europe in the fifteenth century—steeped as that century was in dissimulation and bad faith—that would not have scorned to have made such dishonourable and dishonouring methods as these an acknowledged, regular and integral part of its procedure.

Pegna himself reveals the fact, when he finds it necessary further to justify these practices precisely because they were not in use in the civil courts:

"Perchance the authority of Aristoteles—who out of the bosom of Paganism condemned all manner of dissimulation—may be opposed to us, as well as that of the jurisconsults who disapprove of artifices of which judges may make use to extract the truth. But there are two forms of artifice: one addressed to an evil end, which must not be permitted; the other aiming at discovering truth, which none could blame."[106]

When confession has been obtained it would be idle, Eymeric points out, to grant the delinquent a defence. "For although in civil courts the confession of a crime does not suffice without proof, it suffices here." The reason advanced for this is as specious as any in the "Directorium": "Heresy being a sin of the soul, confession may be the only evidence possible."

Where an advocate was granted to conduct the defence of an accused, we have seen in Art. XVI of Torquemada's "Instructions" that he was under the obligation to relinquish such defence the moment he realized the guilt of his client, since by canon law an advocate was forbidden to plead for a heretic in any court, civil or ecclesiastical, or in any cause whatsoever—whether connected with heresy or any other matter.

On the subject of witnesses, it should be added to what already has been said in the previous chapter that the Inquisition, whilst admitting the testimony of any man, even though he should be excommunicate or a heretic, so long as such testimony was adverse to the accused, refused to admit witnesses for the defence who were themselves tainted with heresy.

Since to bear witness in defence of a person charged with heresy might result in the witness himself becoming suspect, it will be understood that witnesses for the defence were not easily procured by the accused.

CHAPTER XII
THE JURISPRUDENCE OF THE HOLY OFFICE—THE AUDIENCE OF TORMENT

Eymeric's cold-blooded directions for leading an accused who refused to confess into contradictions that should justify his being put to torture have already been considered.

The inquisitors could not proceed to employ the question—as the torture was euphemistically called—save under certain circumstances prescribed by law; and the strict letter of the law, as you have seen, and as you shall see further, was a thing inviolable to these very subtle judges.

These circumstances, as expounded by Eymeric in his "Directorium,"[107] are (a) the inconsistence of the accused's replies upon matters of detail whilst denying the main fact; (b) the existence of semi-plenal proof of his offence.

This semi-plenal proof is considered forthcoming—

> (a) When an accused is "reputed" to be a heretic and there is but one witness against him who can depone to having seen or heard him do or say that which is against the Faith. (Two witnesses were by law required to establish his guilt.)
>
> (b) When in the absence of witnesses there are grounds for vehement or violent suspicion.
>
> (c) When there is no evil "reputation" attaching to the accused, but one witness against him and *grounds* for vehement or violent suspicion—*i.e.* not actual suspicion but indications of it; a suspicion of suspicion, as it were. The distinction is most elusively fine.

The scholiast Pegna adds in his commentaries that this combination of "reputation" (or grounds for suspicion) and one witness is not necessary to justify submitting the accused to the question—

> (a) When to evil reputation are added evil morals, which lead easily to heresy—thus those who are incontinent and very greatly addicted to women persuade themselves that this incontinence is not in itself a sin. (Such an opinion if proclaimed would amount to heresy, therefore one who acts as if he held it lays himself open to suspicion of heresy.)
>
> (b) When the accused who has incurred evil reputation shall have fled. (The circumstance of his flight is accepted as evidence of evil conscience.)[108]

Eymeric further enjoins that the question shall be employed only when all other means of obtaining the truth shall have failed, and he recommends the use of exhortation, gentleness, and ruse to draw the truth from the prisoner.[109]

He observes that, after all, not even the torture can be depended upon always to extract the truth. There are weak men who under the first torments confess even what they have not done; and there are others so stubborn and vigorous that they can suffer the greatest pains; there are those who having already undergone torture are able to endure it with greater fortitude, knowing how to adapt themselves to it; and there are others still who, by having recourse to sorcery, remain almost insensible to the pain and would die before divulging anything.

These last, he warns inquisitors, use passages from the Gospel curiously inscribed upon virgin parchment, intermingling in these the names of angels that are unknown, designs of circles, and magic characters. These charms they bear about their bodies.

"I don't yet know," he confesses, "what remedies are available against these sorceries; but it will be well to strip and closely to examine the patient before putting him to the question."

He recommends that when the accused has been sentenced to torture, and whilst the executioners are making ready to perform it, the inquisitor should continually endeavour to induce the accused to confess. The torturers should strip him with precipitation, but with a sorrowful air and almost as if troubled for him (*quasi turbati*). When stripped, he should be taken aside and once more exhorted to confess. His life may be promised him, provided that the crime of which he is accused is not such as to make it forfeit.

If all proves vain the inquisitor shall proceed to the question, beginning by interrogating him upon the more trivial matters of which he is accused, as he would naturally acknowledge these more readily (and when acknowledged they can be made the stepping-stones to more), the notary being at hand to write down all that is asked and answered.

If he persists in his denials he is to be shown further implements of torture, and assured that he will have to undergo them all unless he speaks the truth.

If he still denies, the question may be *continued* on the second or third day, but not *repeated*.

Here again we have them observing the letter and flagrantly violating the spirit of the law. Torture must not be repeated because it is by law forbidden to put an accused to the question more than once, unless in the meantime fresh evidence has been forthcoming; but it is not forbidden to continue it—not forbidden because those who formulated that law never dreamt of such a quibble being raised.

It is almost incredible that men should juggle with words in this way. But here is the passage itself:

"Ad continuandum non ad iterandum, quia iterari non debent, nisi novis supervenientibus indiciis, sed continuari non prohibentur."

Lest they should be in danger of having to repeat the torture, they took care to suspend it as soon as the patient was at the limit of his endurance, and merely resumed or continued it two or three days later, to suspend again and continue again as often as they might deem necessary.

That it can have made no difference to the wretched patient whether they described the procedure by one verb or the other does not appear to have weighed with them. There was a difference—an important verbal difference.

Upon this point the apologist Garcia Rodrigo, in his "Historia Verdadera de la Inquisicion," very daringly draws attention to the meekness of the courts of the Inquisition as compared with the civil tribunals. He contrasts the methods of the two, and to make out a case in favour of the former, to prove to us that those who preached a gospel of mercy knew also how to practise mercy, he tells us, rather disingenuously, that whilst in civil courts a prisoner might be ordered three times to the torture, in the courts of the Inquisition this could not be imposed upon him more than once—*its rules forbidding repetition.*

He does not consider it worth while to add that the "Directorium" in which he found that rule points out, as we have seen, how it may be circumvented

It is much easier to set up a case for the other side, to show that the greater mercy in the matter of torture was practised by the secular courts. In these, for instance, a nobleman was immune from torture. Not so in the courts of the Inquisition, which proceeded, no doubt, upon the grounds that all are equals in the sight of God. No exception was made there in favour of any man. And in Aragon, where the torture was never applied in civil trials, it was none the less resorted to by the inquisitors.

When the accused shall have endured torture without confessing, the inquisitors may order his release by sentence, stating that after careful examination they are unable to find anything against him on the score of the crime of which he is accused—which, of course, is no acquittal, since he may at any time be re-arrested and put upon his trial once more.

In his commentaries Pegna tells us[110] that there are five degrees of torture. He does not mention them in detail, saying that they are sufficiently well known to all. These five degrees are given in Limborch.[111]

The first four are not so much torture as terror—or mental torture; it is only in the fifth degree that this becomes physical. The conception is of an almost fiendish subtlety; and yet its aim, we must believe, was merciful, since they accounted it more merciful to torture and terrify the mind than to bruise the flesh.

Eymeric's directions are the basis of this, although Eymeric himself does not break up the procedure into degrees. These are:

(1) The threat of torture.

(2) Being conducted to the torture-chamber and shown the implements and their functions.

(3) Stripping and preparing for the ordeal.

(4) Laying and binding upon the engine.

(5) The actual torture.

The actual torture was of various kinds, any of which the inquisitor might employ as he considered most suitable and effective, but Pegna admonishes him not to resort to unusual ones. Marsilius, the scholiast informs us, mentions fourteen different varieties, and adds that he had imagined others, such as that of depriving a prisoner of sleep. In this he appears to have received the approval of other authors, but he does not receive Pegna's. Even the scholiast is shocked at an ecclesiastic's fertility of invention in this branch, and confesses that such researches are better suited to executioners than theologians.

It must be admitted that the records show none of that fiendish invention which is so widely believed to have been exercised. The cruel subtleties of the inquisitors were spiritual rather than physical, and we have just seen Pegna's censure of an inquisitor who gave his attention to the devising of novel and ingenious torments.

It is very clear, from the records we have, that the Holy Office must have been content to depend upon the engines already in existence, or, rather, upon a limited number of the most efficacious. There were exceptions, of course. The torture of fire—which consisted in toasting the feet of the patient after anointing them with fat—appears upon rare occasions to have been employed; and a barbarous piece of supererogative cruelty was practised at a great Auto de Fé held at Valladolid in 1636: ten Jews convicted of having whipped a crucifix were made to stand with one hand nailed to an arm of a St. Andrew's cross whilst sentence of death was being read to them.

As a rule, however, both in torturing and in punishing the inquisitors avoided novelties. For the question they usually resorted to one of three methods: the rack; the *garrucha*, which is the torture of the hoist, the *tratta di corda* of the Italians; and the *escalera*, or *potro*, or ladder, or water torture.

The inquisitors attended in person—as prescribed by Torquemada—to question the patient, accompanied by their notary, who wrote down in fullest detail an account of the proceedings.

The hoist was the simplest of all engines; it consisted of no more than a rope running through a pulley attached to the ceiling of the torture-chamber.

The patient's wrists were pinioned behind him, and one end of the rope was attached to them. Slowly then the executioners drew upon the other end, gradually raising the patient's arms behind him as far as they would go, backwards and upwards, and continuing until they brought him to tip-toe and then slowly off the ground altogether, so that the whole weight of his body was thrown upon his straining arms.

At this point he was again questioned and desired to confess the truth.

If he refused to speak, or if he spoke to no such purpose as his questioners desired, he was hoisted towards the ceiling, then allowed to drop a few feet, his fall being suddenly arrested by a jerk that almost threw his arms out of their sockets. Again was the question put, and if he continued stubborn he was given a further drop, and so on until he had come to the ground once more, or until he had confessed. If he reached the ground without confessing, weights were now attached to his feet, thus increasing the severity of the torture, which was resumed. And so it continued. The weights were increased, the drops were lengthened—or else he might be left hanging— until confession was extracted, or until with dislocated shoulders the patient had reached the limit of his endurance.[112]

In the latter case the torture might be suspended, as we have seen, to be continued two or three days later, when the prisoner should sufficiently have recovered.

The notary made a scrupulous record of the *audiencia*—the weights attached, the number of hoists endured, the questions asked and the answers delivered.

The potro, or water-torture, was more complex, far more cruel, and appears to have been greatly favoured by the Holy Office.

The patient was placed upon a short narrow engine, in the shape of a ladder, and this was slanted a little so that his head was below the level of his feet, for reasons that will soon be apparent. His head was now secured by a metal or leather band which held it rigidly in position, whilst his arms and legs were lashed to the sides of the ladder so tightly that any movement on his part must cause the whipcord to cut into his flesh.

In addition to these bindings garrotes were applied to his thighs and legs and arms. This was a length of cord tied firmly about a limb—upon occasion round the whole torso over the arms; a stick was thrust between the cord and the flesh, and by twisting this stick a tourniquet was formed; first strangury, then the most agonizing pain was thus occasioned, whilst if the twisting was carried far enough the cords would sink through nerve and sinew until they reached the bone.

The mouth of the patient was now distended and held so by a prong of iron—called a *bostezo*. His nostrils were plugged, and a long strip of linen was placed across his jaws, and carried deep into his throat by the weight of water poured into his gaping mouth. Down this *toca*—as the strip was called— water continued to be slowly poured. As this water filtered through the cloth, the patient was subjected to all the torments of suffocation, the more cruel because he was driven by his instincts to make futile efforts to ease his condition. He would constantly exert himself to swallow the water, hoping thus to clear the way for a little air to pass into his bursting lungs. A little would and did pass in—just enough to keep him alive and conscious, but not enough to mitigate the horrible sufferings of asphyxiation, for the cloth was always wet and constantly charged with water.

From time to time the *toca* was brought up, and the gasping wretch would be invited to confess. Further to combat stubbornness on his part, and also, it would seem, to revive him when he was failing, the executioners would give an agonizing turn or two to the garrotes upon his—or her—limbs; for the Holy Office did not discriminate between the sexes in these matters.

To prevent the vomiting which any form of torture might produce, and the *potro* in particular, the inquisitors, with their never-failing attention to detail, provided that no patient should be given food for eight hours before the question was applied. The notary present at this *audiencia de tormento* was required to set down, in addition to questions asked and answers returned, the fullest details of the torture applied, and particularly how many jars of water were administered, these being the measure of the severity of the ordeal.[113]

The rack is too well-known to need describing here, having in its time been used in all European countries. Cruel as it was, it was perhaps one of the least cruel engines of torture that have been employed.

It was required by law that any confession extracted under torture should afterwards be ratified by the prisoner. This was one of the prescriptions of Alfonso XI in the Partidas code. It recognizes that a man might be driven by pain to say that which is not true, and therefore it forbids the courts to accept as evidence what might be declared under torture.

Therefore on one of the three days after the question had been applied—as soon, presumably, as the prisoner was sufficiently recovered to attend—the prisoner was brought once more into the audience-chamber.

His confession, reduced to writing by the notary, was placed before him, and he was invited to sign it—the act being necessary to convert that confession into admissible evidence. If he signed, the proceedings now ran swiftly and uninterruptedly to their end. If he refused to sign, repudiating the statements made, the inquisitors proceeded upon the lines laid down by Torquemada in Article XV of his "Instructions" to meet the case.

Pegna warns inquisitors against delinquents who feign madness to avoid the torture. They should not, he says, delay on that account, for the torture may be the best means of ascertaining whether the madness is real or simulated.[114]

Finally let it be added upon this gruesome subject that it was not only the accused who was liable to be put to the question. A witness suspected of falsehood, or one who had lapsed into contradictions in the course of his evidence, might be put to torture *in caput alienum*.[115]

CHAPTER XIII
THE JURISPRUDENCE OF THE HOLY OFFICE—THE SECULAR ARM

The comparatively light sentences imposed upon those who came forward to abjure heresies which they were suspected of harbouring, and upon those who submitted to canonical purgation to cleanse them of "evil reputation," have already been considered.

It remains to be seen how the Holy Office dealt with *negativos*—*i.e.* those who persisted in refusal to confess a first offence of heresy or apostasy after their guilt had been established to the satisfaction of the court—and with *relapsos*—*i.e.* those who were convicted of having relapsed into error after once having been penanced and pardoned.

Offenders in either of these two classes were to be abandoned to the secular arm—the ecclesiastical euphemism for death by fire. The same fate also awaited impenitent heretics and contumacious heretics.

He who after having been convicted by sufficient witnesses persisted in denying his guilt should, says Eymeric, be abandoned to the secular arm upon the ground that he who denies a crime which has been proved against him is obviously impenitent.[116]

The impenitence is by no means obvious. It is possible, after all, that the accused might deny because he was innocent and a good Catholic. And whilst, as we shall see, this possibility is not altogether ignored, yet it is given very secondary consideration. It was the inquisitor's business to assume the guilt of any one brought before him.

It is true, however, that Eymeric urges the inquisitors to proceed very carefully in the examination of the witnesses against such a man; he recommends them to give the accused time in which to resolve himself to confess, and to employ every possible means to obtain such confession.

He counsels them to confine the prisoner in an uncomfortable dungeon, fettered hand and foot; there to visit him frequently and exhort him to confess. Should he ultimately do so, he is to be treated as a penitent heretic[117]—in other words he is to escape the fire but suffer perpetual imprisonment.

The term perpetual imprisonment, or perpetual immuration, is not to be accepted too literally. It lay at the discretion of the inquisitors to modify and commute part of such sentences, and this discretion they exercised so far as the imprisonment was concerned. But the confiscation of the prisoner's property and the infamy attaching to himself, his children, and his grandchildren—by far the heavier part of the punishment—could not in any way be commuted.

However tardily confession might come from the *negativo*, the inquisitors must accept and recognize it. Even if he were already bound to the stake, and, at last, being taken with the fear of death, he turned to the friar who never left him until the faggots were blazing, admitted his guilt and offered to abjure his heresy, his life would be spared. And this for all that they recognized that a confession in such extremes was wrung from him by "the fear of death rather than any love of truth."

It must naturally occur to any one that, conducted in secret as were the examinations of the witnesses, and no opportunity being afforded the accused of demolishing the evidence offered against him, since he was rarely informed of its extent, many a good Catholic, or, at least, many a man innocent of all heretical practices, must have gone to his death as a *negativo*. For the methods of the Holy Office opened the door extraordinarily wide to malevolence; and human nature being such as it is—and such as it was in the fifteenth century—it is not to be supposed that malevolence never seized the chance, that it never slunk in through that gaping door to vent itself in such close and sheltered secrecy—to strike in the back, in the dark, with almost perfect immunity to itself, at the man who was hated, or envied, or whom it was desired to supplant.

It was not sufficient for the prisoner to protest his innocence. He must prove it categorically. An innocent man might be unable to furnish categorical proof; witnesses for the defence were extremely difficult to obtain by one who was charged with heresy; it was a dangerous thing to testify in favour of such a man; should his conviction none the less follow, the witness for the defence might find himself prosecuted as a befriender, or *fautor*, of heretics. Yet, even when testimony for the defence was obtained, the judges leaned upon principle to the side of the accusers; and since they considered it their mission to convict rather than to judge, they would always assume that the accusers were better informed than the defenders.

Therefore this danger of death to the innocent existed. The inquisitors themselves did not lose sight of it, for they lost sight of nothing. But how did they provide for it? Pegna has a great deal to say upon the subject. He tells us that some authorities pretend that when a *negativus* protests that he staunchly believes all that is taught by the Roman Catholic Church such a man should not be abandoned to the secular arm.

But this is an argument mentioned by the scholiast merely that he may demolish it. It is indefensible, he says with confidence; and, as indefensible, it is almost universally rejected.

Torquemada most certainly did not favour it. He lays it down clearly in Art. XXIV of his first "Instrucciones" that a *negativo* must be deemed an impenitent heretic, however much he may protest his Catholicism. The accused will not satisfy the Church, which demands confession of his fault solely that she may pardon it; and she cannot pardon it until it is confessed. That is the inquisitorial view of the matter.

It is evident that the danger of occasionally burning an innocent man did not perturb the inquisitorial mind. In fact, Pegna reveals to the full the equanimity with which it could contemplate such an accident.

"After all," says he, "should an innocent person be unjustly condemned, he should not complain of the sentence of the Church, which was founded upon sufficient proof, and which cannot judge of what is hidden. If false witnesses condemned him, he should receive the sentence with resignation, and rejoice in dying for the truth."[118]

He is also, we are to suppose, to rejoice with the same lightheartedness at the prospect of his children's destitution and infamy.

Anything, it seems, is possible to argument, and the craziest argument may be convincing to him who employs it. Pegna makes this abundantly clear.

An innocent man might be tempted to save his life by a falsehood, by making the desired confession; and many a man may so have escaped burning. This also the scholiast duly weighs. He propounds the question whether a man convicted by false witnesses is justified in saving his life by a confession of crimes which he has not committed.[119]

He contends that, reputation being an external good, each is at liberty to sacrifice it to avoid torments that are hurtful, or to save his life, which is the most precious of all possessions.

In this contention the scholiast lacks his usual speciousness. He has entirely overlooked that whether an innocent man confesses or not, whether he is burnt or sent to perpetual imprisonment, his reputation is equally blasted. The inquisitors see to that. His silence is interpreted as impenitence.

But it is evident that Pegna himself is not quite satisfied with what he urges. He vacillates a little. Strong swimmer though he is, these swirling waters of casuistry begin to give him trouble. He seems here to turn in an attempt to regain the shore. "Who thus accuses himself," he concludes, "commits a venial sin against the love which he owes himself and a falsehood in confessing a crime which he has not committed. This falsehood is particularly criminal when uttered to a judge who examines juridically, for it then becomes a mortal sin. And even though it were no more than venial, it would not be permitted to commit it for the sake of avoiding death or torture."

"Therefore," he sums up, "however hard it may seem for an innocent man condemned as a *negativus* to die under such circumstances, his confessor must exhort him not to accuse himself falsely, reminding him that if he suffers death with resignation he will obtain the martyr's immortal crown."

In short, to burn at the stake for crimes never committed is a boon, a privilege, a glory to be enjoyed with a profound gratitude towards the inquisitors who vouchsafed it. One cannot help a pang of regret at the thought that the scholiast himself should have been denied that glory.

A person was considered *relapsus*—relapsed into heresy—not only if, as in the case of the self-delator who availed himself of the edict of grace, he had once been pardoned an avowed heresy, but if he had once abjured a heresy of which he had been suspected either vehemently or violently. And it was of no account whether the heresy of which he was now convicted was that particular one of which formerly he had been suspected, or an entirely fresh one. Moreover, to convict as a relapsed heretic one who had already abjured, it was sufficient to show that he held intercourse with heretics.

Further, a person would be dealt with as *relapsus* in the event of formal proof appearing that he had actually committed the heresy which he had abjured as suspect, although his conduct since abjuration might have been entirely blameless. For it was argued that these fresh proofs, although acquired after abjuration, revealed the person's real guilt, and showed that he had been judged too leniently in being allowed to abjure merely upon suspicion.[120]

In fact, it was held that he had acted in bad faith towards the inquisitors; that he had neglected to confess his sin when he was given the opportunity; that he had attempted to defraud the treasury of his property, which was due to it by confiscation. Since he had not made an open and complete confession, it was argued that he was clearly an impenitent heretic, for whom there could be no mercy—or only a very slight one, as we shall see.

Canonical purgation entailed the same sequel as abjuration for one against whom proofs of heresy were afterwards forthcoming. Thus, to quote an instance given by Pegna: if a man should be suspected of thinking that heretics should be tolerated, and if after being canonically purged of the offence against the Faith contained in that sentiment of which he was suspected, it should be proved against him that his acts or words had actually expressed that sentiment, he must be considered a relapsed heretic.

Torquemada further decreed that any who after reconciliation should fail to fulfil the penance imposed upon him, or any part of it, must be deemed relapsed. The argument, obviously, was that a neglect of this penance showed a want of proper contrition, which could only be explained in one way.

A relapsed heretic, once his guilt was thoroughly established, must be "abandoned to the secular arm," and this notwithstanding any repentance he might manifest or any promises he might make for the future. "*Sine audientia quacumque*," says Eymeric.[121] "In effect," adds his commentator, "it is enough that such people should once have defrauded the Church by false confession"[122]—a statement this, diametrically opposed to the injunction of the Founder of Christianity on the score of forgiveness.

All the mercy they vouchsafed a relapsed heretic who confessed and expressed repentance was the mercy of being strangled at the stake before his body was burnt.

Eymeric instructs inquisitors to see that the prisoner is visited and entertained on the subject of contempt for this world, the miseries of this life and the joys of Paradise. He should be given to understand that there is no hope of his escaping temporal death, and he should be induced to put the affairs of his conscience in order. He is to be accorded the sacraments of Penitence and the Eucharist if he solicits them with humility. Further, the inquisitor is advised not to visit him personally, lest the sight of him should excite the sin of anger in the doomed man, and so turn him from the sentiments of patience and penance which are to be inspired in him.

It would seem at least that the inquisitors had no delusions as to the sentiments which the sight of them inspired in their victims, just as it seems that they were able to endure these with Christian resignation—perhaps even with that sense of martyrdom of him who accounts himself misunderstood or misjudged.

After some days thus employed in preparing the prisoner for death, the inquisitor should advise the secular justices of the day and hour and place when and where he would abandon to them a heretic. At the same time an announcement should be made to the people inviting them to attend, as the inquisitor is to preach a sermon of the Faith, and those who are present will gain the usual indulgences.[123]

It is not necessary at present to enter into particulars of the dread ceremonial, the ghastly, almost theatrical, solemnities that went to compose the greatest horror that has sprung from the womb of Christianity: the Auto de Fé.

"An Asiatic," says Voltaire, "arriving in Madrid on the day of an Auto de Fé, would doubt whether here was a festival, a religious celebration, a sacrifice, or a massacre. It is all of these. They reproach Montezuma with sacrificing human captives to God. What would he have said had he witnessed an Auto de Fé?"[124]

Occasion to enter into these details will occur later. We are more concerned at the moment with the words of the inquisitors than with their acts, and it is necessary on the subject of the laws that governed the Auto de Fé to touch upon quite the most extraordinary of all the quibbles by means of which the Holy Office avoided—in the letter—committing an irregularity.

Nothing in the whole of its jurisprudence savours more rankly of hypocrisy than this matter of abandoning a heretic to the secular arm. It is the very last word in that science which it is the fashion to call "Jesuitism," but which we think might quite as aptly and justly be termed "Dominicanism." Yet it would be very rash to say that these men were prompted by conscious hypocrisy. Such is certainly not the inference to be drawn from their jurisprudence. Stupidity—the stupidity of the man of one idea, of the man who is able to perceive but one thing at a time—was, rather than hypocrisy, responsible for what they did.

They were imbued with a passion for formality, for procedure that should be scrupulously correct, scrupulously in accordance with the letter of the law; and they justified their circumvention, their perversion of its spirit, with crazy arguments that must at least have been convincing to themselves, obfuscated as they were by the fanaticism that bubbled through their extraordinary intelligences.

We say that these arguments must have been convincing to themselves, because we find them in books that were never intended to be perused by any but inquisitors and ecclesiastics. Since these books were never meant to be placed before the world, no suspicion can attach to them of having deliberately and hypocritically resorted to sophistries for the purpose of hoodwinking the lay mind.

It was themselves they hoodwinked—by the arguments they themselves conceived—and although it is undeniable that they practised a deception which must provoke the scorn of every thoughtful man, yet it must be remembered that this deception was the self-deception that lies in wait for every fanatic, whatever the subject of his fanaticism. By staring too long and too intently at one object, that object itself becomes blurred and indistinct.

"*Ecclesia abhorret a sanguine.*"

That was the principle that governed them. Conceive it!

The tenet that a Christian must not be guilty of shedding blood or causing the death of a fellow-creature has been touched upon more than once in these pages. It has been seen how in the very dawn of Christianity the Christian's refusal to bear arms in the service of the State gave rise to friction with the Roman authorities, and, being construed into insubordination, was one of the causes of the persecutions to which Christians were subjected in the first and second centuries. As time went on, under stress of the necessities of this world, the Christian was forced to abandon that fine and loftily humanitarian ideal. Soon he had not only abandoned it under pressure of expediency, but he had forgotten it altogether; so that he donned the cross of the crusader, and went forth sword in hand, exultantly, to shed the blood of the infidel in the name of that tender Founder Whose disciple had brought to Rome the great Message of Forbearance.

But however much it might be accounted justifiable and even necessary for the Christian layman to wield the sword, the priest still continued under the prohibition to shed blood or compass the death of any man. And if a priest lay under such an injunction, so must a tribunal that was controlled by priests.

Therefore it follows that not only was it admittedly illicit for the inquisitor to pass a capital sentence, to send a man to his death, but even to be in any way a party to such an act.

This was the letter of the law, and, happen what might, that letter must suffer no violence. Nor did it. When the accused was found guilty of heresy, when he was impenitent, or relapsed, the inquisitor was careful that the sentence he passed contained no single word that could render him responsible for the delinquent's death. Far from it. The inquisitors earnestly implored the secular justiciaries to whom they abandoned him not to do him any hurt whatever.

But consider the actual formula of the sentence as prescribed by Eymeric. It concluded thus:

"The Church of God can do no more for you, since you have already abused its goodness.... Therefore we cast you out from the Church, and we abandon you to the secular justice, beseeching it none the less, and earnestly, so to moderate its sentence that it may deal with you without shedding your blood or putting you in danger of death."[125]

They were careful not so much as to say that they *delivered* him to the secular arm; for delivery suggests activity in a matter in which they must remain absolutely passive. They merely *abandoned* him. Pilate-like, they washed their hands of him. If the secular justiciaries chose to bear him away and burn him at the stake in spite of their "earnest intercessions" to the contrary, that was the secular justiciaries' affair.

Thus was the letter of the law most scrupulously observed, and the inquisitor displayed in his intercession on the heretic's behalf the benignity proper to his sacerdotal office. His conscience was entirely at peace.

For the rest, he knew, of course, that there was a bull of Innocent IV, known as "ad extirpanda," which compelled the secular justiciaries, under pain of greater excommunication, and of being themselves prosecuted as heretics and *fautores*, to put to death within a term of not more than five days any convicted heretic taken within their jurisdiction.

Francesco Pegna recommends inquisitors to be careful not to omit the intercession on the prisoner's behalf, lest they should render themselves guilty of an irregularity. At the same time he raises the interesting question whether an inquisitor can reconcile this intercession with his conscience— not, as you might suppose, upon the score of the dissimulation it entails; but purely on the ground that it is most strictly forbidden to intercede on behalf of heretics; to do so, indeed, is to incur suspicion of being a befriender of heretics—an offence as punishable as heresy itself.

This question he has no difficulty in answering. Thus:

"In truth it would not be permitted to employ for a heretic an intercession that would be of any advantage to him, or which tended to hinder the justice which is to be executed upon his crime, but only an intercession whose aim it is to relieve the inquisitor of the irregularity he might otherwise incur."

He goes on to say that when the heretic has been abandoned to the secular justiciaries, the latter must pronounce their own sentence and conduct him to the place of execution, permitting him to be accompanied by pious men, who will pray for him and not leave him until he shall have delivered up his soul. And he reminds the inquisitors—though it hardly seems necessary— that should the magistrates delay in putting to death a heretic who has been abandoned to them, they must be regarded as *fautores* and themselves prosecuted.

Innocent IV, as we have seen, allowed the magistrates a term of five days in which to do their duty in this matter, and in Italy it was usual to take the heretics back to prison after sentence, and bring them forth again upon a week-day—always within the prescribed term—to be burnt. In Spain, however, the custom was that the magistrates having pronounced their own sentence—as soon as the heretic was abandoned to them—should immediately proceed to execute it.

According to some authorities the sentence, by which was meant the Auto de Fé generally, should not take place in church. Pegna agrees with these, but not upon the score of the desecration of sanctuary, which was their reason. He agrees because in a large open space higher scaffolds can be erected for the Auto, and greater multitudes can assemble to witness this uplifting spectacle of the triumph of the Faith. On the same grounds does he belittle those who maintain that heretics should not be put to death on Sundays. He considers it quite the best day of the week, and excellent the Spanish custom that appoints it for the Auto, "for," he says, "it is good that large multitudes should attend, so that fear may turn them from evil ways; the spectacle being one that inspires the attendance with terror and presents a fearful image of the last judgment."

That it is expedient to put heretics to death no pious authority has ever ventured to dispute. But there have been differences of opinion on the subject of the means by which this should be done. The scholiast is entirely on the side of the large majority that considers fire the proper instrument, and actually cites the Saviour's own authority for this: "If a man abide not in me, he is cast forth as a branch that is withered; and men gather them, and cast them into the fire, and they are burned" (John xv. 6).

If the accused should happen to be a cleric, he must be unfrocked and degraded by a bishop before being arrayed in the hideous *sanbenito* and abandoned to the secular arm, whilst those convicted of contumacy were— if still absent at the time of the sentence—to be burnt in effigy pending their capture, when, without further trial, they would be burnt alive.

In effigy also were burnt those convicted after death, these effigies being cast into the flames together with the remains of the dead man, which were exhumed for the purpose.

Reference has several times been made here to the *sanbenito* which was imposed upon all whom the Holy Office found guilty of heresy, whether reconciled or abandoned, and also upon those who were suspected in the degree *violenter*.

In this garment they attended the Auto de Fé, and went to execution if they were abandoned; or they might be required to wear it for varying periods after reconciliation, and in some instances for as long as they lived, to advertise their infamy.

It was the perversion into a garb of shame and disgrace of the penitential garment originally prescribed by St. Dominic; for whereas once it—or, rather, that from which it was derived—had been worn even by princes as an outward mark of contrition for the sins into which they had fallen, it was now imposed that it might subject its wearer to opprobrium and contempt.

St. Dominic's instructions were that it should be a sackcloth habit, of the kind worn by his own brotherhood, and that its colour might be at the discretion of the wearer so long as it was sombre. As it had ever been the custom of the Church to bless the "sack" or tunic worn by members of religious confraternities or by those upon whom it had been imposed as a penance, such a garment was called a *saco bendito*, which in course of time was contracted into *sanbenito*, though also known by its proper Spanish name of *zamarra*.

When the crusade against the Albigensian heretics was at its height in Southern France, not only did the crusaders wear the cross upon their garments, but all faithful Catholics assumed it for their protection; for—as on the night of the St. Bartholomew, some four centuries later—no man's life was safe if he did not display that device. St. Dominic desired that the penitent should enjoy the same protection, but so that his penance should still be proclaimed, he was ordered to wear two crosses, one on each breast.

Later, when the wars of religion had ceased, and the general wearing of the cross was abandoned, the Council of Toulouse decreed, in 1229, that these penitential crosses should be yellow, whilst the Council of Beziers, four years later, going further into the matter, ordained that they should be two and a half hands long (vertical) by two hands wide (horizontal), and that they should be made of cloth of the width of three fingers. Instead of being worn upon the breast, as hitherto, they were now placed one on the breast and one on the back, with a third on the hood or veil if hood or veil were worn.

For abettors of heresy the following solemn penance was enjoined by the Council of Tarragona in 1242:

"On All Saints', on the First Sunday in Advent, on the feasts of Christmas, the Circumcision, the Epiphany, St. Mary of February (Purification), St. Mary of March, and all Sundays in Lent, the penitents shall go to the Cathedral to take part in the procession. They shall be dressed only in their shirts, barefoot, their arms crossed, and they shall be whipped in the procession by the bishop or parish priest. Similarly shall they repair to the Cathedral on Ash Wednesday in their shirts, barefoot, their arms crossed, and submit to banishment from church for all Lent; so that during that season they must remain at the church door and hear the service thence. On Thursday in Holy Week they shall come to the church to be reconciled in accordance with the canonical provisions, it being understood that this penance of remaining out of the church through Lent and of being whipped in procession on the days appointed shall be performed yearly for the remainder of the penitents' lives."

At first, and down to Eymeric's day, the *sanbenito* preserved its original form—a tunic similar to that worn by the members of regular orders. But in the fourteenth century it was altered to a scapulary or tabard, with an opening at the top through which the head was passed; it was to be of the full width of the body, and to descend no lower than the knees, lest it should too closely resemble the scapulary which the regulars wore in addition to their tunic. Soon after it was resolved that it should be of yellow sackcloth, and that the crosses should be red.

Once this stage was reached, it may be said that the transition from a garment solely of penitence into a garment chiefly of shame and infamy was complete.

Photo by Donald Macbeth.

PROCESSION TO AUTO DE FÉ.
From Limborch's "Historia Inquisitionis."

We have said that the imposition of the *sanbenito* had been falling into desuetude during the fifteenth century. But for Torquemada it might indeed have become entirely obsolete. It happened, however, that the Prior of Holy Cross perceived the virtues of it, the salutary results to be obtained from parading the victims of the Holy Office in that hideous garb. Therefore he revived it, and strongly enjoined its use by all offenders save those against whom there was no more than evil reputation, and who submitted themselves to be purged of this canonically.

It was not, however, until the famous Ximenes de Cisneros, who became Grand Inquisitor some ten years after Torquemada's death—that the *sanbenito* attained its full development, the form which it was to preserve until the extinction of the Inquisition.

Cisneros substituted for the ordinary rectangular cross worn on back and breast of the *sanbenito* an *aspa*, or St. Andrew's cross, and he otherwise disposed that the *sanbenito* might proclaim the offence and sentence of its wearer. Three varieties were devised for those who were abjuring a heresy of which they had incurred suspicion: the suspect of the degree *leviter* wore a perfectly plain *sanbenito* without any cross or other device; the suspect *vehementer* wore upon back and breast one arm only of the St. Andrew's cross; the suspect *violenter* was made to wear the full cross.

Those actually convicted of heresy wore in addition to the *sanbenito* a tall mitre, or pyramidal cap, made of cardboard and covered with yellow sackcloth; and that their precise condition might be distinguished, the following differentiations were prescribed: the heretic who repented before the passing of sentence, and who—not being a relapsed—was not to die by fire, bore upon the breast and back of his *sanbenito* and upon the front and back of his *coroza*, as the mitre was called, a full St. Andrew's cross; the relapsed heretic who had repented before the Auto bore, in addition to the crosses, the device of a bust upon burning faggots on the nether part of his *sanbenito*; further his *sanbenito* and *coroza* were flecked with tongues of flame, which pointed downwards to signify that he was not to die by fire, although his body was to be burnt. He had deserved the charity of being strangled at the stake before the faggots were ignited. And this mercy, be it added, the Holy Office conceded to any heretic who at the eleventh hour confessed his guilt and desired to make his peace with the Church and die, as it were, upon her loving bosom. To this end the condemned was accompanied from the Auto to the stake by two friars, who never ceased to exhort him to make confession, save his body from the temporal torment of physical fire, and his soul from the eternal torment of spiritual fire.

Finally, the impenitent heretic bore the same devices as the relapsed penitent, but in his case the tongues of flame pointed upwards to show that he was to die by them, and his *sanbenito* was further daubed with crude paintings of devils—horrible, grotesque caricatures—to advertise the spirits ruling over his soul.

Something should by now have been gathered of the spirit of the Inquisition as reflected in the pages of Eymeric and his commentator Pegna in that "Directorium" upon which such copious draught has been made for these chapters upon the Jurisprudence of the Holy Office. It is worth while, before proceeding, to cite another author's views upon Justice and Mercy as understood by the Inquisition, and to consider an illuminating passage from the pen of Garcia de Trasmiera.

This Trasmiera—to whom reference has been made already—was an Aragonese, an inquisitor who lived in the seventeenth century—nearly two hundred years after the epoch with which we are here concerned. We might go to a score of other sources, from Paramo downwards, for very similar sentiments, and the only reason for choosing this particular passage from Trasmiera is that it is almost in the nature of an epitome.

He seems to summarize the very arguments with which Torquemada and his delegates convinced themselves not merely of the righteousness, but of the inevitability—if they were to do their duty by God and man, and fulfil the destinies for which they had been sent into this world—of the task to which they had set their hands.

"These two virtues of Mercy and Justice," says the Aragonese writer, with all the authority of an Evangelist, "are so closely united in God, although we imperfectly judge them to be opposed, that Divine Wisdom but avails Itself of the one, the more gloriously to exercise the other. The most proper effect of the Divine Mercy, none doubts, is the salvation of souls, and who can doubt that what in this court of the Inquisition appears to be rigour of Justice is really medicine prescribed by Mercy for the good of the delinquents? Just as it would be a barbarous judgment to attribute to cruelty on the part of the surgeon the cautery of fire which he employs to destroy the contagious cancer of the patient, so it would be crass ignorance to suppose that these laws which appear to be severities are prescribed for any purpose other than that which governs the surgeon in curing his patient, or a father in punishing his child. Says the Holy Ghost: 'Who does not use the rod hates the child,' and elsewhere: 'God punishes whom He loves.'"[126]

Could perversity of interpretation go further? In Rome, in Torquemada's day, the Father of Christianity was granting absolutions, commuting the punishment of hanging to pecuniary penances where such penances were solicited, and justifying such commutation by reminding Christianity that God does not desire the death of a sinner, but rather that he should live and be converted.

It would seem as if Inquisitor and Pontiff did not see eye to eye in this matter of Mercy and Justice. To the credit of the Pontiff be it said.

Trasmiera, echoing the inquisitorial casuistry of centuries, holds that the rigour of Justice is prescribed by Mercy for the good of the delinquents. The impenitent Judaizer was sent to the stake. How could that redound to his good in this world or the next? We could admit a certain logical consummation of their arguments if the inquisitors had confined themselves to burning those who repented, or those who were innocent even; by burning these whilst they were in a state of grace they would have ensured their salvation by abstracting them from all perils of future sin. But to burn the impenitent upon such grounds as they themselves urged, believing, as they did, that just as surely as his mortal part was burnt there at the stake, just so surely would his immortal part burn through all eternity in hell—that was, clearly, by their own lights, to perpetrate the murder of his soul.

CHAPTER XIV
PEDRO ARBUÉS DE EPILA

There is no difficulty in believing Llorente's statement—based upon extracts from contemporary chronicles—to the effect that the Inquisition was not looked upon with favour in Castile. It was impossible that a civilized and enlightened people should view with equanimity the institution of a tribunal whose methods, however based fundamentally upon those of the civil courts, were in the details of their practice so opposed to all conceptions of equity.

In no Catholic country does the cherishing of a fervent faith, in itself, imply respect for the clergy. Nor, for that matter, does the respect of any religion in itself signify respect for those who administer it. It appears to do so; it is even prescribed that it should; but in point of fact it seldom does, other than with simple peasant classes. The ministers, after all, are men; but by virtue of their office they labour under disadvantages greater than the ordinary man's. When they display the failings to which all men are subject, these failings wear a much graver aspect by virtue of the office they hold and the greater purity which that office implies. Holiness is looked upon as the priest's trade, and it is expected that he should conduct that trade honestly, as any layman conducts the affairs by which he earns his livelihood. The only test of honesty in the priest, of whatever denomination, lies in his own conduct; and when this falls short of that high standard in which he claims to deal, he earns a contempt akin to that which overtakes the trader who defrauds his creditors. It is remembered then, to his disadvantage, that under his cassock the cleric is a man, and so subject to all the faults that are man's heritage. But it happens that in addition to these he is subject to other failings that are peculiarly of the cassock, failings which the world has never been slow to discern in him. The worst of these is the ecclesiastical arrogance, the sacerdotal pride which has been manifested by priests of all cults, but which in none is so intolerable as in the Christian, who expounds a gospel of humility and self-abnegation. He is akin to a feudal tyrant who grinds the faces of his serfs whilst he lectures them upon the glories of democracy.

Of such priests Spain of the fifteenth century had an abundant share. She knew them and mistrusted them, and hence she mistrusted any organization of theirs which should transcend the strict limits of their office.

Now, the tribunal of the Inquisition laid itself peculiarly open to this mistrust in consequence of the secrecy of its proceedings—a secrecy, as we know, greatly increased by the enactments of Torquemada. Its trials were not conducted in open court; the examination of witnesses took place in secret and under the veil of anonymity, so that the world had no assurance of the honesty of the proceedings. When it happened that a man was arrested, the world, as a rule, knew him no more until he came forth, candle in hand, arrayed in a *sanbenito* to play his tragic part in an Auto.

By virtue of this secrecy the Inquisition had invested itself with a power far greater, more subtle, and farther-reaching than that of any civil court. The might of the Grand Inquisitor was almost boundless, and he was unanswerable to any temporal authority for the arbitrariness with which he exercised it. Rivalling the sovereign power in much, in much else the Grand Inquisitor's went above and beyond it, for not even the King himself could interfere in matters of the Faith with one who held his office directly from the Pope.

The net which Torquemada cast was of the very widest; the meshes of that net were of the closest, so that no man, however humble, could account himself safe; its threads were of the strongest, so that no man, however powerful, could be sure of breaking through were he once brought within its scope.

What, then, but terror could Torquemada and his grim machinery inspire? It is not difficult to believe the sometime secretary of the Inquisition when he assures us that the Holy Office was not favourably viewed in Spain. The marvel is that whilst the Castilians were chilled by awe into inactivity and meek submission, it should have remained for Aragon, which already had known an inquisition for a century, to rise up in rebellion.

And yet what may seem at first glance a reason why Aragon should have submitted to Torquemada's rule in matters of the Faith, may be the very reason of its rash and futile rebellion. For a hundred years already the court of the Holy Office had been operating there; but its operations, never vigorous, had become otiose. In this inactive form Aragon had suffered it to continue. But of a sudden it was roused from that lethargy by Torquemada. It was bidden to enforce its stern decrees and other sterner decrees which he added to those already in existence, and to follow the course of arbitrary procedure which he laid down. Never welcome in Aragon, it now became intolerable. The New-Christians, who knew the fate of their Castilian brethren, went with fear in their countenances, and despair and its fierce courage in their hearts.

In the spring of 1484 Ferdinand held his Cortes at Tarragona. He was attended on the occasion by Torquemada, and he seized the opportunity to present to his kingdom the gaunt Prior of Holy Cross, its pontifically-appointed Grand Inquisitor.

Torquemada's activity matched his boundless zeal. At once he convened a council composed of the Vice-Chancellor of Aragon, Alonso de Caballeria—himself a New-Christian—the Royal Councillor Alonso Carillo, and some doctors of canon law, that they might decide upon the course to be adopted in Aragon to the end that the Inquisition might be conducted with absolute uniformity there, as in Castile. This done, he proceeded to appoint inquisitors to the Archbishopric of Zaragoza, and his choice fell upon Frey Gaspar Yuglar and Frey Pedro Arbués de Epila, Master of Theology and Canon of the Metropolitan Church of Zaragoza.

After the publication of the "Instructions" drawn up that same year in Seville, Torquemada further appointed to the Holy Office of Zaragoza a fiscal advocate, an apparitor, notaries, and receivers, whereupon that office began immediately to exercise its functions under the new system.

At once the courage of despair roused the New-Christians to opposition. Amongst them were many who held high positions at court, persons of great influence and esteem, and these immediately determined to send a deputation to the Vatican and another to the Sovereigns to voice their protests against the institution of this tribunal in Aragon, and to beseech that it be abolished, or at least curtailed in its powers and inhibited from proceeding to confiscation, which was contrary to the law of the land.

This last was a shrewd request, based no doubt upon the conviction that, deprived of the confiscations upon which it battened, the tribunal must languish and very soon return to its former inoperative condition.

Nor were the *conversos* the only ones to denounce the procedure of the Holy Office. Zurita records that many of the principal nobles of Aragon rebelled against it, protesting that it was against the liberties of the kingdom to confiscate the property of men who were never allowed to learn the names of those who bore witness against them.

As well might they have appealed against death—for death itself was not more irresistible or inexorable than Torquemada. All the fruit borne by their labours was that those who had lent their names to the petition were ultimately prosecuted as hinderers of the Holy Office. But this did not immediately happen.

In the meanwhile Torquemada's delegates, Arbués and Yuglar, went about the business entrusted to them with that imperturbability which the "Directorium" enjoins. They published their edicts, ordered arrests, carried out confiscations, and proceeded with such thoroughness that it was not long before Zaragoza began to present the same lurid, ghastly spectacles that were to be witnessed in the chief cities of Castile.

In the following May (1485) they celebrated with great solemnity the first Auto de Fé, penancing many and burning some. This was followed by a second Auto in June.

The despair and irritation of the New-Christians mounted higher at these spectacles. It is believed to have reached its climax with the sudden arrest of Leonardi Eli, one of the most influential, wealthy, and respected *conversos* of Zaragoza.

Those who had put the petition afoot, abandoning now all hope of obtaining any response either from the Sovereigns or from Rome, met to concert other measures. Their leader was a man of influence named Juan Pedro Sanchez. He had four brothers in influential positions at Court, who had lent their services in the matter of the petition to the Sovereigns.

A meeting took place in the house of one Luis de Santangel, and Sanchez urged a desperate remedy for their desperate ills. They must strike terror into their terrorizers. He proposed no less than the slaughter of the inquisitors, urging with confidence that if they were slain no others would dare to fill their places. In this he seems to have underestimated the character of Torquemada.

The proposal was adopted, an oath of secrecy was pledged, plans were laid, measures were taken, and funds were collected to enable these plans to be executed. Six assassins were chosen, among whom were Juan de Abadia and his Gascon servant Vidal de Uranso, and Juan de Esperandeu. This last was the son of a *converso* then lying in the prisons of the Inquisition, whose property had already been confiscated; so that he was driven by the added spur of personal revenge. There was, too, the further incentive of a sum of five hundred florins promised by the conspirators to the slayer of Arbués, and deposited by them for that purpose with Juan Pedro Sanchez.[127]

Several early attempts to execute this project were baffled by circumstances. It would seem, moreover, that Arbués had received some warning of what was in store for him—or else he was simply conscious of the general hatred he had incurred—for he exercised the greatest prudence, took to wearing body armour, and was careful not to expose himself in any way; all of which does not suggest in him that eagerness for the martyr's crown with which his biographer Trasmiera would have us believe that he was imbued.

At last, however, the assassins found their opportunity. Late on the night of September 15 of that year, 1485, they penetrated into the Metropolitan Church to lie in wait for their victims when these should come to the midnight office imposed by the rule of their order.

Juan de Abadia, with his Gascon servant Uranso and another, entered by the main door. Esperandeu and his companions gained admittance through the sacristy.

About the pillars of the vast church, in the gloom that was scarcely relieved by the altar-lamp, they waited silently, "like bloody wolves," says Trasmiera, "for the coming of that gentle lamb."

Towards midnight there was a stir overhead; lights beat faintly upon the darkness; the canons were assembling for matins in the choir.

A note of the organ boomed through the silence, and then Arbués entered the church from the cloisters.

It seemed that even now chance did not favour them, for Arbués came alone, and their aim was to take both the inquisitors.

The dominican was on his way to join his brethren in the choir. He carried a lantern in one hand and a long bludgeon in the other. Nor did his precautions end in this. He wore a shirt of mail under his white habit, and there was a steel lining to his black velvet skull-cap. He must indeed have gone in fear, that he could not trust himself to matins save armed at all points.

He crossed the nave on his way to the staircase leading to the choir. But as he reached the pulpit on the left he halted and knelt to offer up the prescribed prayer in adoration of the Sanctissimum Sacramentum. He set the lantern down upon the ground beside him, and leant his club against a pillar.

Now was the assassins' opportunity. He was at their mercy. And although to strike now was to leave half their task undone, they must have resolved that rather than postpone the matter again in the hope of slaying both inquisitors, they had better take the one that was delivered up to them.

The chanting overhead muffled the sound of their steps as they crept up behind Arbués, out of the blackness into the faint wheel of yellow light cast by his lantern.

Esperandeu was the first to strike, and he struck clumsily, doing no more than wound the inquisitor in the left arm. But swift upon that blow followed another from Uranso—a blow so violent that it smashed part of the steel cap, and, presumably glancing off, opened a wound in the inquisitor's neck, which is believed to have been the real cause of his death.

It did not, however, at that moment incapacitate him. He staggered up, and turned to the staircase that led to the choir. But now Esperandeu returned to the assault, and drove at the Dominican so furiously with his sword that, despite the shirt of mail with which Arbués was protected, the blade went through him from side to side.

The inquisitor fell, and lay still. The organ ceased abruptly, and the assassins fled.

There was confusion now in the choir. Down the stairs came the friars with their lanterns, to discover the unconscious and bleeding inquisitor. They took him up and carried him to bed. He died forty-eight hours later at midnight on Saturday, September 17, 1485.[128]

By morning all the town had heard of the deed, and the effect which it produced was very different from that for which its perpetrators had hoped. The Old-Christians, some moved by religious zeal, some by a sense of justice, snatched up weapons and went forth to the cry of "To the fire with the *conversos!*"

The populace—an uncertain quantity, ever ready to be swayed by the first voice that is loud enough, to follow the first leader who points the way— took up the cry, and soon Zaragoza was in turmoil. Through every street rang the clamours of the multitude, which threatened to offer up one of those hecatombs in which fire disputes with steel the horrid laurel of the day.

The uproar penetrated to the Palace of Alfonso of Aragon, the seventeen-year-old Archbishop of Zaragoza. It roused that bastard of Catholic Ferdinand from his slumbers. A high-spirited lad, he summoned the grandees of the city and the officers of justice, and rode out at their head to meet and quell the rioters. But only by a promise that the fullest justice should be done upon the murderers did he succeed in dispersing them and restoring order to that distracted city.

"Divine Justice," says Trasmiera, "permitted the deed, but not its impunity."

Rash indeed had been the action of the New-Christians, and terrible was the penalty exacted, terrible the price they were made to pay for the life they had taken. In conceiving that they could intimidate by such an act a man of Torquemada's mettle, they displayed a lamentable want of judgment, as was speedily proved. To fill the place of the dead inquisitor, and to set about the stern business of avenging him, Torquemada instantly dispatched to Zaragoza Fr. Juan Colvera, Fr. Pedro de Monterubio, and Dr. Alonso de Alarcon. For the greater security of themselves and their prisoners, these delegates set up their tribunal in the royal alcazar of the Castle of Aljaferia, and proceeded to institute an active search for the culprits. Several were seized, amongst whom was Abadia's servant, Vidal de Uranso. He was put to the question, and an admission of his own guilt extracted from him. He was tortured further in the endeavour to wring from him the names of his associates in the deed, and finally he was promised "grace" if he would divulge them.

At this price the unfortunate Gascon consented to speak, betraying all whom he had known to be in the plot and all whom he had known to sympathize with it. And Llorente, who saw the records of the proceedings, tells us that when Uranso claimed the promised grace, he was benignly answered that he should receive the grace of not having his hands hacked off—as must the others—before being hanged, drawn, and quartered.

Amongst those taken were Juan de Abadia, Juan de Esperandeu, and Luis de Santangel.

Esperandeu and Uranso suffered together at the Auto of June 30, 1486—the seventh held in Zaragoza that year. Esperandeu was dragged through the city on a hurdle, his hands were hacked off on the steps of the Cathedral, whereafter he was hanged, drawn, and quartered. Five other conspirators suffered in the same Auto, being abandoned to the secular arm and burnt alive. Two others, who had escaped, were burnt in effigy, and one of these was that Juan Pedro Sanchez who had been the leading spirit in the affair. And together with these living men and the grotesque effigies of straw arrayed in *sanbenito* and *coroza* they burnt the corpse of Juan de Abadia. He had cheated in part the Justice of the Holy Office. He had committed suicide in prison by eating a glass lamp.[129]

Autos succeeded one another at such a rate now in Zaragoza that no less than fourteen were held in that year 1486; 42 persons were burnt alive, 14 in effigy, and 134 were penanced in varying degrees from perpetual imprisonment to public whippings. And to the end that the publicity of these Autos might be increased and the salutary lesson inculcated by them might be as far-reaching as possible, Torquemada ordered that a fortnight before the holding of each it should be announced by public proclamation, with great solemnity and parade of mounted familiars of the Holy Office—a matter which upon this precedent became customary throughout Spain.

In his allusion to these Autos Trasmiera[130] advances one of the usual sophistries employed by the Inquisition to justify its constant claim that its proceedings were dictated by mercy.

He assures us that it was a happiness (*dicha*) for the culprits to die so soon, and he explains that to have allowed them to live would have shown a greater rigour of justice—"as witnesseth Cain, upon whom God placed a sign ordering that none should kill him since by the prolongation of his life, his nature being what it was, he must commit more sins, and thus more surely deserve greater degrees of punishment in his eternal damnation."

It is a priest who puts forward this blasphemous assertion that God desires the damnation of a sinner, and suggests that by burning that sinner betimes, God is to be cheated—at least in part—of His unspeakable purpose. It serves excellently to show to what desperate shifts of argument men could be urged in the attempt to justify the practices of the Holy Office.

With precisely the same degree of authority does he assure us that all the murderers died penitent—in consequence of the affectionate prayers offered up for them by Arbués in the hour of his death.

Vidal de Uranso's confession had yielded up to the inquisitors the names not only of participators in the murder of Arbués, but of those who were believed by the Gascon to be in sympathy with the deed. By pursuing the methods peculiarly their own to cause a prosecution to spread like an oil-stain, slowly and surely covering an ever-widening area, the inquisitors were able to cause the indictment of many whose connection with the crime was of the remotest, and of others who, moved by a very Christian pity, had afforded shelter to New-Christians fleeing in terror before the blind vengeance of the Holy Office. Among the latter many were prosecuted where there was no proof that the fugitives they had sheltered were Judaizers or unfaithful. It is believed that sheer panic had driven many perfectly innocent New-Christians to depart from a city where no New-Christian might account himself secure. But in consequence of the clause introduced by the merciless Torquemada into his "Instructions," a man's flight was in itself a sufficient reason for the presumption of his guilt.

A reign of terror was established in Zaragoza. The tribunal of that city became one of the busiest in Spain, and it is computed that altogether some two hundred victims paid in one way and another for the death of Pedro Arbués, so that there was hardly a family, noble or simple, that was not plunged into mourning by the Justice of the Faith.

Amongst those against whom proceedings were instituted were men of the very first importance in the kingdom. One of these was that Alonso de Caballeria, Vice-Chancellor of Aragon, who had been prominent in the council summoned by Torquemada to determine the details of the introduction of the Inquisition into Aragon. Nor did they confine their attention to New-Christians. Amongst those they summoned to render to the Holy Office an account of their deeds we find no less a person than Don Jaime de Navarre, known as the Infante of Navarre or the Infante of Tudela, the son of the Queen of Navarre, and King Ferdinand's own nephew.

A fugitive New-Christian coming to Tudela cast himself upon the mercy of the prince, and found shelter in Navarre for a few days until he could escape into France. The inquisitors, whom nothing escaped, had knowledge of this, and such was their might and arrogance that they did not hesitate to arrest the Infante in the capital of his mother's independent kingdom. They haled this prince of the blood-royal to Zaragoza to stand his trial upon the charge of hindering the Holy Office. They cast him into prison, and subjected him to the humiliating penance of being whipped round the Metropolitan Church by two priests in the presence of his bastard cousin, the seventeen-year old

Archbishop, Alfonso of Aragon. Thereafter he was made to stand penitentially, candle in hand, in view of all during High Mass, before he could earn absolution of the ecclesiastical censure he had incurred.

Alonso de Caballeria is one of the few men in history who was able successfully to defy and withstand the terrible power of that sacerdotal court.

This Vice-Chancellor was a man of great ability, the son of a wealthy baptized Hebrew nobleman, whose name had been Bonafos, but who had changed this to Caballeria upon receiving baptism, in accordance with the prevailing custom. He was arrested not only upon the charge of having given shelter to fugitives, but also upon suspicion of being, himself, a Judaizer.

Presuming upon his high position, and also upon the great esteem in which he was held by his king, Caballeria showed the Inquisition an intrepid countenance. He refused to recognize the authority of the court and of Torquemada himself, appealing to the Pope, and including in his appeal a strong complaint of the conduct of the inquisitors.

This appeal was of such a character and the man's own position was so strong that on August 28, 1488, Innocent VIII dispatched a brief inhibiting the inquisitors from proceeding further against the Vice-Chancellor, and avocating to himself the case. But such was Torquemada's arrogance by now that he was no longer to be intimidated by papal briefs. Under his directions the inquisitors of Zaragoza replied that the allegations contained in Caballeria's appeal were false. The Pope, however, was insistent, and he compelled the Holy Office to bow to his will and supreme authority. On October 20 of that year the minutes of the case were forwarded to the Vatican. As a result of their perusal His Holiness must have absolved Caballeria, for not only was he delivered of the peril in which he had stood, but he continued to rise steadily in honour and consequence until he became Chief Judge and head of the Hermandad of Aragon.[131]

Llorente informs us[132] that he perused the records of some thirty trials in connection with the Arbués affair, and that the publication of any one of them would suffice to render the Inquisition detested, were it not sufficiently detested already in all civilized countries, including Spain.

He mentions, however, two cases of interest and importance,[133] to show how arbitrary was the spirit of the Inquisition, and how far-reaching its arm.

Juan Pedro Sanchez, the leader of the affair, having fled to Toulouse, was, as we have seen, sentenced as contumacious and burnt in effigy pending the seizure of his person.

In Toulouse at this time there was a student named Antonio Agustin, a member of an illustrious family of Aragon and a man destined to rise to great dignity and honour. Under the impulse of fanaticism, and acting in conjunction with several other Spaniards in Toulouse, he petitioned for the arrest of Sanchez. When this had been effected, he indited a letter to the inquisitors of Aragon, and forwarded it to his brother Pedro in Zaragoza for delivery.

Pedro, however, first discussed the matter with Guillerme Sanchez, brother of the fugitive, and three friends, and all were opposed to Agustin's purpose. They decided not to deliver the letter, and they wrote to Agustin begging him to withdraw his plea against Sanchez and consent to the fugitive's being restored to liberty.

Agustin was persuaded, and replied informing his brother that he had done as they had requested. Once Pedro Agustin in Zaragoza was assured of this, he delivered the letters to the inquisitors—though why he should have done so is not by any means clear. Possibly he conceived that this was the wisest course to pursue, lest it should afterwards transpire that he had suppressed such a communication. But from what follows it will be seen how ill-advised he was.

The Holy Office having received the letters, and supposing Juan Pedro Sanchez still under arrest in Toulouse, ordered him to be brought to Zaragoza. The courts of Toulouse replied that he had already been released and that his whereabouts were now unknown.

The inquisitors inquired into the matter with that terrible thoroughness of which they commanded the means. They controlled the most wonderful police system that the world has ever seen. A vast civilian army was enrolled in the service of the Holy Office, as members of the tertiary order of St. Dominic. These were the lay brothers of the family, and as the position conferred upon those who held it certain signal benefits, of which immunity from taxation was one,[134] it will be understood that their number had to be limited, so very considerable were the applications for enrolment.

Originally this had been a penitential order, but very quickly it came to be known as the Militia Christi, and its members as familiars of the Holy Office—*i.e.* part of the family of St. Dominic. They dressed in black, and wore the white cross of St. Dominic upon their doublets and cloaks, and they were made to join the Confraternity of St. Peter Martyr. The inquisitors seldom went abroad without an escort of these armed lay-brothers.

In the ranks of the Militia Christi were to be found men of all professions, dignities, and callings. They formed the secret police of the Inquisition, they were the eyes and ears of the Holy Office, ubiquitous in every stratum of social life.

Through these agents the inquisitors were not long in ascertaining what had taken place in the matter of Juan Pedro Sanchez, and soon the five friends were under arrest and forced to answer the serious charge of hindering the Holy Office.

They were paraded in public in the Auto of May 6, 1487, as suspects— *leviter*—of Judaizing; they were penanced to stand in full view of the people, candle in hand and wearing the *sanbenito*, during Mass, and they were thereafter disqualified from holding any office or benefice or pursuing any honourable profession during the good pleasure of the inquisitors.

As it was, they escaped lightly. That they were suspected *leviter* of Judaizing, shows us how easily that suspicion might be incurred. It was purely constructive in this instance—an inference to be drawn from the fact that they had befriended a Judaizer who was under sentence.

The other case is far more horrible. It shows in operation Torquemada's decree regarding the children of heretics, and reveals in the fullest measure its appalling inhumanity.

Another who had fled to Toulouse, fearing implication in the affair of the murder of Arbués, was one Gaspar de Santa Cruz. It happened that he died there, after having been sentenced as contumacious and burnt in effigy at Zaragoza. It came to the ears of the inquisitors that he had been assisted in his flight by his son; and not content with the heavy punishment of infamy that must fall automatically upon that son for sins that were not his own, not content with having reduced him to destitution by confiscating his inheritance and by disqualifying him from office, benefice, or honourable employment, they now seized his person and indicted him for hindering.

Arrayed in a yellow *sanbenito*, this son, who had discharged by his father the sacrosanct duty which nature and humanity impose, was exhibited to scorn in an Auto, and further penanced by being compelled to come before the court of the Holy Office and testify to his father's contumacious flight. Nor did that ghoulish tribunal count itself satisfied even then. It was further imposed upon him that he must repair to Toulouse, exhume his father's remains, and publicly burn them, returning to Zaragoza with a properly attested report of the performance, when he should receive absolution of the censures incurred.

Santa Cruz carried out that barbarous command, as the only means of saving his liberty and perhaps his life. For it is certain that had he refused, it would have been argued that he had rejected the offered means of reconciliation with the Church he had so grievously offended, and he would have been prosecuted as impenitent; whilst had he availed himself of the only alternative and fled, he must have been sentenced as contumacious and would have gone to the stake if he were ever taken.

From the hour of his death Pedro Arbués de Epila was looked upon as a saint and martyr, the notion being carefully fostered by the members of his order in the minds of the faithful.

And, as is usual in such cases, miraculous manifestations of his sanctity are alleged to have begun in the very hour of his death. Trasmiera tells us that the bells rang of themselves when he died, and he opines that this serves to approve their use in a time when Luther and others were condemning them as vain.

The blood of the inquisitor, we learn from the same source, boiled upon the stones of the church where it had fallen, and continued to do so for a fortnight afterwards; whilst on any of the twelve days immediately following the night of his murder, a handkerchief pressed to the stones upon which his blood had been shed, when removed, was found to be blood-stained.

These, says Trasmiera, were miracles of which all were witnesses. There is much more of the same kind—including an account of the inquisitor's apparitions after death, as testified by Mosen Blanco, to whom the ghost appeared, and with whom it conversed at length—to be found in Trasmiera's "Vida y Muerte del Venerable Inquisidor, Pedro Arbués."

The sword with which he was slain was preserved in the Metropolitan Church of Zaragoza, a relic sanctified by the blood that had embrued it.

He was buried in the same church, and on the spot where he fell Isabella raised a beautiful monument to his memory in 1487. Part of its inscription ran: "Happy Zaragoza! Rejoice that here is buried he who is the glory of the martyrs."

He was beatified two hundred years later by Alexander VII, largely in consequence of the efforts of the Spanish inquisitors, who perceived what an added prestige it would give their order if one of its members were worshipped as a martyr. His canonization followed in the nineteenth century. It was effected by Pope Pius IX, and was the subject of much derisory comment in the Rome of that day, which had just broken the shackles of clerical government that had trammelled it for some fifteen hundred years.

CHAPTER XV
TORQUEMADA'S FURTHER "INSTRUCTIONS"

The intrepid but ineffectual resistance offered by Zaragoza to the Inquisition was emulated by the principal cities of Aragon; one and all protested against the institution of this tribunal under the new form which Torquemada had given it.

But nowhere was resistance of the least avail against the iron purpose of the Grand Inquisitor, armed with the entire force of civil justice to constrain the people into submission to the ecclesiastical will.

Teruel had been thrown into open revolt by the proposal to appoint inquisitors there; and so fierce and determined was the armed resistance, that not until the King's troops made their appearance in the streets of that city, in March 1485, were order and obedience restored.

In Valencia, too, there was a vigorous opposition led by the nobles, and throughout Cataluña the resistance was so resolute that it was not until two years later that the Sovereigns were able to reduce the people to submission.

Barcelona urged an ancient right to appoint her own inquisitors, and refused persistently and angrily to recognize the authority of Torquemada or his delegates, in spite of any bulls that might have been issued by Sixtus IV and Innocent VIII. Nor was this city's obstinacy conquered until 1487, after Pope Innocent had issued his second bull, confirming Torquemada in the office of Grand Inquisitor of Castile, Leon, Aragon, and Valencia, and further extending his jurisdiction so that it included all the Spains—in which bull he formally cancelled the ancient rights of Barcelona to appoint her own inquisitors.

It should be sufficiently clear from this that, notwithstanding the racial antipathy between Spaniard and Jew, notwithstanding the religious spirit so very ardent in the people of Spain, serving to aggravate beyond all reason that hatred of the Israelite, the Inquisition—as Torquemada understood and controlled it—was very far from being desired by them. That this grim institution should have contrived so firmly to establish itself upon Spanish soil and to wield there a power such as it wielded in no other Catholic country of Europe, was due entirely to the brothers of St. Dominic and the fanaticism of Torquemada playing upon the bigotry and acquisitiveness of the Sovereigns.

Assailants of the Roman Church have urged that the Inquisition was a religious institution. Defenders of that same Church, in their endeavour to shift so terrible a burden from her shoulders, have sought to show that the

Inquisition was a political machine. It was neither, and at the same time it was both. But chiefly and primarily it was just a clerical weapon. And clericalism in the Iberian Peninsula, pervaded by the spirit of Torquemada, converted that institution into an instrument far more dreadful and oppressive than was its character in Italy, or France, or any other Roman Catholic country of the world in which the Holy Office held jurisdiction.

In Spain it had set up in the evening of the fifteenth century an absolute reign of terror, depriving men of all liberty of conscience and of speech and spreading a network of espionage over the face of the land.

And in the meantime, practice having brought to light certain shortcomings in the decrees which he had already issued, Torquemada added a further eleven articles in 1485. In the main, however, these are concerned with the internal affairs of the Holy Office rather than with its attitude towards offenders.

Articles I and II provide for the payment of officers of the Inquisition, and decree that no officer shall receive gifts of any nature under pain of instant dismissal.

Article III disposes that the inquisitors shall keep a permanent agent in Rome, who shall be skilled in the law, so that he may attend to matters appertaining to the Holy Office.

From this it is to be inferred that appeals to the Vatican continued to be numerous, notwithstanding the provisions made by the Pope to constitute Torquemada the supreme arbiter in matters of the Faith.

Articles V to XI are entirely concerned with details relating to confiscations. These would be of no particular interest, but that they serve to show how vast by now was the business of confiscation, since the manner of conducting it and disposing of confiscated property should demand so many decrees to govern it.

Article IV is the only one that may be said to concern the actual jurisprudence of the Holy Office. This is intended not so much to soften the rigour as to remove the inconveniences that might arise out of Article X of the "Instructions" of 1484.

By that article it was decreed that confiscation should be retrospective—*i.e.* that a heretic's property should be confiscate not from the day of the discovery of his heresy, but from the date of the offence itself. So that any property that might in the meantime have been alienated—whether in the ordinary way of commerce or otherwise—must be considered as the property of the Holy Office, and was to be seized by the Holy Office, no matter into whose hands it might meanwhile have passed.

Such a decree, as will be seen, was proving a serious hindrance to trade; for it became unsafe to purchase anything from any one, since should either party to the transaction subsequently be discovered to have fallen into the sin of heresy prior to that transaction, the other would be stripped of the acquired property, and might be subjected to the entire loss. Moreover, as proceedings were taken against the dead, and as there was no limit imposed upon the retrospection allowed to inquisitors, no man could account himself safe from confiscations incurred through the sin of some other from whom he or his forbears had acquired the property.

The vagueness of this article urgently demanded amending, and this was the purpose of Article IV of the "Instructions" of 1485. It decreed that all contracts concluded before 1479 should be accounted valid, although it might come to be discovered against either of the contracting parties that he was guilty of heresy at the time of such contract.

This is the only instance in which we find Torquemada promulgating a decree to soften the rigour of any previous enactment, and it is very clear that it is a decree dictated not by clemency but by expediency.

In the event of fraud, or of any one being a party to a fraud to abuse the privilege conferred by this article, Torquemada provided that the offender, if reconciled, should receive a hundred lashes and be branded on the face with a hot iron; whilst, if not reconciled—even though he should be a good Catholic—he must suffer confiscation of all his property.[135]

To justify the punishment of branding on the face, the case of Cain is urged as a proper precedent, and so modern a historian as Garcia Rodrigo does not hesitate to put this seriously forward.[136]

Three years later—in 1488—Torquemada found it necessary to add a further fifteen articles to his "Instructions," and we may anticipate a little by briefly surveying their provisions at this stage.

Complaints to Rome of the injustices and the excessive rigour of the inquisitors—a constant feature of Torquemada's Grand-Inquisitorship— had by that time become so numerous that the Pope found it necessary to order Torquemada to re-edit what Amador de los Rios very aptly terms his "Code of Terror."[137]

The chief ground of these complaints had concerned the delays that so commonly occurred in bringing an accused to trial. When a prisoner's acquittal ultimately chanced to take place, it was after a long term of imprisonment for which there was no compensation or redress; and when the person so treated was a man of position and influence, it is natural that he would protest strongly against the treatment to which he had been subjected before it was discovered that no charge could be sustained against him. The real reason of these delays must not be supposed to lie in dilatoriness or sluggishness on the part of the inquisitors. Indeed, the excessive dispatch with which they conducted the affairs of their tribunal is a matter to the scandal of which Llorente draws attention more than once—and particularly in the course of chronicling the fact that in the year of its introduction into Toledo this court dealt—as we shall see—with no less than some 3,300 cases, 27 of the accused being burnt and the remainder penanced in various degrees. He protests with reason that it is utterly impossible that at such a rate of procedure evidence can properly have been sifted and any sort of justice done.

Where delays took place they were the result of the extreme reluctance on the part of the Holy Office to allow any to go free upon whom its talons had once fastened. Thus, when even the slight degree or evidence necessary to enable the inquisitors to convict was lacking, they would delay in the daily hope that such evidence might be forthcoming, and by repeated examinations they would meanwhile seek to force the unfortunate prisoner into contradictions that should justify them in resorting to torture.

In view of the explicit pontifical command, Torquemada was compelled to amend this state of things, at least in theory, by decreeing (Article III) that there should be no delays in proceeding to trial through lack of proof. Where proof was lacking, the accused should at once be restored to liberty, since he could at any time—when fresh proof was forthcoming—be rearrested.

Similarly, with a view of expediting trials, he ordered (Article IV) that since in all the courts of the Inquisition there were not the necessary lawyers, henceforth, when a case was completed, the *dossier* of the proceedings should be sent to the Grand Inquisitor himself, and he would then submit it to the lawyers of the Suprema, who would advise upon it.

But he amply made up for what softening of rigour might be contained in these articles by the greater severity enjoined in some of the other decrees which he embodied in these "Instructions" of 1488.

Finding that the inquisitors of Aragon had been departing from certain of his enactments of 1484, diluting them with the weaker rules that had obtained under the old Inquisition in that kingdom, he commanded that all inquisitors should proceed in strict obedience to the statutes contained in the past "Instructions."

He provided (Article V) that the inquisitors should themselves visit the prisons once in every fortnight, but that no outsiders should be permitted to communicate with the prisoners, save of course the priests who would go to comfort them. To the end that a still greater secrecy should be observed in the trials, he commanded (Article VI) that when the depositions of the witnesses were being taken none should be present other than those who were by law absolutely necessary; and he enjoined (Article VII) the safe and secret custody of all documents relating to the cases tried.

We are left to gather that the harshness of his enactment concerning the children of heretics had been tempered a little by a natural humane pity which did not at all commend itself to the pitiless Grand Inquisitor; for we now find him (Article XI) enjoining inquisitors to take care that the decree forbidding those unfortunates the use of gold and silver and fine garments, and disqualifying them from honourable employment, should be rigorously enforced.

He provided (Article XIII) that all the expenses of the Holy Office—which must have been enormous by now, considering to what vast proportions he had developed that organization—should be defrayed out of confiscated property before this was surrendered to the Royal treasury; and further (Article XV), that all appointed notaries, fiscals, and constables should discharge their functions in person and not by deputy.

The most interesting of these statutes of 1488, in consequence of the information it conveys on the subject of the activities of the Inquisition and the enormous scale of the prosecutions upon which it was engaged, is contained in Article XIV. The prisons of Spain were becoming so crowded, and the expense of maintaining the prisoners was imposing so heavy a tax upon the Holy Office, that it had become urgently necessary to make some fresh provision that would relieve this burden. Therefore, as this article sets forth, Torquemada enjoined the Sovereigns to order the building in every district of the Inquisition of a quadrangular enclosure of small houses (*casillas*) for the residence of those sentenced to the penance of imprisonment. These houses were to be so contrived that the penitents might pursue in them their business or trade and earn their own livelihood, thus relieving the Inquisition of the heavy expense of supporting them. Each of these quadrangular penitentiaries—for this is the origin of the term—was to be equipped with its own chapel.[138]

CHAPTER XVI
THE INQUISITION IN TOLEDO

Llorente, the historian of the Spanish Inquisition, and M. Fidel Fita, the distinguished contributor to the "Boletin de la Real Academia de la Historia," both had access to and both made use of a record left by the licentiate Sebastian de Orozco, an eyewitness of the establishment of the Inquisition in Toledo. This has been printed verbatim by M. Fidel Fita.[139]

The details afforded by Orozco are so circumstantial that it is worth while to follow them closely, since they may be said to afford a typical picture of what was happening not only in the city with which they are concerned, but throughout the whole of Spain.

It was in May of the year 1485 that the Inquisition was first set up in Toledo, that noble city erected upon a rock that rises sheer from the swirling waters of the Tagus, and is crowned by the royal palace which still bears the Moorish name of Alcazar. It was transferred thither, by Torquemada's orders, from Villa Real, where it had been operating for some months.

"To the end that our Infinite Redeemer Jesus Christ be praised in all that He does, and for the greater power of His Holy Catholic Faith," writes Orozco, "know all who shall come after us that in the year 1485, in the month of May, the Holy Inquisition against heretical pravity was sent to this very noble City of Toledo by our very enlightened Sovereigns, Don Fernando and Donna Isabella.... Of this Inquisition were administrators Vasco Ramirez de Ribera, Archdeacon of Talavera, and Pedro Dias de la Costana, Licentiate of Theology, and with them one of the Queen's Chaplains as fiscal and prosecutor, and one Juan de Alfaro, a patrician of Seville, as chief constable (*alguazil*), and two notaries."

The licentiate Pedro Dias de la Costana preached to the people on the third day of Pentecost (Tuesday, May 24), notifying them of the papal bull under which the inquisitors were acting and of the power vested in these inquisitors to deal with matters of heresy; pronouncing greater excommunication against any who by word or deed or counsel should dare to oppose the Inquisition in the execution of its duty.

At the conclusion of his announcement the Gospels and a crucifix were brought, and upon these all were required to make solemn oath of their desire to serve God and the Sovereigns, to uphold the Catholic Faith, and to defend and shelter the administrators of the Holy Inquisition.

Lastly the licentiate published the usual edict of grace for self-delators. He summons all Judaizers to return to the Faith and become reconciled to the

Church within a term of forty days, as set forth by the edict itself, which by his orders was nailed to the door of the Cathedral.

A week elapsed without any response to this summons. The *conversos* of Toledo had been preparing to resist the introduction of the Inquisition to their city, and under the guidance of one De la Torre and some others they had already matured their plans and laid down the lines which this resistance was to take.

Photo by Donald Macbeth.

THE AUTO DE FÉ.
From Limborch's "Historia Inquisitionis."

The plot was—according to Orozco, who, you will have gathered, was an ardent partisan of the Holy Office—that on the feast of Corpus Christi, which fell that year on June 2, the conspirators should be armed to lie in wait for the procession, falling upon it as it was advancing through the streets, and slaying the inquisitors and their defenders. That done, they were to seize the gates of the city and hold Toledo against the King.

The fine strategic position of the city might have lent itself to so daring a scheme, and presumably the aim of the New-Christians would have been to hold it rebelliously until accorded terms of capitulation that should guarantee the immunity of the rebels from all punishment, and the immunity of Toledo itself from the jurisdiction of the Holy Office. But, on the whole, it was so very crack-brained a conspiracy that we are more than justified in doubting whether it ever had any real existence.

"It pleased our Redeemer," says Orozco, "that this conspiracy was discovered on the eve of Corpus Christi." He does not satisfy our curiosity as to how the discovery was made, and the omission increases our doubts.

The details, we are told, were derived from several of the plotters who were arrested on that day by the Corregidor of Toledo, Gomes Manrique. In view of the information thus obtained, Manrique proceeded to capture De la Torre and four of his friends. One of these captives, a cobbler named Lope Mauriço, the Corregidor hanged out of hand on the morning of the festival, before the procession had issued from the Cathedral. The act may have been intended as a deterrent to any who still entertained the notion of putting the plot into execution.

The procession passed off without any disturbances; and having hanged another of his prisoners Manrique subjected the remainder to heavy fines, whereby they escaped far more lightly than if they had been tried by the court of the Holy Office. Fortunately for themselves, it was deemed that their offence was one that came within the jurisdiction of the secular courts.

Soon thereafter, possibly because they now realized that they had nothing left to hope for, self-delators began to come before the inquisitors to solicit reconciliation.

But when the term of the edict had expired, it was found that the indefatigable Torquemada had prepared a second one to supplement it. He ordered the publication of an entirely fresh measure, commanding that all who knew of any heretics, apostates, or Judaizers, must, under pain of excommunication and of being deemed heretics themselves, divulge to the inquisitors the names of such offenders within a term of sixty days.

There was already in existence an enactment of the Inquisition, which instead of offering, as in all times has been done by secular tribunals, a reward for the apprehension of fugitives from justice, imposed upon those who neglected spontaneously to set about that catchpoll work when the occasion arose, a fine of 500 ducats in addition to excommunicating them. But Torquemada's fresh measure went even beyond that. Nor did it end with the edict we have mentioned. When the sixty days expired, he ordered the prolongation of the term by another thirty days—not only in Toledo, but also in Seville, where he had commanded the publication of the same edict—and now came the cruellest measure of all. He commanded the inquisitors to summon the Rabbis of the synagogues and to compel them to swear according to the Mosaic Law that they would denounce to the inquisitors any baptized Jew whom they found returning to the Jewish cult, and he made it a capital offence for any Rabbi to keep such a matter secret.

Not even now did he consider that he had carried far enough this infamous measure of persecution. He ordained that the Rabbis should publish in their synagogues an edict of excommunication by the Mosaic Law against all Jews who should fail to give information to the inquisitors of any Judaizing whereof they might have knowledge.

In this decree we catch a glimpse of the intensity of the fanatical, contemptuous hatred in which Torquemada held the Israelites. For nothing short of blended hatred and contempt could have inspired him so to trample upon the feelings of their priests, and to compel them under pain of death to a course in which they must immolate their self-respect, violate their consciences, and render themselves odious in the esteem of every right-thinking Jew.

By this unspeakable enactment the very Jews themselves were pressed into the secret service of the Inquisition, and compelled by the fear of spiritual and physical consequences to turn informers against their brethren.

"Many," says Orozco, who no doubt considered it a measure as laudable as it was fiendishly astute, "were the men and women who came to bear witness."

Arrests commenced at once, and were carried on with an unprecedented activity revealed by the records of the Autos that were held, which Orozco has preserved for us.

And already fire had been set to the faggots piled at the stake of Toledo, for the first victims had soon fallen into the eager hands of the Inquisitors of the Faith.

These were three men and their three wives, natives of Villa Real, who had fled thence when first the inquisitors had set up their tribunal there. They reached Valencia safely, purchased there a yawl, equipped it, and set sail. They were on the seas for five days, when, of course, "it pleased God to send a contrary wind, which blew them back into the port from which they had set out"—and thus into the hands of the benign inquisitors, so solicitous for the salvation of their souls. They were arrested upon landing, and brought to Toledo, whither the tribunal had meanwhile been transferred. They were tried; their flight confirmed their guilt; and so—*Christi nomine invocato*—they were burnt by order of the inquisitors.

As a result of the self-delations the first great Auto de Fé was held in Toledo on the first Sunday in Lent (February 12), 1486. The reconciled of seven parishes, numbering some 750 men and women, were taken in procession and submitted to the penance known as *verguenza*—or "shame"—which, however humiliating to the Christian, was so hurtful to the pride of the Jew (and no less to that of the Moor) that he would almost have preferred death itself. It consisted in being paraded through the streets, men and women alike, bareheaded, barefooted, and naked to the waist.

At the head of the procession, preceded by the white cross, and walking two by two, went a section of the Confraternity of St. Peter the Martyr—the familiars of the Holy Office—dressed in black, with the white cross of St. Dominic displayed upon their cloaks. After them followed the horde of half-naked penitents, cruel physical discomfort being added to their mental torture, for the weather was so raw and cold that it had been considered expedient to provide them with sandals, lest they should have found it impossible to walk.

In his hand each carried a candle of green wax—unlighted, to signify that as yet the light of the Faith did not illumine his soul. Anon, when they should have been admitted to reconciliation and absolution, these candles would be lighted, to signify that the light of the Faith had once more entered their hearts—light being the symbol of the Faith, just as "light" and "faith" have become almost convertible terms.

Orozco informs us that among the penitents were many of the principal citizens of Toledo, many persons of eminence and honour, who must deeply have felt their shame at being paraded in this fashion through crowded streets, that they might afford a salutary spectacle to the multitude which had assembled in Toledo from all the surrounding country districts. To ensure this good attendance the Auto had been proclaimed far and wide a fortnight before it was held.

The chronicler of these events tells us that many and loud were the lamentations of these unfortunates. But it is very plain that their condition did not move his pity, for he expresses the opinion that their grief was rather at the dishonour they were suffering than—as it should have been—because they had offended God.

The procession wound its way through the principal streets of the city, and came at last to the Cathedral. At the main doors stood two chaplains, who with their thumbs made the sign of the cross on the brow of each penitent in turn, accompanying the action by the formula: "Receive the Sign of the Cross which you denied, and which, being deluded, you lost."

Within the Cathedral two large scaffolds had been erected. The penitents were led to one of these, where the reverend inquisitors waited to receive them. On the other an altar had been raised, surmounted by the green cross of the Inquisition, and as soon as all the penitents were assembled, the crowd of holiday-makers being closely packed about the scaffolds, Mass was celebrated and a sermon of the Faith was preached.

This being at an end, the notary of the Holy Office rose and called over the long roll of the penitents, each answering to his name and hearing his particular offence read out to him. Thereafter the penance was announced. They were to be whipped in procession on each of the following six Fridays, being naked to the waist, bareheaded and barefooted; they were to fast on each of those six Fridays, and they were disqualified for the rest of their lives from holding office, benefice, or honourable employment, and from using gold, silver, precious stones, or fine fabrics in their apparel.

They were warned that if they relapsed into error, or failed to perform any part of the penance imposed, they would be deemed impenitent heretics and abandoned to the secular arm; and upon that grim warning they were dismissed.

On each of the following six Fridays of Lent they were taken in procession from the Church of San Pedro Martir to a different shrine on each occasion, and when at last they had completed this humiliating penance it was further ordained that they should give "alms" to the extent of one-fifth of the value of their property, to be applied to the holy war against the infidels of Granada.

Scarcely are the penitents of this Auto disposed of—the last procession took place on March 23—than the second Auto was held.

This occurred on the second Sunday in April, and 486 men and women were penanced on this occasion, the procedure and the penance imposed being the same.

At Whitsuntide of that year a sermon of the Faith was preached by the inquisitor Costana, whereafter an edict was publicly read and nailed to the Cathedral door, summoning all who had fled to surrender themselves to the Holy Office within ninety days, under pain of being sentenced as contumaciously absent. Among those cited there were, we learn, several clerics, including three Jeronymite friars.

Finally, on the second Sunday in June—the 11th of that month—we have the last Auto within the period of grace. In this the penitents of four parishes, numbering some 750 persons, were conducted to reconciliation under precisely the same conditions as had already been observed in the two previous Autos.

CHAPTER XVII
AUTOS DE FÉ

The Inquisition of Toledo had now to deal with heretics who must be considered impenitent, since they had not availed themselves of the benign leniency of the Church and spontaneously sought the reconciliation offered. From this moment the proceedings assume a far more sinister character.

The first Auto under these altered conditions was held on August 16, 1486. Among the accused brought up for sentence were twenty men and five women, whose offences doomed them to be abandoned to the secular arm, and one of these was no less a personage than the Regidor—or Governor—of Toledo, a Knight-Commander of the Order of Santiago.

They were brought forth from the prison of the Inquisition at a little before six o'clock on that summer morning, arrayed in the yellow *sanbenito* and *coroza*. Each *sanbenito* bore an inscription announcing the name of the wearer and the nature of his offences against the Faith, and they were smeared in addition with grotesque red images of dragons and devils. A rope was round the neck of each prisoner, and his hands were pinioned with the other end of it. In his hands, thus bound, he carried the unlighted candle of green wax.

Thus they were led in procession through the streets, the procession being headed as usual by a posse of familiars of the Confraternity of St. Peter the Martyr—the Soldiers of the Faith—and preceded now by the green cross of the Inquisition, which was shrouded in a mourning veil of black crape.

The green cross did not merely symbolize, by its colour, constancy and eternity, but it was fashioned as if of freshly-cut boughs, to represent living wood, the emblem of the true faith in contradistinction to the withered branches that are to be flung into the fire.[140]

Following the Soldiers of the Faith, under a canopy of scarlet and gold, borne by four acolytes and preceded by a bell-ringer, came the priest who was to celebrate the Mass, in the crimson chasuble prescribed by the liturgy for these dread solemnities. He bore the Host, and as he advanced the multitude sank down upon their knees, beating their breasts to the clang of the bell.

Behind the canopy walked another posse of familiars, and after these again followed the doomed prisoners, each attended by two Dominican brothers in their white cassocks and black cloaks, fervently exhorting those who had not yet confessed to do so even at this late hour.

The constables of the Holy Office and the men-at-arms of the secular authorities flanked this section of the procession, shouldering their glittering halberts.

They were closely followed by a group of men who bore aloft, swinging from long green poles, the effigies of those who were to be sentenced as contumaciously absent—horribly grotesque mannequins of straw with painted faces and bituminous eyes, tricked out in the *sanbenitos* and *corozas* that should have adorned the originals had not these remained fortunately at large.

Next, mounted upon mules in trailing funereal trappings, rode the reverend inquisitors, attended by a group of mounted gentlemen in black, the white cross upon their breasts announcing them as familiars of the Holy Office, the officers of the tribunal.

They were immediately preceded by the banner of the Inquisition, displaying in an oval medallion upon a sable ground the green cross between an olive-branch (dexter) and a naked sword (sinister). The olive-branch, emblem of peace, symbolized the readiness of the Inquisition to deal mercifully with those who by true repentance and confession were disposed to reconcile themselves with Holy Mother Church. The mercy of which so much parade was made might consist, as we know, of strangulation before burning, or, at best, of perpetual imprisonment, the confiscation of property, and infamy extending to the children and grandchildren of the condemned.

The sword, on the other hand, announced the alternative. Garcia Rodrigo says that it proclaimed the Inquisition's tardiness to smite. If so, it is a curious symbol to have chosen for such a purpose; but in any case the tardiness is hardly perceptible to the lay vision.

The procession was closed by the secular justiciary and his *alguaziles*.

In this order that grim cortège advanced to the Cathedral Square. Here two great scaffolds were draped in black for the ceremony—blasphemously called an Act of Faith.

The prisoners were conducted to one of these scaffolds and accommodated upon the benches that rose from it in tiers, the highest being always reserved for those who were to be abandoned to the secular arm—to the end, we suppose, that they should be fully in the view of the multitude below. Each of the accused sat between two Dominican friars. The poles bearing the effigies were placed so that they flanked the benches.

On the other scaffold, on which an altar had been raised and chairs set for the inquisitors, these now made their appearance, accompanied by the notaries and fiscal and attended by their familiars.

The shrouded green cross was placed upon the altar, the tapers were lighted, the thurible kindled, and as a cloud of incense ascended and spread its sweetly pungent odour the Mass began.

At the conclusion a sermon of the Faith was preached, wherein the sins of the accused were denounced, and those who had incurred the penalty of being abandoned to the secular arm were exhorted fervently to repent and make their peace with Holy Mother Church that they might save their souls from the damnation into which, otherwise, it was the Inquisition's business to hurry them.

As the preacher ceased, the notaries of the Holy Office of Toledo proceeded to the business of reading out the crime of each accused, dwelling in detail upon the particular form which his Judaizing was known to have taken. As the name of each was called, he was brought forward, and placed upon a stool,[141] whilst the reading of the lengthy sentence took place.

It requires no great imaginative effort to form a mental picture of these proceedings, and of the poor livid wretch, horror-stricken and bathed in the sweat of abject terror which that long-drawn agony must have extorted from the stoutest, sitting there, perhaps half-dazed already by the merciful hand of Nature, in the glaring August sun, under the stare of a thousand eyes, some pitiful, some hateful, some greedy of the offered spectacle. Or it might be some poor half-swooning woman, steadied by the attendant Dominicans, who seek to support her fainting courage, to mitigate her unutterable anguish with comfortless words that hold out the promise of pitiless mercy.

And all this, *Christi nomine invocato!*

The reading of the sentence is at an end. It concludes with the formula that the Church, being unable to do more for the offender, casts him out and abandons him to the secular arm. Lastly comes the mockery of that intercession, *efficaciter*—to preserve the inquisitors from irregularity—that the secular justice shall so deal with him that his blood may not be shed, and that he may suffer no hurt in life or limb.

Thereupon the doomed wretch is removed from the scaffold; the *alguaziles* of the secular justiciary seize him; the Regidor mutters a few brief words of sentence, and he is thrust upon an ass and hurried away, out of the city to the burning-place of La Dehesa.

A white cross has been raised in this field, where twenty-five stakes are planted with the faggots piled under each, and a mob of morbid sightseers surges, impatient to have the spectacle begin.

The condemned is bound to the stake, and the Dominicans still continue their exhortations. They flaunt a crucifix before his dazed, staring eyes, and they call upon him to repent, confess, and save his soul from Eternal Hell. They do not leave him until the fire is crackling and the first cruel little tongues of bluish flame dart up through the faggots to lick the soles of his naked feet.

If he has confessed, wrought upon by spiritual or physical terror, the Dominican makes a sign, and the executioner steps behind the stake and rapidly strangles the doomed man. If his physical fears have not sufficed to conquer his religious convictions, if he remains firm in his purpose to die lingeringly, horribly, a martyr for the faith that he believes to be the only true one, the Dominican withdraws at last, baffled by this "wicked stubbornness," and the wretch is left to endure the terrible agony of death by slow fire.

Meanwhile, under that limpid sky—*Christi nomine invocato*—the ferocious work of the Faith goes on; accused succeeds accused to hear his or her sentence read, until the last of the twenty-five victims has been surrendered to the tireless arm of the secular justice. In the meadows of La Dehesa there is such a blaze of the fires of the Faith, that it might almost seem that the Christians have been avenging upon their enemies those human torches which an enemy of Christianity is alleged to have lighted once in Rome.

Six mortal hours, Orozco informs us, were consumed in that ghastly business,[142] for the Court of the Holy Office must in all things proceed with stately and pompous leisureliness, with that calm equanimity enjoined by the "Directorium"—*simpliciter et de plano*—lest by haste it should fall into the unpardonable offence of irregularity.

Not until noon did the proceedings conclude with the hurrying away to La Dehesa of the last of those twenty-five.

The inquisitors and their followers descended at length from their scaffold, and withdrew to the Casa Santa to rest them from these arduous labours of propagating Christianity.

There was more to be done upon the morrow—very important business, demanding an entirely different ceremonial, wherefore it had been set apart and allotted a day to itself.

The accused on this occasion were only two, but they were two clerics. One was the parish priest of Talavera; the other occupied the distinguished position of a royal chaplain. Both had been found guilty of Judaizing. They were conducted to the Auto in full canonicals, as if about to celebrate Mass, each carrying his veiled chalice. Led to the scaffold of the condemned, they found themselves confronted from the other scaffold not only by the inquisitors and their attendants and familiars, but further by the Bishop, who was attended by two Jeronymites—the Abbot of the Convent of St. Bernard and the Prior of the Convent of Sisla.

The notary of the Holy Office read out the crimes of the accused, and pronounced them cast out from the Church. Thereupon each was brought in turn before the Bishop, who proceeded to degrade him, since the law could not without sacrilege lay violent hands upon an ecclesiastic.

Beginning by depriving each of his chalice, the Bishop passed on to divest the priestly offender of his chasuble; stole, maniple, and alb were removed in succession, the Bishop pronouncing the prescribed formula for each stage of the degradation, and defacing the tonsure by clipping away a portion of the surrounding fringe of hair.

At last the doomed clerics stood stripped of all insignia of their office. And now the *sanbenito*—that chasuble of infamy—was flung upon the shoulders of each; their heads were crowned with the tragically grotesque *coroza*, a rope was put about each neck, and their hands were pinioned. The sentence was fulfilled at last by their being abandoned to the secular authorities, who seized them and bore them away to the stake.

On Sunday, October 16, a proclamation was read in the Cathedral, pronouncing several deceased persons to have been heretics, and setting forth that, although dead themselves, their reputations lived as those of Christians. Therefore it became necessary to publish their heresy, and their heirs were summoned to appear within twenty days and render to the inquisitors an account of their inheritances, from the enjoyment of which they were disqualified, since all property that had belonged to the deceased was, by virtue of Torquemada's decree, confiscate to the royal treasury.

On December 10 900 persons were admitted to public reconciliation. They were self-delators from remote country districts who had responded to a recent edict of grace published in those districts.

The notary announced the forms of Judaizing of which each had been guilty and proclaimed it as their intention henceforth to live and die in the faith of Christ. He then read out the Articles of Faith, and they were required to say "I believe" after each, and lastly to make oath upon the Gospels and the crucifix never again to fall into the error of Judaism, to denounce any whom they knew to be Judaizers, and ever to favour and uphold the Holy Inquisition and the Holy Catholic faith.

The penance imposed was that they should be scourged in procession for seven Fridays, and thereafter on the first Friday of every month for a year. This in their own districts. In addition, they were required to come to Toledo and be scourged in procession on the Feast of St. Mary of August and on the Thursday of Holy Week. Two hundred of them were further ordered to wear a *sanbenito* over their ordinary garments for a year from that date, and never to appear in public without it under pain of being deemed impenitent and punished as relapsed.

Another 700 came to be reconciled on January 15, 1487, and yet another 1,200 on March 10. These last, Orozco says, were from the districts of Talavera, Madrid, and Guadalajara; and he adds that some amongst them were penanced to the extent of being condemned to wear the *sanbenito* for the remainder of their lives.

In the Auto of May 7 fourteen men and nine women were burnt. Amongst the former was a Canon of Toledo who was accused of horrible heresies, and who, writes Orozco, had confessed under torture to abominable subversions of the words of the Mass. Instead of the prescribed formula of the consecration, he had stated that he was in the habit of uttering the absurd and almost meaningless gibberish—"Sus Periquete, que mira la gente."

On the following day there was held a supplementary Auto, especially for the purpose of dealing with deceased and fugitive heretics, conducted with a ceremony of an unusual and singularly theatrical order, which is not so much typical—as are the other Autos described—of what was taking place throughout Spain, as indicative of a morbid inventiveness on the part of the Toledan inquisitors.

On the scaffold usually occupied by the accused a sepulchral monument of wood had been erected and draped in black. As each accused was cited by the notary, the familiars opened the monument and drew out the effigy of the dead man dressed in the grave-clothes peculiar to the Jews.

To this dummy of straw the detailed account of his crimes and the sentence of the court whereby he was condemned as a heretic were solemnly read out. When all the condemnations had thus been proclaimed, the effigies were flung into a bonfire that had been kindled in the square; and together with the effigies went the bones of the deceased, which had been exhumed to that end.

After that the next Auto of importance was held on July 25, 1488, when twenty men and seventeen women were sent to the stake, with a supplementary Auto upon the morrow in which they burnt the effigies of over a hundred dead and fugitive heretics.

And so it goes on, as recorded by the licentiate Sebastian Orozco, and cited by Llorente[143] and Fidel Fita.[144] From now onwards the burnings increase in number. Indeed, all edicts of grace having expired, and no new ones being permissible, sentencing to the flames—through the medium of the secular arm—and to perpetual imprisonment becomes the chief business of the Inquisition in Toledo and elsewhere.

The *sanbenitos* of the burnt were preserved in the churches of the parishes where they had lived. They were hung in these churches as banners won in battle are hung—trophies of victory over heresy.

CHAPTER XVIII
TORQUEMADA AND THE JEWS

During that first year of the Inquisition's establishment in Toledo, twenty-seven persons there convicted of Judaizing were burnt and 3,300 were penanced. And what was taking place in Toledo was taking place in every other important city in Spain.

Numerous now and vehement were the protests against the terrible and excessive rigour of Torquemada. Already, upon the death of Pope Sixtus IV, a vigorous attempt had been made by some Spaniards of eminence to procure the deposition of the Prior of Holy Cross from the office of Grand Inquisitor. It was argued that as his appointment had been made by Sixtus, so it was automatically determined by that Pope's decease. But whatever hopes may have been founded upon such an argument were very quickly overthrown. Innocent VIII, as we have already seen, not only confirmed Torquemada in his office, but considerably increased his powers and the scope of his jurisdiction.

Indeed, not only was he given jurisdiction over all the Spains, but Innocent's bull of April 3, 1487, *motu proprio*, commanded all Catholic princes that, upon being requested by the Grand Inquisitor so to do, they should arrest any fugitives he might indicate and send them captive to the Inquisition under pain of excommunication.[145]

Notwithstanding the threat by which it was backed, this command from the Vatican appears to have been generally disregarded by the Governments of Europe.[146]

That such a bull should have been solicited gives us yet another glimpse of the terrible rancour against the Jews which fanaticism had kindled in the soul of Torquemada. Had his aim been merely, as expressed, to weed the tares of heresy from the Catholic soil of Spain, the self-imposed exile of those wretched fugitives would fully have satisfied him, and he would not have thought it necessary to hound them out of such shelter as they had found abroad that he might have the satisfaction of hurling them into the bonfire he had kindled.

His position being so greatly strengthened by the wider and ampler powers accorded to him by the new Pontiff, Torquemada gave a still freer rein to the terrible severity of his nature, and thus occasioned those frequent and very urgent appeals to the Vatican.

Many New-Christians who secretly practised Jewish rites, being repelled from taking advantage of the edict of grace by the necessity it imposed of undergoing the horrible *verguenza* already described, applied now to the

Pontiff for secret absolution. This required special briefs. Special briefs brought money into the papal coffers, and procured converts to the Faith. Two better reasons for granting these requests it would have been impossible to have urged, and so the Curia acceded.

But the result of this curial interference with the autonomous jurisdiction of the Holy Office in Spain was to provoke the resentment of Torquemada. Wrangles ensued between the Grand Inquisitor and the Pontifical Court— wrangles which may be likened to those of two lawyers over a wealthy client.

Torquemada arrogantly demanded that this Roman protection of heretics should not only cease in future but be withdrawn where already it had been granted in the past, and his demand had the full support of Catholic Ferdinand, who did not at all relish the spectacle of the gold of his subjects being poured into any treasury other than his own. Rome, having meanwhile pocketed the fees, was disposed to be amenable to the representations of the Catholic Sovereigns and their Grand Inquisitor; and the Pope proceeded flagrantly to cancel the briefs of dispensation that had been granted.

There was an outcry from the swindled victims. They protested appealingly to the Pope that they had confessed their sins against the Faith, and that absolution had been granted them. Very rightly they urged that this absolution could not now be rescinded—for not even the Pope had power to do so much—and they argued that, being in a state of grace, they could not now be prosecuted for heresy.

But they overlooked the retrospective power which—however unjustifiable by canon or any other law—the Inquisition had arrogated to itself. By virtue of this, as we have seen, the inquisitors could take proceedings even against one who had died in a state of grace, at peace with Holy Mother Church, if it were shown that an offence of heresy committed at some stage of his life had not been expiated in a manner that the Holy Office accounted condign.

These protests of the unfortunate Judaizers, who by their own action had achieved—as they now realized—no more than self-betrayal, were met by the priestly answer that their sins had been absolved in the tribunal of conscience only, and that it still remained for them to seek temporal absolution in the tribunal of the Holy Office. This temporal absolution would accord them, as we know—and as they knew—the right to live in perpetual imprisonment after the confiscation of their property and the destitution and infamy of their children.

The answer, crafty and sophistical as it was, did not suffice to silence the protests. Clamorously these continued, and the Pope, unable to turn a deaf ear upon them, fearful lest a scandal should ensue, effected a sort of compromise. With the royal concurrence, Innocent VIII issued several bulls, each commanding the Catholic Sovereigns to admit fifty persons to secret absolution with immunity from punishment. These secret absolutions were purchased at a high price, and they were granted upon the condition that in the event of the re-Judaizing of a person so absolved, he would be treated as relapsed, the secret absolution being then published.

These absolutions were particularly useful in the case of persons deceased, several of whom, at the petition of the heirs, were included among the secretly reconciled—the inheritance being thereby secured from confiscation.

Altogether Pope Innocent granted four of these bulls in 1486.[147] In the last one issued he left it at the discretion of the Sovereigns to indicate those who should be admitted to this grace, and they were permitted to include the names even of persons against whom proceedings had already been initiated.

With what degree of equanimity Torquemada viewed these bulls of absolution we do not know. But very soon we shall see him vexed by papal interference of a fresh character.

Simoniacal practices were never more rampant in Rome than under the rule of Innocent VIII. His greed was notorious and scandalous, and a number of alert baptized Jews bethought them that this might be turned to account. They slyly submitted to the Holy Father that although they were good Catholics, such was the harshness of the Grand Inquisitor towards men of their blood that they lived in constant dread and anxiety lest the mere circumstance of their having originally been Jews should be accounted a sufficient reason to bring them under suspicion or should lay them open to the machinations of malevolent enemies. Hence they implored his Holiness to grant them the privilege of exclusion from inquisitorial jurisdiction.

At a price this immunity was to be obtained; and soon others, seeing the success that had attended the efforts of the originators of this crafty idea, were following their example and setting a drag upon the swift wheels of Torquemada's justice.

That it stirred him to righteous anger is not to be doubted, however subservient and injured the tone in which he addressed his protest to the Pontiff.

Innocent replied by a brief of November 27, 1487, that whenever the Grand Inquisitor found occasion to proceed against one so privileged, he should inform the Apostolic Court of all that might exist against the accused, so that his Holiness should determine whether the privilege was to be respected.[148]

It follows inevitably that if there was heresy, or the suspicion of it, the Pope must allow the justice of the Holy Office to run its course. So that the Jews who had purchased immunity must have realized that they were dealing with one who understood the science of economics (and the guile to be practised in it) even better than did they, famous as they have always been for clear-sightedness in such matters.

Meanwhile, with the power that was vested in him, Torquemada was amassing great wealth from the proportion of the confiscations that fell to his share. But whatever his faults may have been, he was perfectly consistent in them, just as he was perfectly, terribly sincere.

Into the sin of pride he may have fallen. We see signs of it. And, indeed, it is difficult to conceive of a man climbing from the obscurity of the monastic cell to the fierce glare of his despotic eminence and remaining humble at heart. Humble he did remain; but with that aggressive humility which is one of pride's worst forms and akin to self-righteousness—the sin most dreaded by those who strive after sanctity.

We know that he unswervingly followed the stern path of asceticism prescribed by the founder of his order. He never ate meat; his bed was a plank; his flesh never knew the contact of linen; his garments were the white woollen habit and the black mantle of the Dominican. Dignities he might have had, but he disdained them. Paramo says[149] that Isabella sought to force them upon him, and that, in particular, she would have procured his appointment to the Archbishopric of Seville when this was vacated by the Cardinal of Spain. But he was content to remain the Prior of Holy Cross of Segovia, as he had been when he was haled from his convent to direct the affairs of the Holy Office in Spain. The only outward pomp he permitted himself was that whenever now he went abroad he was attended by an escort of fifty mounted familiars and two hundred men on foot. This escort Llorente admits[150] was imposed by the Sovereigns. It is possible, as is suggested, that it was to defend him from his enemies, since the death of Arbués had shown to what lengths the New-Christians were prepared to go. But it is more probable that this escort was accepted as an outward sign of the dignity of his office, and perhaps also to serve the terrorizing purpose which Torquemada considered so very salutary.

That he practised the contempt for worldly riches which he preached is beyond all doubt. We cannot discover that any of the wealth that accrued to him was put to any worldly uses or went in any way to benefit any member of his family. Indeed, we have already seen him refusing suitably to dower his sister, allowing her no more than the pittance necessary to enable her to enter a convent of the Tertiary Order of St. Dominic.[151]

He employed the riches which his office brought him entirely to the greater honour and glory of the religion which he served with such terrible zeal. He spent it lavishly upon such works as the rebuilding of the Dominican Convent of Segovia, together with the contiguous church and offices. He built the principal church of his family's native town of Torquemada and half of the great bridge over the River Pisuerga.[152]

Fidel Fita quotes an interesting letter of Torquemada's, dated August 17, 1490, in which he thanks the gentry of Torquemada for having sent him a sumpter-mule, but rather seems to rebuke the gift.

"To me," he writes, "it was not, nor is necessary to send such things; and it is certain that I should have sent back the gift but that it might have offended you; for I, praised be our Lord, possess nine sumpter-mules, which suffice me."[153]

In sending the gift they had asked him for assistance towards the work being carried out in the church of Santa Ollala, the contribution he had already made not having proved sufficient. He replies regretting that he can do nothing at the moment, as he is not with the Court, but promises that upon his return thither he will do the necessary with the Sovereigns so as to be able to send them the further funds they require.[154]

As early as 1482 he began to build at Avila the church and monastery of St. Thomas. This pleasant little country town, packed within its narrow red walls and flanked with towers so that it presents the appearance of a formidable castle, stands upon rising ground in the fertile plain that is watered by the River Adaja. Torquemada built his magnificent monastery beyond the walls, upon the site of a humbler edifice that had been erected by the pious D. Maria de Avila. It was completed by the year 1493, and what moneys came to him thereafter appear to have gone to the endowment of this vast convent—a place of handsome, spacious, cloistered courts and splendid galleries—which became at once his chief residence, tribunal, and prison.[155]

Again his fanatical hatred of the Israelites displays itself in the condition he laid down—and whose endorsement he obtained from Pope Alexander VI—that no descendant of Jew or Moor should ever be admitted to these walls, upon which he engraved the legend:

PESTEM FUGAT HÆRETICAM.[156]

In this monastery the amplest provisions were made, not only for the tribunal of the Inquisition, but also for the incarceration of its prisoners.

Garcia Rodrigo, anxious to refute the widespread belief that the prisons of the Inquisition were unhealthy subterranean dungeons, draws attention to the airy, sunny chambers here set apart for prisoners.[157] It is true enough in this instance, as transpires from certain records that are presently to be considered.[158] But it is not true in general, and it almost seems a little disingenuous of Garcia Rodrigo to put forward a striking exception as an instance of the rule that obtained.

Whatever the simplicity of Torquemada's life, and whatever his personal humility, it would be idle to pretend that he was not imbued with the pride and arrogance of his office, swollen by the increase of power accorded him, until in matters of the Faith he did not hesitate to dictate to the Sovereigns themselves, and to reproach them almost to the point of menace when they were slow to act as he dictated, whilst it was dangerous for any under Sovereign rank to come into conflict with the Grand Inquisitor.

As an instance of this, the case of the Captain-General of Valencia may be cited. The Inquisition of Valencia had arrested, upon a charge of hindering the Holy Office, one Domingo de Santa Cruz, whose particular offence, in the Captain-General's view, came rather within the jurisdiction of the military courts. Acting upon this opinion, he ordered his troops to take the accused from the prison of the Holy Office, employing force to that end if necessary.

The inquisitors of Valencia complained of this action to the Suprema, whereupon Torquemada imperiously ordered the Captain-General to appear before that council and render an account of what he had done. He was supported in this by the King, who wrote commanding the offender and all who had aided him in procuring the release of Santa Cruz to submit themselves to arrest by the officers of the Inquisition.

Not daring to resist, that high dignitary was compelled humbly to sue for absolution of the ecclesiastical censure incurred, and he must have counted himself fortunate that Torquemada did not subject him to a public humiliation akin to that undergone by the Infante of Navarre.

The brilliant and illustrious young Italian, Giovanni Pico, Count of Mirandola, had a near escape of falling into the hands of the dread inquisitor. When Pico fled from Italy before the blaze of ecclesiastical wrath which his writings had kindled, Pope Innocent issued a bull, December 16, 1487, to Ferdinand and Isabella, setting forth that he believed the Count of Mirandola had gone to Spain with the intention of teaching in the universities of that country the evil doctrines which he had already published in Rome, notwithstanding that, having been convinced of their error, he had abjured them. (Another case of the "*e pur si muove*" of Galileo.) And since Pico was noble, gentle, and handsome, amiable and eloquent of speech (*Pseudopropheta est; dulcia loquitur et ad modicum placet*), there was great danger that an ear might be lent to his teachings. Wherefore his Holiness begged the Sovereigns that in the event of his suspicions concerning Pico's intentions being verified, their highnesses should arrest the Count, to the end that the fear of corporal pains might deter him where the fear of spiritual ones had proved insufficient.

The Sovereigns delivered this bull to Torquemada that he might act upon it. But Pico, getting wind of the reception that awaited him, and having sufficient knowledge of the Grand Inquisitor's uncompromising methods to be alarmed at the prospect, took refuge in France, where he wrote the apologia of his Catholicism, which he dedicated to Lorenzo de' Medici.[159]

We have said, on the subject of the Inquisition's introduction into Spain, that to an extent and after a manner this must be considered the most justifiable—by which we are to be taken to mean the least unjustifiable—of religious persecutions, inasmuch as it had no concern save with deserters from the fold of the Roman Church. Liberty was accorded to all religions that were not looked upon as heretical—*i.e.* that were not in themselves secessions from Roman Catholicism—and Jew and Moslem had nothing to fear from the Holy Office. It was only when, after having received baptism, they reverted to their original cults, that they rendered themselves liable to prosecution, being then looked upon as heretics, or, more properly speaking, as apostates.

But this point of view, which satisfied the Roman See, did not at all satisfy the Prior of Holy Cross. His bitter, fanatical hatred of the Israelites—almost rivalling that of the Dean of Ecija in the fourteenth century—urged him to violate this poor remnant of equity, drove him to overstep the last boundary of apparent justice, and carry the religious war into the region of complete and terrible intolerance.

The reason he advanced was that as long as the Jews remained undisturbed in the Peninsula, so long would a united Christian Spain be impossible. Despite penances, imprisonments, and burnings, the Judaizing movement went on. New-Christians were seduced back into the error of the Mosaic Law, whilst conversion amongst the Jews was checked by respect for the feelings of those who remained true to their ancient faith. Nor did the Hebrew offences against Christianity end there. There were the indignities to which holy things were subjected at their hands. There were criminal sacrileges in which—according to Torquemada—they vented their hatred of the Holy Christian Faith.

Such, for instance, was the outrage upon the crucifix at Casar de Palomero in 1488.

On Holy Thursday of that year, in this village of the diocese of Coria, several Jews, instead of being at home with closed doors at such a season, as the

Christian law demanded, were making merry in an orchard, to the great scandal of a man named Juan Caletrido, who there detected them.

The spy, moved to horror at the mere thought of these descendants of the crucifiers daring to be at play upon such a day as that, went to inform several others of what he had witnessed. A party of young Spaniards, but too ready to combine the performance of a meritorious act with the time-honoured sport of Jew-baiting, invaded the privacy of the orchard, set upon the Jews, and compelled them to withdraw into their houses.

Smarting under this indignity—for, when all is said, they had been more or less private in their orchard, and they had intended no offence by their slight evasion of the strict letter of the law—they related the event to other members of the synagogue, including the Rabbi.

From what ensued it seems plain that they must there and then have determined to avenge the honour of their race, which they conceived had been affronted.

Llorente, basing himself upon the chronicler Velasquez and the scurrilous anti-Jewish writings of Torrejoncillo, supposes that their aim was to repeat as nearly as possible the Passion of the Nazarene upon one of His Images. That, indeed, may have been the prejudiced view of the Grand Inquisitor.

But it is far more likely that, to spite these Christians who had added this insult to the constant humiliations they were putting upon the Israelites, the latter should simply have resolved to smash one of the public symbols of Christianity. The details of what took place do not justify the supposition that their intentions went any deeper.

On the morrow, which was Good Friday, the circumstance of the day contributing perhaps to the more popular version of the story, whilst the Christians were in church for the service of the Passion, a party of Jews repaired to an open space known as Puerto del Gamo, where stood a large wooden crucifix. This image they shattered and overthrew.

It is alleged that before finally breaking it they had indulged in elaborate insult, "doing and saying all that their rage dictated against the Nazarene."

An Old-Christian, named Hernan Bravo, having watched them, ran to bear the tale of their sacrilegious deed. The Christians poured tumultuously out of church, and fell upon the Jews. Three of the latter were stoned to death on the spot; two others, one of whom was a lad of thirteen, suffered each the loss of his right hand; whilst the Rabbi Juan, being taken as an inciter, was put to the question with a view to inducing him to confess. But he denied so stoutly the things he was required to admit, and the inquisitors tortured so determinedly, that he died upon the rack—an irregularity this for which each inquisitor responsible would have to seek absolution at the hands of the other.

All those who took part in the sacrilege suffered confiscation of their property, whilst the pieces of the crucifix, which had become peculiarly sanctified by the affair, were gathered up and conveyed to the Church of Casar, where, upon being repaired, the image was given the place of honour.[160]

It is extremely likely that the story of this outrage, exaggerated as we have seen, would be one of the arguments employed by Torquemada when first he began to urge upon the attention of the Sovereigns the desirability of the expulsion of the Jews. He would cite it as a flagrant instance of the Jewish hatred of Christianity, which gave rise to his complaint and which he contended rendered a united Spain impossible as long as this accursed race continued to defile the land. Further, there can be very little doubt that it would serve to revive and to lend colour to the old stories of ritual murder practised by the Jews and provided for by one of the enactments in the "Partidas" code of Alfonso XI.

The reluctance of the Sovereigns to lend an ear to any such arguments is abundantly apparent. Not Ferdinand in all his bigotry could be blind to the fact that the chief trades of the country were in the hands of the Israelites, and to the inevitable loss to Spanish commerce, then so flourishing, which must ensue on their banishment. Of their ability in matters of finance he had practical and beneficial experience, and the admirable equipment of his army in the present campaign against the Moors of Granada was entirely due to the arrangements he had made with Jewish contractors. Moreover, there was this war itself to engage the attention of the Sovereigns, and so it was not possible to lend at the moment more than an indifferent attention to the fierce pleadings of the Grand Inquisitor.

Suddenly, however, in 1490 an event came to light, to throw into extraordinary prominence the practice of ritual murder of which the Jews were suspected, and to confirm and intensify the general belief in the stories that were current upon that subject. This was the crucifixion at La Guardia, in the province of La Mancha, of a boy of four years of age, known to history as "the Holy Child of La Guardia."

A stronger argument than this afforded him for the furtherance of his aims Torquemada could not have desired. And it is probably this circumstance that has led so many writers to advance the opinion that he fabricated the whole story and engineered the substantiation of a charge that so very opportunely placed an added weapon in his hands.

Until some thirty years ago all our knowledge of the affair was derived from the rather vague "Testimonio" preserved in the sanctuary of the martyred child, and a little history of the "Santo Niño," by Martinez Moreno, published in Madrid in 1786. This last—like Lope da Vega's drama upon the same subject—was based upon a "Memoria" prepared by Damiano de Vegas of La Guardia in 1544, at a time when people were still living who remembered the incident, including the brother of a sacristan who was implicated in the affair.[161]

Martinez Moreno's narrative is a queer jumble of possible fact and obvious fiction, which in itself may be responsible for the opinion that the whole story was an invention of Torquemada's to forward his own designs.

But in 1887 the distinguished and painstaking M. Fidel Fita published in the "Boletin de la Real Academia de la Historia" the full record, which he had unearthed, of the proceedings against Yucé (or José) Franco, one of the incriminated Jews.

A good deal still remains unexplained, and must so remain until the records of the trials of the other accused are brought to light. It may perhaps be well to suspend a final judgment until then. Meanwhile, however, a survey of the discovered record should incline us to the opinion that, if the story is an invention, it is one for which those who were accused of the crime are responsible—an unlikely contingency, as we shall hope to show—and in no case can the inventor have been Frey Tomás de Torquemada.

CHAPTER XIX
THE LEGEND OF THE SANTO NIÑO

The extravagant story related by Martinez Moreno, the parish priest of La Guardia, in his little book on the Santo Niño, is derived, as we have said, partly from the "Testimonio" and partly from the "Memoria" by de Vegas; further, it embodies all those legendary, supernatural details with which the popular imagination had embellished the theme.

Either it is one of those deliberate frauds known as "pious," or else it is the production of an intensely foolish mind. When we consider that the author was a doctor of divinity and an inquisitor himself, we prefer to incline to the former alternative.

This mixture of fact and fiction sets forth how a party of Jews from the townships of Quintana, Tenbleque, and La Guardia, having witnessed an Auto de Fé in Toledo, were so filled with rage and fury, not only against the Holy Tribunal, but against all Christians in general, that they conspired together to encompass a complete annihilation of the Faithful.

Amongst them was one Benito Garcia, a wool-comber of Las Mesuras, who was something of a traveller, and who had learnt upon his travels of a piece of sorcery attempted in France for the destruction of the Christians, which had miscarried owing to a deception practised upon the sorcerers.

The story is worth repeating for the sake of the light it throws upon the credulity of the simple folk of Spain in such matters, a credulity which in remote districts of the peninsula is almost as vigorous to-day as it was in Moreno's century.

The warlocks, in that earlier instance of which Benito had knowledge, were alleged to be a party of Jews who had fled from Spain on the first institution of the Inquisition in Seville in 1482. They had repaired to France bent upon the destruction of all Christians, to the end that the Children of Israel might become lords of the land, and that the Law of Moses might prevail. For the sorcery to which they proposed to resort they required a consecrated wafer and the heart of a Christian child. These were to be reduced to ashes to the accompaniment of certain incantations, and scattered in the rivers of the country, with the result that all Christians who drank the waters must go mad and die.

Having obtained the wafer, they now approached an impoverished Christian with a large family, and tempted him with money to sell them the heart of one of his numerous children. The Christian, of course, repudiated the monstrous proposal. But his wife, who combined cunning with cupidity, drove with the Jews the bargain to which her husband refused to be a party, and having killed a pig she sold them the heart of the animal under obviously false pretences.

As a consequence, the enchantment which the deluded Jews proceeded to carry out had no such effect as was desired and expected.

Armed with his full knowledge of what had happened, Benito now proposed to his friends that they should have recourse to the same enchantment in Spain, making sure, however, that the heart employed was that of a Christian boy. He promised them that by this means, not only the inquisitors, but all the Christians would be destroyed, and the Israelites would remain undisputed lords of Spain.

+ EXURGE DOMINE ET JUDICA CAUSAM TUAM. PSALM 73.

Photo by Donald Macbeth.

BANNER OF THE INQUISITION.
From Limborch's "Historia Inquisitionis."

Amongst those who joined him in the plot was a man named Juan Franco, of a family of carriers of La Guardia. This man went with Benito to Toledo on the Feast of the Assumption, intent upon finding a child for their purpose. They drove there in a cart, which they left outside the city while they went separately about their quest.

Franco found what he sought in one of the doorways of the Cathedral, known as the Puerta del Perdon—the door, adds Moreno, through which the Virgin entered the church when she came from heaven to honour with the chasuble her votary St. Ildefonso. The Jew beheld in this doorway a very beautiful child of three or four years of age, the son of Alonso de Pasamontes. His mother was near at hand, but she was conveniently blind—*i.e.* conveniently for the development of Moreno's story, this blindness serving not only the purpose of rendering the child's undetected abduction easily possible, but also that of affording the martyred infant scope for the first miraculous manifestation of his sanctity.

Juan Franco lured the boy away with the offer of sweetmeats. He regained his cart with his victim, concealed the latter therein, and so returned to La Guardia. There he kept the child closely and safely until Passion Week of the following year, or, rather, until the season of the Passover, when the eleven Jews—six of whom had received Christian baptism—assembled in La Guardia. They took the child by night to a cave in the hills above the river, and there they compelled him to play the protagonist part in a detailed parody of the Passion, scourging him, crowning him with thorns, and finally nailing him to a cross.

On the subject of the scourging, Moreno tells us that the Jews carefully counted the number of lashes, aiming in this, as in all other details, at the greatest historical fidelity. But when the child had borne without murmuring upwards of five thousand strokes, he suddenly began to cry. One of the Jews—finding, we are to suppose, that this weeping required explanation—asked him: "Boy, why are you crying?"

To this the boy replied that he was crying because he had received five lashes more than his Divine Master.

"So that," says this doctor of divinity quite soberly, "if the lashes received by Christ numbered 5,495, as computed by Lodulfo Cartujano in his 'In Vita Christi,' those received by the Holy Child Christoval were 5,500."[162]

He mentions here the child's name as "Christoval," to which he informs us that it was changed from "Juan," to the end that the former might more aptly express the manner of his death. There is no doubt that some such consideration weighed when the child was given that suggestive name; but the real reason for it was that no name was known (for the identity of the boy did not transpire), and it was necessary to supply him with one by which he might be worshipped.

When he was crucified, his side was opened by one of the Jews, who began to rummage[163] for the child's heart. He failed to find it, and he was suddenly checked by the child's question—"What do you seek, Jew? If you seek my heart, you are in error to seek it on that side; seek on the other, and you will find it."

In the very moment of his death, Moreno tells us, the Santo Niño performed his first miracle. His mother, who had been blind from birth, received the gift of sight in the instant that her child expired.[164]

This interpolation appears to be entirely Moreno's own, and it is one of the justifications of our assumption that the work is to be placed in the category of pious frauds. But he is, of course, mistaken, by his own narrative, in announcing this as the first of the child's miracles. He overlooks the miracle entailed in the capacity to count displayed by a boy of four years of age, and the further miracle of the speech addressed by the crucified infant to the Jew who had opened his side.

Benito Garcia was given the heart, together with a consecrated wafer which had been stolen by the sacristan of the Church of Sta. Maria de La Guardia, and with these he departed to seek out the mage who was to perform the enchantment. It happened, however, that in passing through Astorga, Benito—who was himself a *converso*—pretending that he was a faithful Catholic, repaired to church, and, kneeling there, the more thoroughly to perform this comedy of devoutness, he pulled out a Prayer Book, between the leaves of which the consecrated wafer had been secreted.

A good Christian kneeling some little way behind him was startled to see a resplendent effluence of light from the book. Naturally he concluded that he was in the presence of a miracle, and that this stranger was some very holy man. Filled with reverent interest, he followed the Jew to the inn where he was lodged, and then went straight to the father inquisitors to inform them of the portent he had witnessed, that they might investigate it.

The inquisitors sent their familiars to find the man, and at sight of them Benito fell into terror, "so that his very face manifested how great was his crime." He was at once arrested, and taken before the inquisitors for examination. There he immediately confessed the whole affair.

Upon being desired to surrender the heart, he produced the box in which it had been placed, but upon opening the cloth that had been wrapped round it, the heart was discovered to have miraculously vanished.

Yet another miracle mentioned by Moreno is that when the inquisitors opened the grave where it was said that the infant had been buried, they found the place empty, and the Doctor considers that since the child had suffered all the bitterness of the Saviour's Passion, it was God's will that he should also know the glories of the Resurrection, and that his body had been assoomed into heaven.

The "Testimonio" from the archives of the parochial church of La Guardia, printed on tablets preserved in the Sanctuary of the Santo Niño, is quoted by Moreno,[165] and runs as follows:

"We, Pedro de Tapia, Alonso Doriga and Matheo Vazquez, secretaries of the Council of the Holy and General Inquisition, witness to all who may see this that by certain proceedings taken by the Holy Office in the year 1491, the Most Reverend Frey Tomás de Torquemada being Inquisitor-General in the Kingdoms of Spain, and the inquisitors and judges by him deputed in the City of Avila being the Very Reverend Dr. D. Pedro de Villada, Abbot of San Marcial and San Millan in the Churches of Leon and Burgos, the Licentiate Juan Lopez de Cigales, Canon of the Church of Cuenca, and Frey Fernando de Santo Domingo of the Order of Preachers, inquisitors as is said against heretical pravity, and with power and special commission from the Very Reverend D. Pedro Gonzalez de Mendoza, Cardinal of Santa Cruz, Archbishop of Toledo, Primate of Spain, Grand Chancellor of Castile, and Bishop of Siguenza.

"It transpires that the said inquisitors proceeding against certain Jews and some New-Christians converted from Jews, of the neighbourhood of La Guardia, Quintanar, and Tenbleque, ascertained that amongst other crimes by these committed was that: one of the said Jews and one of the newly-converted being in Toledo and witnessing a burning that was being done by the Holy Office in that city, they were cast down by this execution of justice. The Jew said to the convert that he feared the great harm that might come and did come to them from the Holy Inquisition, and having treated of various matters germane to this subject, the Jew said that if they could obtain the heart of a Christian boy all could be remedied. And so, after his wide practice in this matter, the Jew from the neighbourhood of Quintanar undertook to procure a Christian boy for the said purpose.

"And it was agreed that the said New-Christian should go to Quintanar as soon as bidden by the Jew; and upon this understanding each of the aforesaid left the City of Toledo and returned to his own district.

"A few days later the said Jew summoned the New-Christian to come to him in the village of Tenbleque, where he awaited him in his father's house. There they foregathered, and agreed upon a day when they should meet at Quintanar, whither the New-Christian now returned, and informed, as he had agreed, a brother of his own, who like himself was also a New-Christian, and he related fully all that had been arranged, his brother being of the same mind.

"The better to execute their accursed project, they arranged a place to which the child should be brought, and what was to be done—that this should be in a cave near La Guardia, on the road to Ocaña, on the right-hand side. And thus to execute the matter, the said New-Christian went to Quintanar on the day arranged together with the said Jew.

"The better to dissemble, he went to a tavern, where presently he was able to communicate with the Jew, and as a result of what passed between them, the New-Christian went out to await him on the road to Villa Palomas in a ravine, where presently he was joined by the said Jew on an ass with the child before him—of the age of three or four years.

"They went on together, and arrived after nightfall at the said cave, whither came, as was arranged, the brother of the New-Christian, and with him other newly-converted Jews, with whom it appears that the aforesaid matter had been treated.

"Being all assembled in the cave, they lighted a candle of yellow wax, and so that the light should not be seen they hung a cloak over the mouth of the cave. They seized the boy, whom the said Jew had taken from the Puerta del Perdon in Toledo—which boy was named Juan, son of Alonso Pasamontes and of Juana La Guindera. The said New-Christians now made a cross out of the timbers of a ladder which had been brought from a mill. They threw a rope round the boy's neck and they set him on the cross, and with another rope they tied his legs and arms, and they nailed his feet and hands to the cross with nails.

"Being thus placed (*puesto*), one of the New-Christians from the neighbourhood of La Guardia bled the child, opening the veins of his arms with a knife, and he caught the blood that flowed in a cauldron; and with a rope in which they had tied knots some whipped him, whilst others set a crown of thorns upon his head. They struck him, spat upon him, and used opprobrious words to him, pretending that what they were saying to the said child was addressed to the Person of Christ. And whilst they whipped him, they said: '*Betrayer, trickster, who, when you preached, preached falsehood against the Law of God and Moses; now you shall pay here for what you said then. You thought to destroy us and to exalt yourself. But we shall destroy you.*' And further: '*Crucify this betrayer who once announced himself King, who was to destroy our temple....*' etc. etc.[166]

"After the ill-treatment and vituperation, one of the New-Christians from La Guardia opened the left side of the child with a knife and drew out his heart, upon which he threw some salt; and so the child expired upon the cross. All of which was done in mockery of the Passion of Christ; and some of the New-Christians took the body of the child and buried it in a vineyard near Sta. Maria de Pera.

"A few days later the said Jew and New-Christians met again in the cave and attempted certain enchantments and conjurations with the heart of the child and a consecrated Host obtained through a sacristan who was a New-

Christian. This conjuration and experiment they performed with the intention that the inquisitors of heretical pravity and all other Christians should enrage and die raging (*rabiendo*), and the Law of Jesus Christ our Redeemer should be entirely destroyed and superseded by the Law of Moses.

"When they saw that the said experiment did not operate nor had the result they hoped, they assembled again elsewhere, and having treated of all that they desired to effect, by common consent one of them was sent with the heart of the said child and the consecrated Host to the Aljama of Zamora, which they accounted the principal Aljama in Castile, to the end that certain Jews there, known to be wise men, should with the said heart and Host perform the said experiment and sorcery that the Christians might enrage and die, and thus accomplish what they so ardently desired.

"And for the greater ascertaining of the crime and demonstration of the truth, the said inquisitors having arrested some of the said offenders, New-Christians and Jews, they set the accused face to face, so that in the confession of their crimes there was conformity, and these confessions consisted of what has been here set down. In addition other further steps were taken to verify the places where the crimes were committed and the place where the child was buried; and they took one of the principal accused to the place where the child was buried, and there they found signs and demonstration of the truth of all.[167] Some of the said accused, and some already deceased, being prosecuted, they were sentenced and abandoned to the secular arm, all that we have set down being in accordance with the records of the proceedings to which we refer.

"The said 'Testimonio' written upon three sheets bearing our rubrics, we the said secretaries deliver by request of the Procurator-General of the village of La Guardia, by order of the Very Illustrious Señores of His Majesty's Council of the Holy Inquisition in the City of Madrid in the Diocese of Toledo, on the 19th day of September of the year of the birth of our Lord Jesus Christ, 1569.

"ALONSO DE DORIGA = Nec auro frangenda fides.
MATHEO VAZQUEZ = In cujus fide fœdera consistunt.
PEDRO DE TAPIA."

This "Testimonio" does not afford us the name of any one of the offenders—presumably that the holy place in which the tablets were exposed should not be desecrated. When it is compared with the account left by Moreno and the discrepancies between the two become apparent, when, further, the extravagances of Moreno's story are considered, it is not surprising that the conclusion should have been reached that the whole affair was trumped up to forward that campaign against the Jews to which Torquemada was employing his enormous energies.

But the records of the trial of Yucé Franco discovered by Fidel Fita throw a very different light upon the matter. And whilst we know that Torquemada did avail himself to the utmost of this affair of the Santo Niño to encompass the banishment of the Jews from Spain, we must consider all notion that he himself simply invented the story to that end as completely dispelled by the evidence that is now to be examined.

From the records of the trial of Yucé Franco we are to-day not only able very largely to reconstruct the event, but also to present a complete instance of the application of the jurisprudence of the Inquisition. Indeed, had the archives of the Holy Office been ransacked for an entirely typical prosecution, embodying all the features peculiar to that terrible court, no better instance than this could have been forthcoming.

CHAPTER XX
THE ARREST OF YUCÉ FRANCO

In May or June of 1490—the time of year being approximately determined by the events that follow—a baptized Jew of Las Mesuras named Benito Garcia put up at an inn in the northern village of Astorga. He was an elderly man of some sixty years of age, a wool-comber by trade and a considerable traveller in the course of his trading.

In the common-room of the tavern where he sat at table were several men of Astorga, who, either in a drunken frolic or because they were thieves, went through the contents of his knapsack, and discovered in it some herbs and a communion wafer, which they at once assumed to be consecrated (and which it was grossest sacrilege for a layman so much as to touch).

Uproar followed the announcement of the discovery. With cries of "Sacrilege!" these thieving drunkards fell upon the Jew. They beat him. They flung a rope about his neck, dragged him from the inn and haled him into the presence of the Provisor of Astorga, Dr. Pedro de Villada. The reverend doctor discharged there the functions of an agent of the Holy Office. He was fully experienced in inquisitorial affairs, and he was upon the eve of being promoted to the dignity of inquisitor in the court of Avila.

Villada received the wafer, heard the accusation, and took a short way with Benito when the latter refused to explain himself. He ordered him two hundred lashes, and finding the man still obdurate after this punishment, he submitted him to the water-torture. Under this the wretched fellow at last betrayed himself. Of precisely what he said we have no record taken at the time; but we have his own word for it—as reported afterwards by Yucé Franco to whom he uttered it—that "he had said more than he knew, and enough to burn him."[168]

Having, as is clear, obtained from him an admission of his own guilt, Villada now proceeded, as prescribed by the "Directorium," to induce him to incriminate others. We know the methods usually employed; from these and from what follows it is quite reasonable to assume that recourse was had to them now.

Following Eymeric's instructions, Villada would, no doubt, admonish him with extreme kindness, professing to cast no blame upon Benito himself but rather upon those evil ones who had seduced him into error, and he would exhort the prisoner to save himself by showing a true penitence, pointing out that the only proof of his penitence he could advance would be a frank and free delation of those who had led him so grievously astray.

From the occasional glimpses of this Benito Garcia vouchsafed us in the records of the trial of Yucé Franco, we perceive a rather reckless personality, of a certain grim, sardonic humour, gleams of which actually pierce through the dehumanization of the legal documents to ensnare our sympathy.

He is imbued with contempt for these Christians whose religion he embraced forty years ago, in what he accounts a weak moment of his youth, and from which he secretly seceded again some five years before his arrest. He is weighed down by remorse for having been false to the Jewish faith in which he was born; he believes himself overtaken by the curse which his father launched upon him when he took that apostatizing step; he is out of all conceit with Christianity; since seeing the bonfires of the Faith he has come to the conclusion that as a religion it is an utter failure; it has been his habit to sneer at Jews who were inclining to Christianity.

"Get yourselves baptized," was the gibe he flung at them, "and go and see how they burn the New-Christians."[169]

In the prison of Avila—when he gets there—his one professed aim is to die in the faith of his fathers.

But it would seem that when first taken in the toils of the Inquisition, and having experienced in his own person the horrors of its methods, he realizes the sweetness of life, and eagerly avails himself of the false loophole so alluringly exposed by the reverend doctor.

In his examination of June 6 he betrays to Villada the course of his re-Judaizing. He relates that five years ago, whilst in talk with one Juan de Ocaña, a converso whom he believes to be a Jew at heart under an exterior of Christianity, the latter had urged him to return to the Jewish faith, saying that Christ and the Virgin were myths, and that there is no true law but that of Moses. Lending an ear to these persuasions, Benito had done many Jewish things, such as not going to church (although he whipped his children when they stayed away, lest their absence should betray his own apostasy) nor observing holy-days, eating meat on Fridays and fast-days at the house of Mosé Franco and Yucé Franco—Jews of the neighbourhood of Tenbleque—and wherever else he could eat it without being detected. Indeed, for the past five years, he admits, he has been a Jew at heart, and if during that time he did not more completely observe Jewish rites and practices, it was because he dared not for fear of being discovered; whilst all the Christian acts he had performed had been merely a simulation, that he might appear to be a Christian still. The confessions he had made to the priest of La Guardia had been false ones, and he had never gone to Communion—"believing that the Corpus Christi was all a farce (*creyendo que todo era burla el Corpus Christi*)." He even added that whenever he saw the

Viaticum carried through the streets, it was his habit to spit and to make *higas* (a gesture of contempt).[170]

In these last particulars his confession is of an extreme frankness, and we can only suppose that he is merely repeating what the torture had already extracted from him. Completely to elucidate the matter as it concerns Benito Garcia, we should require to be in possession of the full records of his own trial (which have not yet been discovered), whereas at present we have to depend upon odd documents from that *dossier* which are introduced in Yucé Franco's as relating to the latter.

Questioned more closely concerning these Jews he has mentioned—Mosé and Yucé Franco—Benito states that they lived with their father, Ça Franco, at Tenbleque, that he was in the habit of visiting them upon matters of business, and that he had frequently eaten meat at their house on Fridays and Saturdays and other forbidden days, and had often given them money to purchase oil for the synagogue lamps.

We know that, as a consequence of these confessions, Ça Franco, an old man of eighty years of age, and his son Yucé, a lad of twenty who was a cobbler by trade, were arrested on July 1, 1489, for proselytizing practices—*i.e.* for having induced Benito Garcia to abandon the Christian faith to which he had been converted.

Ça's other son, Mosé, was either dead at the time or else he died very shortly after arrest and before being brought to trial.

Juan de Ocaña, too, was arrested upon the same grounds.

They were taken to Segovia, and thrown into the prison of the Holy Office in that city. In this prison Yucé Franco fell so seriously ill that he believed himself at the point of death.

A physician named Antonio de Avila, who spoke either Hebrew or the jargon of Hebrew and Romance that was current among the Jews of the Peninsula, went to attend to the sick youth. Yucé implored this doctor to beseech the inquisitors to send a Jew to pray with him and to prepare him for death— *"que le dixiese las cosas que disen los Judios quando se quieren morir."*

The physician, who, like all the family of the Inquisition, was himself a spy, duly conveyed the request to the inquisitors. They seized the chance to put into practice one of the instructions advanced by Eymeric. They sent a Dominican, one Frey Alonso Enriquez, disguised as a Jew, to minister to the supposed moribund. The friar had a fluent command of the language spoken by the Jews of Spain. He introduced himself to the lad as a Rabbi named Abraham, and completely imposed upon him and won his confidence.

He pressed Yucé to confide in him, and in his manner of doing so he proceeded along the crafty lines advocated by the "Directorium."

Eymeric, as will be remembered, enjoins that when a prisoner is examined, the precise accusation against him should not be disclosed; rather he should be questioned as to why he conceives that he has been arrested and by whom he supposes himself to have been accused, with the object of perhaps discovering further and hitherto unsuspected matters against him.

Against Yucé Franco and the other prisoners there was at this stage no charge beyond that—serious enough in itself—of having induced Benito Garcia to re-Judaize. But the disguised friar now pressed him with probing questions, asking him what he had done to get himself arrested.

Yucé—who did not yet know what was the charge—entirely duped, and believing that his visitor was a Rabbi of his own faith, replied that "*he had been arrested on account of the* mita *of a* nahar, *which had been after the manner of* Otohays."[171]

We have left the Hebrew words untranslated to illustrate the unintelligibility of the phrase to the general.

Mita means "killing," *nahar* means "a boy," whilst *Otohays*—literally "that man"—is startling because it is identical with the term used in St. Luke (xxiii. 4) and in the Acts of the Apostles (v. 28) to designate Christ.

Yucé begged the false Rabbi Abraham to go to the Chief Rabbi of the Synagogue of Segovia,[172] a man of very considerable importance and influence, and to inform him of this fact, but otherwise to keep the matter very secret.

The Dominican repaired to the inquisitors who had sent him with this very startling piece of information, which was corroborated by the physician, who had remained well within earshot during the entire interview.

By order of the inquisitors Frey Alfonso Enriquez returned to Yucé's prison a few days later to attempt to elicit from the young Jew further particulars of the matter to which he had alluded. But the lad—probably considerably recovered by now, and therefore more alert—evinced the greatest mistrust of the physician Avila, who was hovering near them, and would not utter another word on the subject.[173]

The matter was of such gravity that we are quite safe in assuming—and we have evidence to warrant the assumption—that it was instantly communicated to Torquemada, who at the time was at his convent of Segovia, practically upon the spot.

We know—as will presently transpire—that it was by order of Torquemada that Yucé Franco and the others came to be in the prison of the Holy Office at Segovia, instead of in that of the extremely active Inquisition of Toledo, within whose jurisdiction the accused dwelt and the crime had been committed. We are unable to give an absolutely authentic reason for this. But we gather that the examination of Ça Franco, or of Ocaña, or perhaps of Benito himself—who had said "more than he knew"—must have yielded disclosures of such a nature that upon learning them the Grand Inquisitor had desired that the trial should be conducted immediately under his own direction.

The Sovereigns, who had been in Andalusia since May of the previous year, about the war upon Granada, now wrote to Torquemada—in July 1490— bidding him join them there.

From Segovia the Grand Inquisitor replied, urging very pressing business to which he proposed to give his personal attention, wherefore he begged them to permit him to postpone his response to their summons.[174]

He quitted Segovia at about this time to repair to Avila, where the work upon the church and monastery of St. Thomas was well advanced; so well advanced, indeed, that already he was able to take up his residence in the monastery.

We may assume that the pressing business he had urged to the Sovereigns as an excuse for postponing his journey into Andalusia was the business of inquiring into the alleged crimes of these Hebrew prisoners. For we know that he had intended having them brought before himself at Avila, but that being unable to dispose of the matter before the end of August or to postpone beyond that time his departure to rejoin the Court, he was compelled to entrust the matter to his delegates—the Dominican Frey Fernando de Santo Domingo, and the sometime Provisor of Astorga, Dr. Pedro de Villada, with whom, no doubt, he would leave—as he says himself—the fullest instructions.

So much we are justified in assuming from the tenor of the following letter, which he delivered to them under date of August 27, to serve them as their warrant to remove the prisoners from Segovia and bring them to Avila for trial.

He wrote as follows:

"We, Frey Tomás de Torquemada, Prior of the Monastery of Holy Cross of Segovia, of the Order of Preachers, Confessor and Councillor to the King and Queen, our Sovereign lords, Inquisitor-General of heretical pravity and apostasy in the Kingdoms of Castile and Aragon and all other Dominions of their Highnesses, so deputed by the Holy Apostolic See,

Make known to you,

Reverend and Devout Fathers, D. Pedro de Villada, Doctor of Canon Law ... Juan Lopes de Cigales, Licentiate of Holy Theology ... and to you, Frey Fernando de Santo Domingo ... Inquisitors of heretical pravity in the said City and Bishopric of Avila,

That we, by certain and legitimate information received, ordered the arrest of the persons and bodies of Alonso Franco, Lope Franco, Garcia Franco, and Juan Franco of the neighbourhood of La Guardia in the Archbishopric of Toledo, and of Yucé Franco, a Jew of the neighbourhood of Tenbleque, and of Mosé Abenamias, a Jew of the City of Zamora, and of Juan de Ocaña and Benito Garcia, of the neighbourhood of the said place of La Guardia, and the sequestration of all their property for having practised heresy and apostasy and for having perpetrated certain deeds, crimes, and offences against our Holy Catholic Faith, and we ordered them to be taken to and held in the prison of the Holy Inquisition of the City of Segovia until their cases should be fully known to and decided by us or by such person or persons to whom we consign them upon being so acquainted.

"But inasmuch as we are now occupied with other and arduous matters, and therefore may not personally acquaint ourselves with the said cases or with any one of them, trusting in the legality, learning, experience, and sound conscience of you, the said Reverend Father Inquisitors and of each of you, and that you are such persons as will well and faithfully discharge what we entrust to you by these presents we commit to you, the said Reverend Father Inquisitors, and to each of you, *in solidum*, the said proceedings against and trials of the aforementioned and of any of them, whether they may have been participators or accessories before or after the fact of the said crimes and offences in any way committed against our Holy Catholic Faith, and likewise of the abettors, counsellors, defenders, concealers, those who had knowledge of the facts and offenders of whatsoever degree, to the end that concerning them you may receive and obtain any information from any part of the said Kingdoms, and seize and examine any witness, and inquire, learn, proceed, imprison, sentence, and abandon to the secular arm such as you may find guilty, absolve and liberate those without guilt, and do concerning them all things and any thing that we ourselves should do being present....

"And by these presents we order the Father Inquisitors of the City of Segovia and each and any of them in whose power are the said prisoners to deliver them immediately in safe custody to you.

"Given in the Monastery of St. Thomas of the said Order of Preachers, which is beyond and near the walls of the said City of Avila."[175]

At what stage of the affair the four brothers Franco of La Guardia—Alonso, Lope, Garcia, and Juan—had been arrested, and upon whose information, we do not know. But we do know—for the *dossier* of Yucé's trial is complete—that they were not betrayed by Yucé.

That their names had been divulged is a confirmation of the surmise that the examinations of Ocaña, or Ça Franco, or even Benito Garcia, had already yielded further information on the subject of the affair of La Guardia.

It must be understood that the record of any examination of these prisoners in which the name of Yucé Franco was not mentioned would find no place in the *dossier* of the latter's trial.

The four Francos of La Guardia were brothers, as we have said; but they were nowise related to the Francos of Tenbleque—Ça and Yucé. They were dealers in cereals—possibly millers—as we shall see, and they owned a number of carts which they appear to have further employed in a carrier's business. They were baptized Jews, as is already made clear in Torquemada's letter by the fact that he does not describe them—as he does the others—as Jews.

All concerned in the affair, with the exception of one Ribera, who does not at present enter into consideration, were men drawn from a humble class of life—a class which through ignorance has always been credulous and prone to belief in sorcery and enchantments.

A curious circumstance is the omission in Torquemada's letter of all mention of the octogenarian Ça Franco, whom we know to have been already under arrest.

Having thus entrusted the conduct of the affair to his subordinates, the Grand Inquisitor set out to join the Sovereigns in Andalusia.

The prisoners were soon afterwards brought to Avila, secrecy being so well observed that each remained in ignorance of the arrest of the others. But before being transferred from Segovia Yucé was taken before the Holy Office there for examination on October 27 and 28. And from the nature of the questions—as revealed by the depositions made—we are left to assume that the inquisitors aimed at further incriminating the Francos of La Guardia, proceeding upon information extracted from them, or else obtained from one of the other prisoners.

In answer to the questions set him, Yucé Franco deponed that some three years earlier he had gone to La Guardia to buy wheat for the unleavened bread of the Passover from Alonso Franco, having been told that the latter had wheat of good quality for sale. He sought Alonso in the market, and thence accompanied him to his house. Talking as they went, Alonso asked him why they made this unleavened bread, to which Yucé replied that it was to commemorate God's deliverance of the Children of Israel out of Egypt.

The question may certainly seem an odd one from a man who had been born a Jew. But it should be remembered that ignorance and lack of education might easily account for it.

Yucé further deponed that in the pursuit of this conversation Alonso not only betrayed nostalgic leanings towards his original faith, but actually admitted that together with some of his brothers he had crucified a boy one Good Friday in the manner that the Jews had crucified Christ.

Continuing, he said that Alonso had asked him whether the Paschal lamb eaten by the Jews at the time of leaving Egypt had been *terefa* (slaughtered and bled in the Jewish manner), to which Yucé had replied that it had not, as at that time the Law had not yet been made.

These replies were construed by the inquisitors into admissions of proselytizing on the part of Yucé, and when subsequently at Avila (January 10, 1491) he was reminded of what he had said at Segovia concerning what had passed between Alonso Franco and himself, and asked whether he could remember anything further, he confirmed all that he had already deponed, but could only add a question on the subject of circumcision which had been addressed to him by Alonso.[176]

The fiscal advocate, or prosecutor of the tribunal, prepared his case against Yucé Franco, and on December 17, 1490, he came before the court at the audience of vespers to open the prosecution.

CHAPTER XXI
THE TRIAL OF YUCÉ FRANCO

The Fiscal, D. Alonso de Guevára, announces to their Reverend Paternities that his denunciation of Yucé Franco is prepared, and he solicits them to order the prisoner to be brought into the audience-chamber that he may hear it read.

The apparitor of the court introduces the accused into the presence of the inquisitors and their notary, to whom Guevára now hands his formal accusation. This the notary proceeds to read. Thus:

"Most Reverend and Virtuous Sirs,—I, Alonso de Guevára, Bachelor of Law, Fiscal Prosecutor of the Holy Inquisition in this City and Diocese of Avila, appear before your Reverend Paternities in the manner by law prescribed, to denounce Yucé Franco, Jew, of the neighbourhood of Tenbleque, who is present.

"Not content that, in common with all other Jews, he is humanely permitted to abide and converse with the faithful and Catholic Christians, he did induce and attract some Christians to his accursed Law with false and deceptive doctrines and suggestions, telling them that the Law of Moses is the true one, in which there is salvation, and that the Law of Jesus Christ is a false and fictitious Law never imposed or decreed by God.

"And with infidel and depraved soul he went with some others to crucify a Christian boy, one Good Friday, almost in the manner and with that hatred and cruelty with which the Jews, his ancestors, crucified our Redeemer Jesus Christ, mocking and spitting upon him, striking and wounding him with the aim of vituperating and deriding our Holy Catholic Faith and the Passion of our Saviour Jesus Christ.

"Item, he contrived, as principal, together with others, to obtain a consecrated Host to be outraged and mocked in vituperation and contempt of our Holy Catholic Faith, and because amongst the other Jews— accomplices in the said crime—there were certain sorcerers who on the day of their Passover of unleavened bread were to commit enchantments with the said Host and the heart of a Christian boy. And if this were done, as said, all Christians were to enrage and die. The intention moving them was that the Law of Moses should be more widely kept and honoured, its rites and precepts and ceremonies more freely solemnized, that the Christian Religion should perish and be subverted, and that they, themselves, should become possessed of all the property of the Catholic and Faithful Christians, and there should be none to interfere with their perverse errors, and their generation should grow and multiply upon the earth, that of the Faithful Christians being entirely extirpated.

"Item, he committed other crimes concerning the Holy Office of the Holy Inquisition, as I shall state and allege in the course of these proceedings as far as I may consider necessary.

"Wherefore I beg you, Reverend Sirs, that you pronounce the said Yucé Franco, for the said crimes, to be a malefactor, abettor of heretics, and a subverter and destroyer of the Catholic and Christian Law; and that he shall be deemed to have fallen into and incurred all the penalties and censures prescribed by canon and civil law for those who commit these crimes, and the confiscation and loss of all his property, which shall be applied to the royal treasury, and that he may be abandoned to the secular arm and justice that it may do with him as by law befits with a malefactor, an abettor of heretics, and an extirpator of the Catholic Faith....

"Wherefore I petition your Reverences to proceed against the said Yucé Franco *simpliciter et de plano et sine estrepitu judicii*, as runs the formula prescribed by law in such cases,[177] to the end that justice may be fulfilled.

"And I swear to God on this Cross on which I set my hand, that this petition and denunciation which I bring against Yucé Franco I do not bring maliciously, but because I believe him to have committed all that I have stated, and to the end that justice may be done and the wicked and the abettors of heretics be punished, that the good men may be known and that our Holy Catholic Faith may be exalted."[178]

It will be seen presently that at this stage of the proceedings Yucé had not the slightest suspicion that the pretended Rabbi Abraham who had visited him in his prison of Segovia when he lay sick was other than he had announced himself. Nor did the accusation afford him the least hint that any of his associates had been taken, or that Benito Garcia had been examined under torture. So carefully had they managed things that he was not even aware of the arrest of his old father.

Therefore it must have come as something of a shock to him to hear this matter of the crucifixion of the child at La Guardia included in the indictment. Nevertheless he unhesitatingly pronounced the denunciation to be the "greatest falsehood in the world."

Guevára answered this denial by petitioning the court to receive the proofs which he was prepared to present.

Being asked whether in the preparation of his defence he would require the services of counsel, Yucé replied in the affirmative, and the tribunal appointed as his attorney the Bachelor Sanç,[179] and as his advocate Juan de Pantigoso. The usual form of oath was imposed upon these lawyers, and Yucé empowered them to act for him within the narrow limitations imposed by the Holy Office, which afforded them no opportunity to cross-examine the witnesses for the prosecution or even to be present at their examination.

The notary of the court was ordered to supply the defendant with a copy of the indictment, and Yucé was allowed a term of nine days within which to prepare his answer.

Five days later the accused successfully petitions the court that to the advocate appointed him be added one Martin Vazquez, to whom he gives the necessary powers. And it is this same Martin Vazquez who on that very day—December 22, 1490—presents to the court the written repudiation of the indictment, prepared by the Bachelor Sanç, in his client's name.

The advocate begins by respectfully submitting that this court has no jurisdiction over his client on the score of the crimes alleged against him, since their Paternities are inquisitors appointed—*Auctoritate Apostolica*—for the Diocese of Avila only, and only over persons of that diocese. Yucé is of the Diocese of Toledo, where there are inquisitors of heretical pravity, before whom he is ready to appear to answer any charges. Therefore his case should have been referred to that court of Toledo, and their Paternities should never have received Guevára's denunciation.

He proceeds to reprove their Paternities for having done so upon sounder grounds, when he protests that the accusation is too vague and general and obscure. It does not state place or year or month or day or hour in which, or persons with whom, it is alleged that his client committed the crimes set forth.

Further, he objects that since his client is a Jew, he cannot with justice be accused of having fallen into the crime of heresy or apostasy; and therefore it is not right that—as may be done in the case of a heretic—the full expression and elucidation of what is charged against him should be withheld, since thus it is impossible for his client to defend himself, not knowing what precisely are the charges made.

The advocate very rightly denounces it as against all equity that the Fiscal should thus prejudice Yucé without particularizing his accusation, and he warns their Paternities that it may prove hurtful to their consciences if, as a result of Guevára's generalizations, Yucé should come to suffer and die undefended.

It is very unsatisfactory equity which says to a man, "You are accused of such-and-such crimes. Prove your innocence of them, or we punish you." But it is not equity at all that can say, "You are accused of something; no matter what. Prove to us that you are innocent of all the offences for which this tribunal may proceed against you, or we find you guilty and send you to death."

This, however, was precisely the method of the Holy Office, and being aware of it, the advocate is forced to confess that in a case of heresy secretly committed the Inquisition may admit an accusation that does not specify time or place of the alleged offence.

But this, he insists, does not apply to his client, who, being a Jew and not having a baptized soul, may not truly be denounced as a heretic. He appeals to the consciences of the inquisitors not to admit the accusation, and finally he threatens that if they do so, he will lodge a complaint where by right he may.

From all this it appears that so completely—as completely as his client—is the advocate in ignorance of the mainsprings of the prosecution that he does not even know that the trial has been ordered by Torquemada, himself, to take place in Avila. That warrant-letter of the Grand Inquisitor's has not been divulged to the defendant, lest in learning the names of his fellow-accused he should learn too much, be put upon his guard, and equipped to set up a tenable defence.

But in any case, and to be on the safe side, the advocate offers a categorical and eloquent denial of every count in the Fiscal's indictment.

He scoffs at the absurdity of accusing Yucé Franco of seeking to seduce Christians into embracing the Law of Moses. He urges the lad's youth, his station in life, his general ignorance (even of that same Law of Moses by which he lives), and the fact that he has to work hard to make a living by his cobbler's trade; and he adduces that his client has neither the time nor the knowledge necessary to attempt any such proselytizing as that with which he is charged.

He declares that if at any time Yucé did expound any part of the Mosaic Law in answer to questions addressed to him (this being obviously inspired by Yucé's recollection of the statements he has made under examination concerning Alonso Franco) he did so simply and frankly, with no thought of proselytizing, nor could it so be construed. In fact, save for the answers returned by him to questions asked by Alonso Franco, the lad does not remember ever to have done even so much, which would have been no real offence in any case.

Full and formal, too, is the denial of Yucé's participation in the crucifixion of any boy, and of having procured or attempted to procure a Host. The advocate ridicules the notion of this cobbler-lad being a sorcerer, or having knowledge of, or interest in, sorcery.

Finally—burrowing ever in the dark, and seeking to undermine possibilities, since he is given no facts that he may demolish—he suggests that the depositions received against Yucé are perhaps susceptible of being interpreted in different ways, and may refer equally to good or evil, and that since he is accused and arrested the things he has, himself, deponed (i.e. concerning Alonso Franco's Judaizing tendencies) should be interpreted in his favour, and not against him.

Therefore he petitions their Reverend Paternities to order the witnesses to declare with whom, where, when, and how Yucé committed these things which are deponed against him. Failing that, he begs them to declare his client acquitted, to release him, restoring him his good fame and all property that may have been confiscated by order of their Paternities or any other judges of the Inquisition.[180]

The court commanded the notary to prepare a copy of this plea, and to deliver it to the Fiscal, who was instructed to reply to it within three days. And they further commanded that at the time of the delivery of the said reply, Yucé Franco should again be brought before them that he might learn what was determined concerning him.

The only matter of interest in the next sitting[181]—and this from the point of view of the illustration which these proceedings afford us of inquisitorial methods—is the Fiscal's repudiation of any obligation on his part to precise the time or place of the crimes with which Yucé Franco is accused, and his insistence that, in spite of all that has been advanced by the defendant, the case must be considered one of heresy.

The court evidently takes the same view, for it commands both parties to the action to proceed to advance proof of their respective contentions within thirty days. Meanwhile, to clear up the matter of the venue, the court communicates with the Cardinal of Spain. The Primate very promptly grants the requisite permission to transfer the action to Avila from his own Archbishopric of Toledo within whose jurisdiction it had lain. This was the merest formality; for considering the explicit commands in the matter left by the supreme arbiter, Torquemada, the Cardinal could hardly have proceeded otherwise.

The methods now adopted by the Fiscal to obtain the proofs which he requires, or at least to build a more complete and overwhelming case—for we cannot but suppose that already he had sufficient material upon which to have obtained a conviction—are eminently typical.

We know that Ça Franco, Benito Garcia, Juan de Ocaña, and the four Francos of La Guardia were all at this time in the hands of the inquisitors; and it is not to be doubted that these men would be undergoing constant examination. But it is obvious, from the absence in the *dossier* with which we are concerned of any document relating to this particular period, that no avowals were made by his fellow-prisoners to increase the incrimination of Yucé.

Without wishing to set up too many hypotheses to bridge the *lacunæ* that result from the absence of the records of the proceedings against the other accused, we would tentatively suggest that in preparing that portion of his denunciation relating to the crucifixion of the child, Guevára had simply adapted details extracted from Benito to Yucé's vague admission in the prison of Segovia. This conclusion is eminently justifiable. It is based upon the fact that Guevára altogether overstepped the limits of any evidence brought to light in the whole course of the proceedings when he said that Yucé "contrived *as principal* ... to obtain a consecrated Host." Further it is based upon the circumstance already mentioned that if in any deposition of Benito or of any other of the accused, Yucé's slightest participation in the affair of La Guardia had been mentioned, such a deposition—or at least the respective extract from it—must have found a place in the *dossier* of his trial. And we know that no such document is present.

Still further, we have the fact that the month prescribed by the court for the submission of proof was allowed to expire and another month after that, and still Guevára had no proofs to lay before their Reverend Paternities, beyond the depositions we have already seen. Meanwhile, Yucé continued to languish in prison.

And here the following question suggests itself: In view of the admission made by Yucé to the false Rabbi in Segovia, why was he not closely and directly questioned upon that matter? and in the event of his withholding details, why was he not put to torture as by law prescribed?

Instead of that direct method of procedure, he was left in complete ignorance of his self-betrayal and of the source whence the inquisitors had derived their knowledge of his association with the affair of La Guardia.

The only answer that suggests itself is that Torquemada desired the matter to be very fully elucidated, that the net should be very fully and carefully spread—as we shall see—so that nothing and no one should escape. And yet this answer is hardly entirely satisfactory.

If Guevára allowed months to pass without being able to lay the required proofs of Yucé's guilt before the court, on the other hand Yucé himself had been similarly unable to supply his counsel with any proof of his innocence— as indeed was impossible in the absence of all particulars of the charges against him.

Thus for a season the case remains in suspense.

Attempts to extract incriminating evidence from the other prisoners having meanwhile failed by ordinary judicial methods, the tribunal now has recourse to other means. Having failed to compel or induce the prisoners into betraying one another, the inquisitors now seek to lure them into self-betrayal.

A well-known scheme is employed.

Benito is moved into a chamber immediately under Yucé's. To while away the tedium of his imprisonment, and with a light-heartedness that is a little startling in a man in his desperate position, Yucé sits by his window thrumming a viol or guitar one day towards the end of March or in early April. The instrument may have been left with him by the gaoler who was in the plot.

What was no doubt expected comes to pass. Yucé's music is abruptly interrupted by a voice from below, which asks:

"Can you give me a needle, Jew?"

Yucé replies that he has no needle other than a cobbler's.[182]

The speaker is Benito Garcia, and it is certain that spies have been set to overhear what passes. We know that their conversation took place through a hole in the floor contrived by the gaoler, who was acting upon the instructions of the inquisitors.[183]

Yucé is very circumspect in all that he says; but Benito is entirely reckless during those first days of their intercourse. And yet, whilst he admits that he considers himself lost already through what "that dog of a doctor" (by which he means the Reverend Inquisitor, Dr. Villada) extracted from him under torture in Astorga, he shows himself at other times not without hope of regaining his freedom.

He mentions a man named Peña, who is the Alcalde of La Guardia. This man, he says, is interested in him, and has—or so Benito fancies—influence at Court which he would exert on Benito's behalf did he but know of the latter's position.

At another time he vows that, if ever he gets out of prison, he will quit Spain and take himself off to Judea. He is convinced that all this trouble has come upon him as a punishment for having abandoned the Law of Moses and denied the true God to embrace the religion of the Begotten God (*Dios Parido*).

But apart from these, there are no lamentations from him; more usually he is sardonic in his grievances, as when he complains that all he got in return for the money he gave for the souls in purgatory were the fleas and lice that all but devoured him alive in the prison of Astorga; or that all the recompense he enjoyed for having presented the Church with a holy-water font was to be subjected to the water-torture by "that dog of a doctor in Astorga."

He vows that he will die a Jew, though he should be burnt alive. He inveighs bitterly against the inquisitors, dubbing them Antichrists, and Torquemada the greatest Antichrist of all; and he alludes derisively to what he terms the frauds and buffooneries of the Church.

It was from Benito that Yucé, to his surprise, received news of his father's arrest and of the fact that Ça Franco lies in that same prison of Avila. He was informed of this during their first talk, when Benito reproved his music.

"Don't thrum that guitar," Benito had said, "but take pity on your father who is here and whom the inquisitors have promised to burn."[184]

In the course of another later conversation between the prisoners Yucé asks Benito what has brought about the latter's arrest. And when Benito has related the happening in the inn at Astorga, Yucé questions him on the subject of the consecrated wafer—and his questions certainly betray the fact that the young Jew had previous knowledge of it and generally of the affair that was afoot. He becomes so importunate in his questions that Benito— perhaps finding them awkward to answer without betraying the extent to which he has incriminated his associates—sharply bids Yucé to leave the matter alone, assuring him at the same time that he has never mentioned Yucé's name to the inquisitors.

Photo by Donald Macbeth.

SANBENITO OF PENITENT ADMITTED TO RECONCILIATION.
From Limborch's "Historia Inquisitionis."

At first glance this statement appears untrue. But it is obvious that Benito means that he has never mentioned Yucé's name in connection with the Host or in any other way that could incriminate him. And in this he is truthful enough as far as he knows, for he could not suppose that what he had said about his own offences against the Faith committed in Yucé's house at Tenbleque could in any way be construed against the lad or his father.

Passing on to other matters, they refer to a certain widow of La Guardia, of whom Benito says that he knows her to be a Judaizer, because she never ate anything containing lard or ham, and he has frequently seen her eat *adafinas* (the Jewish food prepared on the Friday for the Sabbath) and drink *Caser* wine.[185]

In the *dossier* of Yucé Franco there are no depositions of the spy set to overhear his conversations with Benito. But it is probable that some such depositions will be found in the record of the trial of the latter, where they must belong, since from the frankness which he used he incriminated himself to an extraordinary degree and Yucé not at all. And it is not to be doubted that the inquisitors made use of information thus obtained when they came to examine Yucé Franco on April 9 and 10[186] and in a subsequent examination of August 1,[187] when they drew from him a deposition which embodies all the foregoing.

On the margin of the last of these depositions there is a note drawing attention to what was said by Benito concerning the widow of La Guardia, which shows that the inquisitors do not intend that this piece of chance information shall be wasted.

Acting no doubt upon the report of the spy, and having at last obtained information upon which they could go to work, the inquisitors, Villada and Lopes, accompanied by their notary, pay Yucé Franco a surprise visit in his cell on the morning of Saturday, April 9. Having obtained his ratification of what he has already deponed at Segovia and in this prison of Avila, they draw from him by vague and subtle questionings the following additions to those admissions:

About three years ago he was told by a Hebrew physician, named Yucé Tazarte, since deceased, that the latter had begged Benito Garcia to obtain him a consecrated wafer, and that Benito had stolen the keys of the church of La Guardia and so contrived to obtain a Host; that in consequence of that theft, Benito was arrested—upon suspicion, we suppose—two years ago last Christmas (*i.e.* 1488), and detained in prison for two days.

Tazarte told Yucé that the wafer was required "to make a cord with certain knots," which cord, together with a letter, Tazarte gave the witness for delivery to the Rabbi Peres of Toledo, with which request Yucé had complied.

But beyond this, he adds, he has no knowledge of what became of the Host, nor did Tazarte tell him; and that not only Tazarte, but also Benito Garcia, Mosé Franco—his own brother, since deceased—and Alonso Franco of La Guardia, were mixed up in the affair, according to what had been related by Mosé to his wife Jamila. In this last particular he presently corrected himself: it was not, he says upon reflection, to Jamila that Mosé had related this, but to Yucé himself.

It is a curious statement, and would no doubt be made in answer to the trend of the questions set him as to what he knew of a certain Host that had been used for purposes of magic. And there is reason to believe that—as we shall see presently—Yucé was deliberately lying, in the hope of putting the inquisitors off the scent of the real affair.

But it is noteworthy that in this, as in other depositions, he is careful to betray no Jews whom his evidence can hurt. His brother and Tazarte are dead; Alonso and Benito Garcia are already under arrest, and the latter has admitted to Yucé that he has already said enough to burn him. Moreover, they are Christians—having received baptism—and their betrayal cannot be to Yucé as serious a matter as would that of a faithful Jew. Particularly is this emphasized by his retraction of what he had said concerning the slight connection of his sister-in-law Jamila with the affair, having perhaps bethought him that even so little might incriminate her—as undoubtedly it would have done.

The inquisitors withdraw, obviously dissatisfied, and later on that same day they order Yucé to be brought before them in the audience-chamber. There they recommence their questions, and they succeed in extracting from him a considerable portion of what passed between him and Benito in prison— matters of which, beyond all doubt, they would be already fully informed.

Twice on the following day, which was Sunday, was he haled before their Reverend Paternities. At the first audience his statement of yesterday is read over to him, and when he has ratified it he is again pressed with stealthy questions to add a little more of what passed in those conversations with Benito. But in the course of the second examination on that Sunday, Yucé is at last induced or betrayed into supplying the inquisitors with information nearer their requirements.

He says that four years ago he was told by his brother Mosé that the latter, with Tazarte, Alonso Franco, Juan Franco, Garcia Franco, and Benito Garcia had obtained a consecrated wafer, and that by certain incantations they were to contrive that the justice of the Christians and the inquisitors should not have power to touch them. Mosé invited him to join in the affair, but he refused to do so, having no inclination, and being, moreover, on his way to Murcia at the time. And he knows, from what Mosé told him, that about two years ago the same men repeated the same enchantment with the same Host.[188]

We do not know whether Yucé is now left in peace for a whole month, but we cannot suppose it. And we have to explain the absence of any report of an examination during that period by the assumption that whatever examinations did take place were entirely fruitless and brought no fresh particulars to light. As the *dossier* does not anywhere contain a single record of a fruitless examination, this assumption—although we admit its negative character—does not seem unreasonable.

Anyway, on May 7 it is Yucé himself who begs to be taken before the inquisitors to tell them that he remembers having asked Mosé where he and his associates assembled to do what they did, so that the wives of the latter— who were Christian women—should have no knowledge of the affair, and Mosé had answered him that they assembled in the caves between Dosbarrios and La Guardia, on the road to Ocaña.[189]

It is difficult to suppose such a statement to be entirely spontaneous as following upon depositions made a month earlier. Much rather does it appear to be the result of some fruitless questionings such as we suggest may have taken place in the interval. Similarly we assume that the examinations steadily continue, but another month passes before we get the next recorded one, and this—on June 9[190]—contains a really important admission.

He says that *he doesn't remember whether* he has mentioned that some four years ago, being ill at Tenbleque and the physician Tazarte having come to bleed him, he overheard a conversation between his brother and Tazarte, from which he learnt that the latter, together with the Francos of La Guardia, had performed an enchantment with a Host and the heart of a Christian boy, by virtue of which the inquisitors could take no proceedings against them in any way, or, if they did, the inquisitors themselves would die.

His statement that he doesn't remember whether he had mentioned a matter of so grave a character is either a foolish attempt to simulate guilelessness, or else, in itself, it suggests a bewildered state of mind resulting from the multiplication of examinations in which this matter of the heart of a Christian boy—contained, as we know, in Guevára's indictment—has been persistently thrust forward.

THE DISTRICT OF LA GUARDIA.

He is asked whether he heard tell whence they procured the Host, and where they killed the boy to obtain the heart. But he denies having overheard anything, or having otherwise obtained any knowledge of these particulars.

We have seen Eymeric's prescription for visiting a prisoner and assuring him that the inquisitors will pardon him if he makes a frank and full confession of his crime and of all that is known to him of the crimes of others. Although it is not positively indicated, there is reason to suppose from what follows that this course was now being pursued in the case of Yucé Franco. To play the part of the necessary mediator, the inquisitors have at hand the gaoler who must have been on friendly terms with the prisoner, having contrived for him a means of communication with Benito at the time when the latter had occupied the cell immediately beneath Yucé's. That Benito no longer occupies this cell may safely be assumed; for having served his turn, he would of course be removed again.

Whatever the steps that were taken to bring it about, on July 19—a little over a year after his arrest—Yucé is brought before Villada and Lopes,[191] at his own request, for the purpose of making certain additions to *what he has already deponed*.

He begins by begging their Paternities to forgive him for not having earlier confessed all that he knew, protesting that such is now his intention, provided that they will pass him their word assuring him of pardon and immunity for himself and his father for all errors committed.[192]

It certainly seems that without previous assurance that some such consideration was intended towards him, he would never have ventured to prefer a request of this nature, at once incriminating—since it admitted his possession of knowledge hitherto withheld—and impudent in its assumption that such information would be purchased at the price he named.

The inquisitors benignly answered him that they agreed to do so upon the understanding that in all he should tell them the entire truth, and they warned him that they would soon be able more or less to perceive whether he was telling the truth.[193]

(This pretence of being already fully informed is the ruse counselled by Eymeric to persuade the person under examination of the futility of resorting to subterfuge.)

Reassured by this answer, and deluded no doubt by the apparent promise of pardon conditional upon a full confession, Yucé begins by offering, as an apology for his past silence upon the matters he is about to relate, the statement that this has been due to an oath which he swore not to divulge anything until he should have been in prison for a year.

Thereupon he is sworn in the Jewish manner to speak the entire truth without fraud or evasions or concealment of anything known by him to concern the Holy Office of the Inquisition, and he addresses himself to the task of amplifying and rectifying what he has previously said.

His confession is that once some three years ago he had been in a cave situated a little way back from the road that runs from La Guardia to Dosbarrios, on the right-hand side as you go towards the latter place, and midway between the two villages. There were present, in addition to himself, his father, Ça Franco, his brother Mosé, since deceased, the physician Yucé Tazarte and one David Perejon—both deceased—Benito Garcia, Juan de Ocaña, and the four Francos of La Guardia—Juan, Alonso, Lope, and Garcia.

Alonso Franco had shown him a heart, which he said had been cut out of a Christian boy, and from its condition Yucé judged that this had been lately done. Further, Alonso had shown him a wafer, which he said was consecrated. This wafer and the heart Alonso enclosed together in a wooden box which he delivered to Tazarte, and the latter took these things apart, saying that he went to perform an enchantment so that the inquisitors could not hurt any of them, or, if they attempted to do so, they must themselves go mad and die within a year.

At this point the inquisitors interpolate two questions:

"Does he know whence the Host was obtained?"

"Does he know whether they sacrificed any boy to procure the heart?"

His answer to the first is in the negative—he has no knowledge.

To the second question he replies that he remembers hearing Alonso Franco state that he and some of his brothers crucified a Christian boy whose heart this was.

Resuming his statement, he says that some two years ago all the above-mentioned assembled again between La Guardia and Tenbleque, and that on this occasion it was agreed to send a consecrated wafer to Mosé Abenamias of Zamora, and that such a Host was delivered to Benito Garcia enclosed in parchment tied with red silk. This, Benito was to take to Abenamias, together with a letter which had first been written in Hebrew, but which—lest this should excite suspicion in the event of the letter's being discovered—was replaced by another one written in Romance.

The interpretation to place upon this seems to be that, doubts having arisen as to the efficacy of the enchantments performed by Tazarte, it was deemed expedient to have recourse to a magician of greater repute, and to send a consecrated wafer to Abenamias in Zamora, that he might accomplish with it the desired sorcery.

The inquisitors press Yucé to say whether he knows if Benito did actually deliver the wafer to Abenamias. He replies that he doesn't know what Benito did with it; but that he has been told by Benito [in the course of their conversations in the prison of Avila] that he went upon a journey to Santiago, and that in passing through Astorga he was arrested by order of Dr. Villada, who was the provisor there at the time.

As for the heart, he doesn't know what happened to it; but he believes that it remained in the possession of Tazarte, who performed his enchantments with it.

Questioned as to who was the leading spirit in the affair, he replies that Tazarte invited him together with his father and his brother Mosé, and that they all went together to the cave, whilst he believes that the Christians (*i.e.* Ocaña, the Francos, and Benito Garcia) and David Perejon from La Guardia were also summoned by Tazarte.

Finally he is asked whether Tazarte received any money for his sorceries, and whether Benito Garcia was paid to convey the Host to Zamora; and he answers that money was given by Alonso Franco to Tazarte, and that Benito too would be paid for his trouble.

From a ratification on the next day (July 20) of a confession made by the octogenarian Ça Franco, it becomes clear that immediately upon dismissing Yucé, his father was introduced into the audience-chamber for examination.

The inquisitors are now possessed of the information that Ça was present in the cave when Alonso Franco produced the heart of a Christian child. Working upon this and upon the other details obtained from Yucé, they would now be able, by a clever parade of these—and a seemingly intentional reticence as to the rest—convincingly to feign the fullest and completest knowledge of the affair. Thus does the "Directorium" enjoin the inquisitor to conduct his examination.

Believing that all is betrayed, and that further concealment will, therefore, be worse than useless, Ça at last speaks out. He not only confirms all that his son has already admitted, but he adds a great deal more. He confesses that he himself, his two sons and the other Jews and Christians mentioned, assembled in a cave on the right-hand side of the road that runs from La Guardia to Dosbarrios, and he says that some of them brought thither a Christian boy who was there crucified upon two timbers rectangularly crossed, to which they bound him. Before proceeding to do this, the boy was stripped by the Christians, who whipped and otherwise vituperated him.

He protests that he, himself, took no part in this beyond being present and witnessing all that was done. Pressed as to what part was taken by his son Yucé, he admits that he saw the latter give the boy a light push or blow.

It is to this mention of Yucé that we owe the inclusion in the present *dossier* of this extract from Ça's ratification of his confession, which reveals to us so clearly the method pursued by the tribunal.

Ça is removed, and Yucé is forthwith brought back again. Questions recommence, shaped now upon the further information gained, and betraying enough of the extent of that information to compel Yucé to amplify his admissions.

No doubt they would question him directly upon the matter of the crucifixion of the boy, insisting upon this—now the main charge—and depending upon Yucé's replies to supply them with further details than they already possess, so as to enable them to probe still deeper.

Unable to persist in denial in the face of so much obvious knowledge on the part of his questioners, Yucé admits having witnessed the actual crucifixion in the cave some three or four years ago. He says (as his father had said) that it was the Christians who crucified the child, and that they whipped him, struck him, spat upon him, and crowned him with thorns.

So far he merely confirms what is already known. But now he adds to the sum of that knowledge. He states that Alonso Franco opened the veins of the boy's arms and left him to bleed for over half an hour, gathering the blood in a cauldron and a jar; that Juan Franco drew a Bohemian knife (*i.e.* a curved knife) and thrust it into the boy's side, and that Garcia Franco took out the heart and sprinkled it with salt.

He admits that all who were present took part in what was done, and he is able to indicate the precise part played by each, with the exception of his father: he doesn't remember having seen his father do anything beyond just standing there while all this was going on; and Yucé reminds the inquisitors that his father is a very old man of over eighty years of age, whose sight is so feeble that he couldn't so much as see clearly what was being done.

When the child was dead, he continues, they took him down from the cross. (They untied him, he says.) Juan Franco seized his arms, and Garcia Franco his legs, and thus they bore him out of the cave. Yucé didn't see where they took him, but he heard Juan Franco and Garcia Franco informing Tazarte that they had buried him in a ravine by the river Escorchon.

The heart remained in the possession of Alonso until their next meeting in the cave, when he gave it, together with the consecrated wafer, to Tazarte.

"Did this," they ask him, "take place by day or by night?"

"By night," he answers, "by the light of candles of white wax; and a cloak was hung over the mouth of the cave that the light might not be seen outside."

He is desired to say when precisely was this; but all that he can answer is that he thinks it was in Lent, just before Easter, three or four years ago.

They ask whether he had heard any rumours of the loss of a child at about that time in that district, and he says that he heard rumours of a child lost in Lillo and another in La Guardia; the latter had gone to a vineyard with his uncle, and had never been seen again. But he adds that, in any case, the Francos came and went between La Guardia and Murcia, and that on one of their journeys they might easily have found a child and carried it off, because they had sardine barrels in their carts, and some of those would be empty— by which he means that they could have concealed the child in one of these barrels.

Urged to give still further details, he protests that he can remember no more at present, but promises to inform the court if he does succeed in recalling anything else.

He is dismissed upon that with an injunction from Dr. Villada—which may have been backed by a promise or a threat—to reflect and to confess all that he knows to be the business of the Holy Office concerning himself or any others.

CHAPTER XXII
THE TRIAL OF YUCÉ FRANCO (*Continued*)

It is not difficult to conjecture with what fresh energies the court—armed with such information as it now possessed—proceeded to re-examine the other seven prisoners accused of complicity in the crime of La Guardia, pressing each with the particular share he was himself alleged to have borne in the affair, and continuing to play off one accused against another.

It is regrettable that the records of these proceedings should not at present be available, so that all conjecture might be dispensed with in reconstructing step by step this extraordinary case. And it is to be hoped that M. Fidel Fita's expectations that these records will ultimately be brought to light may come to be realized.

A week later, on July 28, Yucé is again brought into the audience-chamber for further examination. But he has nothing more to add on the subject of the actual crime. All that he has contrived to remember in the interval are scraps of conversation that took place when the culprits assembled—on that later occasion—for the purpose of sending the consecrated wafer to Abenamias. Nevertheless, what he says is, from the point of view of the inquisitors, as damaging to those who uttered the things which he repeats as their actual participation in the crucifixion of the boy, and it is hardly less damaging to Yucé himself, since it shows him to have been a *fautor*, or abettor of heretics—a circumstance which he may very well entirely have failed to appreciate.

He depones that Alonso Franco had said that the letter they were dispatching to Abenamias was better than the letters and bulls [of indulgence] that came from Rome and were offered for sale. Ocaña agreed by launching an imprecation upon all who should spend money on such bulls, denouncing such things as sheer humbug (*todo es burla*), and protesting that there is no saviour other than God. But Garcia Franco reproved him with the reminder that it was good policy to buy one now and then, as it gave them the appearance of being good Catholics.

On this same subject of appearances, Alonso grumbled at the trouble to which they were put by the fact of their being married to Old-Christian women who would not even permit the circumcision of their children.

Three days later Yucé has remembered that it was Benito who crowned the child with thorns. He is again questioned as to what he knows about the boy, and he admits having heard Tazarte say that the child was obtained "from a place whence it would never be missed."

They press him further on the subject, but he can only repeat what he has already said—that as the Francos travel a great deal with their carts, they may have found the boy on one of their journeys.

As no more is to be extracted from him on the subject, they now change the line of examination, and seek information concerning other Judaizing practices of the Francos of La Guardia, asking Yucé what he knows upon this matter.

He answers that about six years ago the Francos, to his own knowledge, kept the Feast of the Tabernacles and gave the beggar Perejon money to buy a trumpet which was to be sounded on the seventh day of the feast, as is proper. He knows, further, that they sit down to meat prepared in the Jewish manner, over which they utter Jewish prayers—the *Beraká* and the *Hamoçi*—and that they are believed to have kept the great fast and to give money for the purchase of oil for the synagogue.[194]

Asked further to explain the oath of secrecy which he says was imposed upon him and to which he has said that his past silence has been due, he states that all were solemnly sworn by Tazarte that under no circumstances would they utter a word of what was done in the cave between Dosbarrios and La Guardia until they should have been one year in the prison of the Inquisition, and that even should the torture betray them into infidelity to their oath, they must refuse to ratify afterwards, and deny what they might have divulged.

M. Isidore Loeb clung so tenaciously to the theory that the affair of the "Santo Niño" was trumped up by Torquemada that he would not permit his convictions to be shaken by the revelations contained in these records of Yucé's trial when they came to light. He fastens upon this statement of Yucé's and denounces such an oath as a flagrant absurdity, concluding thence that here, as elsewhere, Yucé is lying.[195]

M. Loeb's criticisms of this *dossier* are worthy of too much attention to be lightly passed over, and we shall return presently to the consideration of them.

In the meanwhile we may permit ourselves a digression here to consider just this point upon which he bases so much argument for the purpose of proving false the rest of the story.

If we were to agree with M. Loeb that Yucé is lying in this instance, that would still prove nothing as to the rest—and it would be very far from proving that Torquemada is the inventor of the whole affair. Assuming that this tale of an oath of silence to endure for one year after arrest is a falsehood, it may very well be urged that it is employed by Yucé in the hope that it will excuse his having hitherto withheld information and that it will induce the inquisitors to deal leniently with him for that same silence. Let it be observed that he prefaces his confession with that excuse at the time of asking the inquisitors to give him an undertaking that they will pardon him if he divulges all that he knows.

But is he really lying?

It seems to us that in arriving at this conclusion, M. Loeb has either overlooked or else not sufficiently weighed the following statement in Yucé's confession: "*Yucé Tazarte ... went to perform an enchantment so that the inquisitors could not hurt any of them, or if they attempted to do so they must, themselves, go mad and die* within a year." This means, of course, within a year of attempting to hurt any of them, which again means *within a year of the arrest of any of them.*

Now, the fact of our not believing to-day in the efficacy of Tazarte's incantations and in the power of his magic spells with the heart and the Host to accomplish the things he promised, is no reason to suppose that Tazarte himself was not firmly persuaded that his enchantments would take effect. Indeed, he and his associates must firmly have believed it, or they would never have gone the length of imperilling their lives in so dangerous a business.

Tazarte's belief was that these sorceries would invest them all with an immunity from inquisitorial persecution, and that should any inquisitors attempt to violate that immunity, such inquisitors must go mad and die within a year of arresting any of Tazarte's associates. Therefore in the event of arrest, all that would be necessary to procure ultimate deliverance would be stubbornly to withhold from the inquisitors all information on the subject of this enchantment until the period within which it was to work should have expired.

When this is sufficiently considered, it seems to us that such an oath as Yucé says was imposed by Tazarte becomes not only likely but absolutely inevitable. Some such oath must have been imposed to ensure the efficacy of the enchantment in the event of the arrest of any of them.

It is difficult to think that Tazarte was a mere charlatan performing this business with his tongue in his cheek for the sake of the money he could extract from his dupes; difficult, because he was dealing with comparatively poor people, from whom the remuneration to be obtained would be out of all proportion to the risk incurred. But even if we proceed upon that assumption, are we not to conclude that, being a deliberate charlatan, Tazarte would be at great pains to appear sincere and to impose an oath which he must have imposed if he were sincere?

It is rather singular and it seems to ask some explanation, which it is not in our power to afford, that not until now do the inquisitors make any use of that grave admission of Yucé's to the supposed Rabbi Abraham in Segovia. It is true that it was extremely vague, but in Ça's admissions of July 19—if not before—they had obtained the connecting link required.

But not until September 16, when they pay Yucé a visit in his cell, do they touch upon the matter. They then ask him whether he recollects having talked when under arrest in Segovia, upon matters concerning the Inquisition, and with whom.

His answer certainly seems to show that even now he has no suspicion that the "Rabbi Abraham" was an emissary of the Holy Office. He says that being sick in prison and believing that he was about to die, he asked the physician who tended him to beg the inquisitors to allow him to be visited by a Jew to pray with him, and his further admissions as to what passed between himself and the "Rabbi" entirely corroborate the depositions of Frey Alonso Enriquez and the physician Antonio de Avila.

The inquisitors ask him to explain the three Hebrew words he used on that occasion: *mita, nahar,* and *Otohays.* He replies that they referred to the crucifixion of the boy, as related by him in his confession.[196]

At this stage it would almost seem to transpire that Benito's admissions under torture at Astorga, when, as he has said, he admitted enough to burn him, must have been confined to matters concerning the Host found upon him, and that until now he has said nothing about the crucifixion of the boy.

This assumption is one that deepens the mysterious parts of the affair rather than elucidates them, for it leaves us without the faintest indication of how the Fiscal Guevára was able to incorporate in his indictment nine months ago the particulars of "enchantments with the said Host and heart of a Christian boy."

From what Benito has said to Yucé in prison we might be justified in supposing that the former is the delator; but in view of the turn now taken by the proceedings this supposition seems to become untenable. It is of course possible that the particulars in question may have been wrung out of one of the other prisoners, or it is possible that Benito himself may have confessed and afterwards refused to ratify. But beyond indicating these possibilities we cannot go.

The fact remains that on September 24 the inquisitors found it necessary to put Benito Garcia to torture that they might obtain his evidence relating to the crucifixion.

And on the rack he confesses that he and Yucé Franco and the others crucified a boy in one of the caves on the road to Villapalomas on a cross made of a beam and the axle of a cart lashed together with a rope of hemp; that first they tied the boy to the cross and then nailed his hands and feet to it; and that as the boy was screaming they strangled or stifled him (*lo ahogaron*); that all was done at night, by the light of a candle which Benito himself had procured from Santa Maria de la Pera; that the mouth of the cave was covered with a cloak, so that the light should not be seen outside; that the boy was whipped with a strap and crowned with thorns—all in mockery and vituperation of our Lord Jesus Christ; and that they took the body away and buried it in a vineyard near Santa Maria de la Pera.[197]

There are some slight discrepancies between the details of the affair afforded by Benito and those given by Yucé. The latter has not mentioned that the child's hands and feet were nailed to the cross; according to him they were merely tied. Nor has he said that the boy was strangled; his statement seems to be that the child was bled to death, as a consequence of opening the veins of his arms—a matter which Benito does not mention. But on the score of the strangling, it is possible that by the word employed—*ahogaron*—Benito merely means that the boy's cries were stifled, a detail which would be confirmed by Yucé's statement that the child was gagged.

The prisoners are evidently permitted to learn that Benito has been tortured. Very possibly they are given the information to the end that it may strike terror into them and so induce them to betray themselves without more ado. But it does not seem that they are very greatly frightened by the prospect of having to undergo the same suffering, if we are to judge by Garcia Franco. This prisoner is permitted on the following day (which is Sunday), by contrivance of the Holy Office, to get into communication with Yucé. In the course of their conversation Garcia strongly urges a policy of denial under torture, should they be subjected to it,[198] from which it seems plain that he has no notion of the extent to which Yucé's tongue has been loosened already.

On the following Wednesday it is Juan Franco's turn to be put to the torture.

Under it he gives a general confirmation of what has already been extracted from the others. He confesses that he and Yucé Franco and the other Christians and Jews crucified a boy in the cave of Carre Ocaña, which is on the right going from La Guardia to Ocaña; that they crucified him on a cross made of two beams of olive-wood lashed together by a rope of hemp; that they whipped him with a rope; and that Yucé was present when the deponent himself cut out the boy's heart—as is more fully contained in the deponent's confession (of which, again, this is no more than an extract relating to Yucé's share in the crime). He states that an enchantment was performed with the heart, so that the Inquisition might not proceed against them.

This confession was duly ratified upon the morrow.[199]

On the Friday of the same week they torture Juan de Ocaña and extract from him a confession that is, in the main, in agreement with those already obtained. He relates how he and the others crucified a boy in the caves of Carre Ocaña; that they whipped him with ropes when he was crucified; that they cut out his heart and caught his blood in a cauldron; that it was night and that they had a light; and that when they took the body down they buried it near Santa Maria de la Pera, as fully set forth in his confession.[200]

As a consequence of his having in the course of this confession spoken of the Host that was sent to Zamora for delivery to Abenamias, Ocaña is questioned again—on October 11—touching this particular. He is asked how he knows that this was done. He replies that he heard Alonso Franco and the Jews—i.e. Ça Franco and his sons (Yucé and Mosé), Tazarte and Perejon—say that such was the intention, but he doesn't know whether the Host was actually delivered or otherwise disposed of.

The persistence with which this apparently trivial question arises—particularly when it is remembered that the inquisitors were, themselves, in possession of the Host found upon Benito at the time of his arrest—leads us to suppose that they were probing to discover whether this consecrated wafer was the identical one dispatched upon the occasion to which the confessions refer. Considering the lapse of time between the dispatch of that wafer and Benito's arrest, they may reasonably have been concluding that the Host found upon the latter relates to some similar, later affair. Such an impression is confirmed by the fact that no letter—such as was addressed to Abenamias—had been discovered upon Benito.

The question again crops up in an examination to which Yucé is submitted on that same day.

"Did any of the Jews or Christians," he is asked, "go to Zamora to Abenamias in this matter?"

He answers precisely as he has answered before: that he doesn't know what became of the Host beyond the fact that he saw them dispatching it together with a letter to the said Abenamias, as deponed, and that all were present when this took place.

They seek to learn who was the instigator of the affair, but Yucé cannot answer with certainty on that point. What he knows he tells them—that Tazarte meeting him when he was on his way to Murcia, the physician asked him would he join in a matter to be performed with a consecrated wafer to ensure that the Inquisition could not harm the Christians in question. Before they met to crucify the boy, Tazarte told the deponent and his brother Mosé that he had arranged for it; and although Yucé protests that he had no inclination to have anything to do with the affair, he and his brother allowed themselves in the end to be persuaded to be present, and they went with Tazarte that same night to the cave. There they were joined by the Christians, who brought the child with them.

So far, it will be seen, the evidence collected from Yucé's fellow-prisoners, whilst admitting that he had been present in the cave when the boy was crucified—an admission in itself grave enough and quite sufficient to procure his being abandoned to the secular arm—did not charge him with any active participation in the proceedings. In his own depositions Yucé had insisted that he and his father had been no more than spectators and that they had gone to the cave more or less in ignorance, as if hardly understanding what they were to witness.

Moreover before relating the happenings in that cave of Carre Ocaña, Yucé had made a sort of bargain with the inquisitors that his confession should not be used against himself or his father. And it is noteworthy that the other Jews whom he incriminated were all dead, and that he suppressed the name of the only surviving Jew—Hernando de Ribera—who had taken part in the affair. Of betraying the New-Christians he would, as we have already said, have less concern, as these by their apostasy must have become more or less contemptible in the sight of a faithful Jew.

Whether the inquisitors conceived that in view of his passivity in the matter, combined with the promise they had made him before obtaining his confession, they were not justified in proceeding to extremes with him, we do not know. It is difficult to suppose any such hesitation on their part. Whatever their object, it is fairly clear that they did not account themselves satisfied yet, and for the purpose of probing this matter to the very bottom they now adopted a fresh method of procedure which appears particularly to aim at the further incrimination of Yucé.

Just as the court was in the habit of suppressing evidence entirely or in part, or the names of witnesses, when this course best served its purposes, so, when the depositions were obtained from co-accused, there must obviously come a moment when the publication of the evidence and of the witnesses by confrontation must further the aims of the tribunal.

The anger aroused in each prisoner by the discovery that his betrayer is one of his associates must spur him to reprisals, and drive him to admit anything he may hitherto have concealed. There is, of course, the danger that he may be urged to embark upon inventions to damage in his turn the man who has destroyed him. But inquisitorial justice was not deterred by any such consideration. Pegna—as we have seen—tells us plainly enough that the point of view of the Holy Office was that it was better that an innocent man should perish than that a guilty one should escape.

In pursuit of this policy, then, Benito Garcia is brought before the inquisitors on October 12, and he is asked whether in the matter of the crucifixion and the Host he will repeat in the presence of any of the participators in the crime what he has already deponed. He replies in the affirmative. Thereupon he is taken out. Yucé Franco is introduced and asked the same question with the same result. Benito is brought in again, and, the two being confronted, each repeats in the presence of the other the confession he has already made.

They are now asked whether they will repeat these statements once more, in the presence of Juan de Ocaña, and they announce themselves ready to do so. They are removed. Ocaña is introduced, and having similarly obtained his agreement to repeat before others whom he has accused of complicity what he has already confessed, the inquisitors order the other two to be brought back.

The notary records that they actually manifest pleasure at seeing one another.

Ocaña now repeats his confession, and Yucé and Benito again go over theirs. The three agree one with the other, and it is now further elicited that it was six months after the crucifixion, more or less, when they assembled between Tenbleque and La Guardia to give Benito the letter and the Host which he was to convey to Abenamias in Zamora.

On October 17 there is another confrontation—of Juan Franco with Ça and Yucé Franco. In this each repeats what he has already confessed, which we now learn for the first time. Juan Franco admits that it was he himself who opened the boy's side and took out his heart, and in this as in other particulars the depositions agree one with another.

Juan Franco goes on to say that they next met in the cave some time after the crucifixion, and that his brother Alonso brought the heart and the Host in a box which he gave to Tazarte, who withdrew with them to a corner of the cave to carry out his enchantments. Later on they assembled between Tenbleque and La Guardia—at a place which, according to this witness, was called Sorrostros—and gave Benito a letter to take to Zamora, this letter being tied with a coloured thread.

So far he is completely in accord with the other deponents; but now there occurs a startling discrepancy. He says that at this last meeting (which, we are told, took place some six months after the crucifixion), in addition to the consecrated wafer and the letter for Abenamias, they also gave Benito the heart to take to Zamora.

Now all the other depositions lead us to suppose that the heart and the first wafer were employed—presumably consumed in some way—by Tazarte in the enchantment performed at the first meeting after the crucifixion, and that as doubts afterwards arose touching the efficacy of the spells performed by the physician, another Host was obtained some six months later, which they forwarded to Zamora.

Is the explanation the simple one that Juan Franco is mistaken on the subject of the heart? It seems possible, because he adds that he did not actually see the Host (on this particular occasion), but that he understood that it was given to Benito. Similarly he may have understood—erroneously taking it for granted—that the heart accompanied it.

And now you may see the confrontation bearing fruit, and yielding the results which we must suppose are sought by the inquisitors—the further incrimination of Yucé Franco.

Juan de Ocaña is examined again on October 20 and questioned as to Yucé's participation in the crime. He now adds to his former confession that Yucé and the others used great vituperations to the child, which vituperations were really aimed at Jesus Christ; he cites the expressions, and in the main they are those we have already quoted from the Testimonio[201]; these, he says, were used by Ça Franco and his two sons. He says that they all whipped the boy, and that it was Yucé himself who drew blood from the arms of the victim with a knife.

"Whence was the child?" they ask him.

He replies that it was the dead Jew Mosé Franco who had brought the boy from Quintanar to Tenbleque on a donkey, and that, according to Mosé's story, he was the son of Alonso Martin of Quintanar.[202] From Tenbleque several of them, amongst whom were Yucé and his father, brought him on the donkey to the cave where he was crucified, and it was Yucé who went to summon the brothers Franco of La Guardia, Benito Garcia, and the witness himself.

So that from having been a more or less passive spectator of the scene, Yucé is suddenly—by what we are justified in accounting the vindictiveness of

Ocaña—thrust into the position of one of the chief actors, indeed, almost one of the instigators of the crime.

On the same day Benito Garcia is re-examined. His former depositions are read over to him, and he is asked if he has anything to add to them. He has to add, he finds, that Yucé—whom he has hardly mentioned hitherto—had whipped and struck the boy, and that he was an active participant in all that was done, his avowed aim being the destruction of Christianity, which he spoke of as buffoonery and idolatry.

On the morrow Ocaña is brought back to ratify his statements of yesterday. He is asked if he has anything to add that concerns the participation of Yucé, and his answer is so very much in the terms of the latest additions made by Benito that one is left wondering whether, departing from their usual custom, the inquisitors put their questions in a precise and definite form—founded upon what Benito has said—and obtained affirmative replies from Ocaña. For Ocaña, too, remembers that Yucé said that Christianity was all buffoonery and that Christians were idolaters.

CHAPTER XXIII
THE TRIAL OF YUCÉ FRANCO—(*Concluded*)

It might now be said that, thanks to the patient efforts which the inquisitors themselves have been exerting for close upon a year, the prosecutor is at last furnished with the evidence necessary to support his original charge against Yucé Franco.

To this end he appears before the court on that same October 21, 1491, to present in proof of his denunciation the entire *dossier*, as taken down by the notary of the tribunal. He begs that Yucé be brought into the audience-chamber to hear the additions which he has to make to the original charge. These additions are the matters lately extracted from Ocaña and Benito Garcia: that Yucé used vituperative words to the child when he was being crucified, and that these vituperations were really aimed at our Lord Jesus Christ and His Holy Catholic Faith; that he struck the boy many times, and that he drew blood from the boy's arm with a penknife. Wherefore, he begs the inquisitors to abandon the prisoner to the secular arm, as is right and proper.[203]

He does not, however, add that Yucé's brother had procured the child, and that Yucé was one of those who brought him to the cave and who summoned the Francos to attend—an omission which shows the credit attached to Ocaña's statement and its lack of corroboration.

Yucé's answer is a denial of all that is alleged and added by the Fiscal, the lad protesting that he never did or said anything beyond what he has, himself, confessed.

Guevára, thereupon, petitions the court to permit him to submit his proofs of the matters of which he accuses the prisoner, and the court having accorded him this petition, he puts in as evidence the entire *dossier* from which we have drawn these pages on the subject.[204]

Five days later both parties are again before the court, Guevára now petitioning their Reverend Paternities to pass to the publication of witnesses, that the trial may be brought to its conclusion. Dr. Villada announces his readiness to do so, but accords the defendants three days within which to lodge any objection to any of the matter contained in the depositions.

Yucé begs through his advocate that copies be given him of all the depositions of those who were present at the crucifixion, with the name of each hostile witness and a statement of the day, month, year, and place in which anything alleged against him is said to have taken place.

But Guevára immediately objects, urging that in the copies of the depositions to be given defendant, no names shall appear of any of the witnesses who had deponed, and no circumstances shall be included which might enable Yucé to conjecture the names. It seems a purely formal objection; for after the confrontations there have been it appears to serve very little purpose. But some purpose it does serve, because those confrontations after all were limited to Ocaña and Benito, and from the moment that it was not considered necessary to proceed to confrontation with any of the other prisoners it would seem that they had needed no such spur to drive them into depositions hostile to Yucé.

However, the reverend inquisitor replies loftily enough that he will do what justice demands, and he orders the notary to deliver to Yucé copies of all the depositions against him. But from Yucé's advocate's plea on October 29—upon the expiry of the three days appointed—it is plain that the particulars claimed have been withheld.

From the fact that the advocate Sanç has drawn up so strong an objection on behalf of his client, it is perfectly clear that even at this date Yucé's guilt of heresy cannot be considered as established. If that were the case, Sanç, in obedience to the oath imposed upon him when entrusted with the defence, would have been compelled to lay down his brief and withdraw.

Yucé denies all the allegations against him which charge him with having taken any active part in the crucifixion of the boy, and he protests that he is unable properly to defend himself because the copies of the depositions supplied him do not mention time or place of the alleged offences nor yet the names of the witnesses by whom these allegations are made. Upon the assumption, however, that these deponents are Benito Garcia, Juan Franco, and Juan de Ocaña, he proceeds to answer the charges as best he can.

This answer consists of a repudiation of those depositions as inadmissible upon the grounds that they do not agree one with another, and that each refers to a separate circumstance, no two confirming any one particular accusation, and all being contrary to what the same witnesses had stated in confrontation with the defendant, when each had acknowledged that Yucé's relation of the events was the true one. Hence it is established that on one or the other of these occasions they must have lied, from which it follows that they are perjured and unworthy of faith.

Further, he claims that they may not be admitted as witnesses because they were, themselves, participators in the crime committed. Finally, he declares that their implication of himself is an act of spite and vengeance upon him. It is his full and faithful confession which has placed the inquisitors in possession of the facts of the case and the names of the offenders, and the latter are determined that since they themselves must die, Yucé shall die with them—out of which malice and enmity they have accused him.

Upon these grounds, and insisting that he has told them the utter and complete truth, and that he himself was no more than a witness of the events, and in no way a participator, Yucé bases his defence, and begs that the depositions should cease to weigh against him.[205]

Guevára's answer, if it inclines to the grotesque, is quite typical, and is certainly more to the taste of the court.

He denies that the witnesses are inspired by any such animosity as Yucé suggests, and he asserts that they have deponed "with devout zeal of faith, and to deliver their souls from peril." And amongst these, be it remembered, was Benito Garcia, who conceived that the worst thing he had ever done in his life had been to get himself baptized a Christian, and who continued firm in his resolve to die a Jew at all costs. Only at the very stake itself—as we shall see—did he recant again, that he might earn the mercy of strangulation. Yet Guevára does not hesitate to say—what he must know to be untrue— that these men have confessed "with devout zeal of faith."

On these grounds Guevára urges that the depositions must be admitted as made in good faith and as proof; and since the said Yucé Franco would not spontaneously confess all that he had done, their Reverend Paternities should put him to the question of torture, as by law prescribed in such circumstances as the present.[206]

The court agrees with its Fiscal and proceeds to draw up a list of fifteen questions to be put to the accused.[207]

With this list the inquisitors Villada and Santo Domingo, accompanied by their notary, go down into the prisons of the Inquisition on November 2, and order Yucé Franco to be brought before them.

"Very lovingly and humanely" they admonish him to tell the whole truth of the things known to him that are the business of the Holy Office, and particularly in answer to the questions they have prepared. These questions being summed up amount to the following: Whence was the child that was crucified? Whose child was it? Who brought it to the cave? Who first set on foot this affair?

They promise him that if he makes truthful answer they will use him as mercifully as the law and their consciences permit.

Yucé has cause to mistrust any such promises. His first confession was made three months ago under a promise of pardon, and he has every reason to suppose that it has been the ruin of him.

He says, however, that being in the cave on the occasion when they foregathered there for the enchantment—about fourteen days after the crucifixion—he heard Tazarte inquire whence was the child, and Juan Franco replied before all that it was from a place whence it would never be missed, "as stated in his confession."

(When last asked this question—at the time of making his confession—he had attributed these words to Tazarte.)

He protests that he can remember no more than he has already confessed.

Their Reverend Paternities deplore his stubbornness. They tell him that since he will not speak the entire truth of what he knows—as they have proof—they must proceed to other measures. They summon Diego Martin, the torturer, and into his hands they deliver the prisoner, with orders to take him to the torture-chamber, strip him naked, and bind him to the *escalera*—intending, if necessary, to proceed to the water-torture.

This is done, and Yucé is stretched naked and cruelly bound with ropes that bite into his flesh as a foretaste of the *garrote* by which his torments will commence. The inquisitors enter—possibly after a delay sufficient to allow the mental torture of anticipation to terrorize the patient into a more amenable frame of mind.

Again they admonish him for his own sake to speak what he knows, and they even point out to him that it is his duty as a God-fearing Jew to speak the truth. Again they promise to deal mercifully with him if he will answer their questions fully and truthfully; and lastly they protest that if his blood is shed in the course of what is to follow, or should he suffer any other harm, or mutilation of limb, or even death, the blame must fall entirely upon himself and nowise upon their reverences.

Fully intimidated by this skilful accumulation of terrorizing agents, Yucé implores them to repeat their questions, which he will do his best to answer.

"Whence," they ask him again, "was the boy who was crucified at La Guardia?"

"Juan Franco," he replies, "brought him from Toledo." He adds that Juan Franco announced this before them all, and told them that he had kept the child concealed in La Hos de La Guardia for a day before bringing him to the cave to be crucified.

Photo by Donald Macbeth.

SANBENITO OF PENITENT RELAPSED.
From Limborch's 'Historia Inquisitionis.'

What is not to be explained is why Yucé should have waited until he was strapped to the *escalera* before making this statement. Why did he not make it when the question was asked him at his last examination—if not in his original confession? It cannot be pretended that he was endeavouring to screen Juan Franco, because he has very amply betrayed him in other ways. Is the explanation that under fear of torture he felt the need to invent an answer likely to satisfy the inquisitors? It can hardly be that, because Juan Franco himself is to admit—as we shall see—the truth of this detail. It only remains to be supposed that the lively fear of torture had sharpened the young Jew's memory. But that again seems hardly satisfactory as an explanation.

"Where," they ask him next, "is La Hos?"

"It is," he replies, "a meadow by the River Algodor," and he goes on to explain that Juan Franco had told them all that he had taken a load of wheat to Toledo to sell, and that, having sold it, he went to an inn, and later on he found the boy in a doorway and coaxed him away with *nuégados* (a sweetmeat composed of flour, honey, and nuts—nougat). Thus he got him into his cart and brought him to La Guardia.

Yucé doesn't know who were the child's parents, nor in what street of Toledo he was taken by Juan Franco, as the latter did not mention those particulars.

"Who were the first to propose the affair? Did the Jews engage the Christians in it, or the Christians engage the Jews?"

He answers that the Francos of La Guardia, fearing the Inquisition, performed an enchantment in the first instance with a consecrated wafer, as he has already confessed (October 11), and then repaired to Tazarte asking him to do something more efficacious, as the sorcery with the wafer had had no result. Tazarte agreed, and bade them procure a Christian boy for the purpose. When Juan Franco brought him, it was decided to cut out his heart, that with this heart and a wafer a stronger enchantment might be performed.

"Why was he done to death by crucifixion rather than in any other way?"

Yucé believes that the crucifixion was preferred in vituperation of Jesus Christ. But again he protests that his own share was no more than he has confessed already.

"What were the particular vituperations used to the child, and by whom?"

His answer to this question incriminates all those who were present at the affair; the vituperations which he tells the inquisitors were employed were rather indecent, and include a scurrilous version of the Incarnation which would, no doubt, be current at the time among Jews and other enemies of Christianity in Spain and elsewhere—a story, it is needless to add, entirely idle and foolish, and rather the obvious thing to be conceived in those days against any historical character who might be detested.

He says that Tazarte was the leader in all the vituperations (which sounds likely enough, as Tazarte was the celebrant), that the others uttered them after him, and he admits that he himself said some of the things which he has mentioned, but he doesn't enter into particulars.

"For what purpose were the heart and the Host required, and what good purpose was expected to be served by these sorceries?"

He replies that these things were done to the end that the inquisitors or any others who should aim at molesting these Christians concerned should die of rabies.

"What advantage did the Jews look to gain?"

He states that Tazarte had assured them that as a consequence of the enchantment all Christians in the land must either perish or become Jews, so that the Law of Moses should triumph and prevail.

"To whom were the heart and the Host to be delivered for the said enchantment?"

"To Mosé Abenamias at Zamora."

"Was Abenamias himself to perform the enchantment?"

"No; he was to give orders for its performance to a wizard of Zamora."

"Does he, or do any of the others, know the said wizard, and what is his name?"

He cannot answer the question, beyond telling them that he had heard Tazarte say that he knew Abenamias and the wizard, and that he had been to school with the latter.

"How many times did they assemble to decide upon the crucifixion?"

He knows that all (with the exception of himself) assembled in the same cave to perform an enchantment with a Host on an occasion previous to that of the boy's crucifixion. He knows this because he was invited to the gathering; he did not wish to go, and so stayed away, but he was told afterwards by the others what had been done.

"What Christians does he know to have kept the Sabbath, the Passover, and to have performed Jewish rites?"

He says that Benito once came to their house at Tenbleque and spent a Sabbath with them, doing no work, eating *adafinas* and drinking *Caser* wine; and that he came upon another occasion and asked them when was the fast of *Tisabeaf* (the eve of Purim), and that he believes that, being informed of this, he kept that fast.

He can remember no others, excepting one Diego de Ayllon and three of his daughters and a son, all of whom kept the Sabbath and observed the law of Moses in secret; and the widow of one Juan de Origuela, deceased, who sometimes kept Jewish fasts; and Juan Vermejo of Tenbleque, whom he knows once to have kept the great fast.

These names are duly noted on the margin of the notary's document as matters of importance which need inquiring into.

"Whence was the wafer procured, and how does he know that it was consecrated?"

He answers that when they assembled, a fortnight after the crucifixion, he heard Alonso Franco say that he had taken it from the monstrance in the Church of Romeral, replacing it by an unconsecrated wafer.

"Was this the wafer given to Tazarte with the heart?"

He believes so, but he is not sure, nor does he know what became of it.

"Who brought the other wafer given to Benito, and whence was it obtained?"

Alonso brought it, and said that he had obtained it in the church of La Guardia, and that it was consecrated. But Yucé doesn't know if anyone gave it to him.[208]

This confession Yucé ratified two days later, adding now that Juan and Garcia Franco together had brought the boy, and that one had remained at La Hos with him whilst the other had come to La Guardia. Further, he adds that the letter to Abenamias at Zamora bore six signatures—Tazarte's, Alonso Franco's, Benito Garcia's, Yucé Franco's own, his brother's, and one other which he can't recall.[209]

We have already indicated that a mystery attaches to this letter. What has become of it? We are told that Benito bore it together with the Host. How does it happen that it was not taken together with the Host when he was arrested at the inn at Astorga? Possibly it was. But in that case, and since it bore Yucé's signature, why is it not included in the *dossier*, and why can we find no trace of any use having been made of it by the inquisitors? The only plausible explanation—and it may be forthcoming when the *dossiers* of the other accused are discovered—is that the Host found upon Benito Garcia was not the one sent with the letter by his hand some time in 1487 or 1488.

On November 3 the octogenarian Ça is examined in the torture-chamber, strapped, as was his son, to the *escalera*. But the mere fear of torture is not sufficient to loosen the tongue of this aged Jew. He resists their questions, and will add nothing to what he has confessed, until the executioner has submitted him to that frightful torment and given him one jar of water. He then affords them, at last, the further information they require, telling them the precise vituperations that were addressed to the crucified boy, and admitting that this was done in mockery of the Passion of Jesus Christ. He says that Tazarte uttered the insults, and that the others—first the Jews, and after them the Christians—repeated them. Further, he confesses that the child was crucified and the sorceries performed that the inquisitors and all Christians should enrage and die.[210]

On the same day Juan Franco was tied to the *escalera*, beyond which it was not necessary to proceed with him, for he there satisfied the inquisitors by confessing to the vituperations employed against the crucified boy.[211]

On the 4th further confirmation of this is obtained from Juan de Ocaña, who confesses to the vituperations, and says that they were first uttered by the Jews, who then compelled the Christians to repeat them. He does not remember the terms used, nor would he ever have known them but for the Jews.[212]

Benito is next examined, and warned by the inquisitors to answer truthfully, as the truth is already fully known to them. He admits that many vituperations were used; he cites them, and in the main they agree with what has already been deponed.

"Who," he is asked, "were the first to utter these things?"

He replies that Ça Franco, his sons, and Tazarte (*i.e.* the Jews) were the first, and that he and the other Christians repeated them afterwards.

Lastly, on November 5, Alonso Franco affords the fullest confirmation to all this that has been confessed by the other accused.[213]

The trial is now rapidly drawing to a close. On the 7th Yucé is again before the court, and—sinister feature—this time he comes alone. His counsel has vanished, in acknowledgment of the fact that it is no longer tenable with his duty to God that he should continue to defend one of whose "heresy" he is himself convinced. Yucé himself, in view of this, must realize that he is lost, and must abandon his last shred of hope.

Guevára, the prosecutor, is there, and Dr. Villada announces that additional proof is now before the court. He orders copies of the latest depositions, obtained in the torture-chamber, to be delivered to the defendant, and he accords the latter three days within which he must lodge any objection to anything contained in them.

But Yucé does not require so long. He realizes that all is lost, and he forthwith confesses that what has been deponed by the witnesses against him concerning the vituperations he used is true with certain exceptions, and these were the most blasphemous and insulting.

Upon that the fiscal Guevára formally petitions the court to pass sentence. The inquisitor Santo Domingo declares the trial to be at an end, and dismisses both parties, requiring them to come before the court again in three days' time to hear the sentence.[214]

Yet, before proceeding to this, on the 14th day of that month of November, the inquisitors ordered all the prisoners (with the exception of Juan Franco) to be introduced together into the audience-chamber. There, in the presence of his co-accused, each was bidden to recite what he had already confessed, this being done with the aim of obtaining a greater unanimity upon details.

Last of all, Juan Franco is brought in, and he now admits that it is true that he brought the boy from Toledo, that they had crucified him as he has confessed, that he himself had opened the boy's side and taken out his heart, and that his brother Alonso had opened the veins of the child's arms, etc.—all as confessed—and further that it is true that he and his brother Alfonso had afterwards buried their victim.

He now corroborates Benito's statement that on the day they stole the child he and Benito went together to Toledo, and that they agreed that one should seek in one quarter of the city whilst the other sought in another. And further, he says that he found the child in the doorway—known as the Puerta del Perdon—of the cathedral, as he has already stated in his confession (which is not before us).[215]

On the next day Guevára appears before the inquisitors to petition that in view of what has been deponed against the deceased Mosé Franco, Yucé Tazarte, and David Perejon, their Paternities should order it to be recorded *ad perpetuam rei memoriam*, to enable the execution of the deceased in effigy, the confiscation of their property, and the infamy of their heirs.

That is on November 15. On the 16th the last scene of this protracted trial is played in the market-square of Avila.

There, near the church of St. Peter, the scaffolds have been erected for the Auto de Fé. On one, in their hideous yellow *sanbenitos*, are grouped the eight prisoners and the three effigies. On the other are the inquisitors, Dr. Pedro de Villada and Frey Antonio de Santo Domingo, with all the *personnel* of the Holy Office, their notaries, the fiscal Guevára, familiars, and apparitors. Round the scaffolds thronged the greater part of the inhabitants of Avila and many who had come in from the surrounding country districts, whence it is clear that the Auto had been announced some days before. The popular feeling against the Jews runs high, and it is an angry, turbulent mob that witnesses the Auto. Avila, indeed, is in uproar, and no Jew dare show himself abroad without risk of being insulted or assaulted in the street.[216]

The sentences are read by the notary Antonio Gonçales, commencing with a very full narrative of the crimes of each of the accused, which we need not render here as it is a summary of all that has been gone through and practically a repetition of the matter contained in the "Testimonio."

They are sentenced all to be abandoned to the secular arm of the Corregidor Don Alvaro de Sant' Estiban, who, advised some days before, is in attendance with his lieutenants and *alguaziles*.

The usual exhortation being duly pronounced, they are seized by the men of the Corregidor and led away out of the city to the burning-place. The inquisitors order their notaries to accompany the doomed men, that they may record their final confessions at the stake.

In Yucé's *dossier* are included not only his own confession—made at the last moment—but also Benito Garcia's, Juan de Ocaña's, and Juan Franco's, all recorded by the notary Gonçales. Further, this *dossier* contains a letter written on the morrow of the event by the same notary of the Holy Office to the authorities of La Guardia, accompanying a relation of the crime and the sentences pronounced, for publication in La Guardia, where the offences were committed.

From this we learn that Benito, in spite of his protestations that he would die a Jew betide what might, accepted at the stake the spiritual comforts of the Church, and thus earned the mercy of being strangled before the faggots were fired.[217]

Similarly Juan de Ocaña and Juan Franco accepted the ministrations of the attendant friars and returned to the Church from which they had secretly seceded. But the Jews—the stalwart old man of over eighty and his son— held staunchly to their faith, and refused to avoid by apostasy any part of the agony prepared them. Wherefore, in a spite that seems almost satanic, their flesh was torn with red-hot pincers before they were consumed over slow fires.

"They refused," writes the reverend notary, "to call upon God or the Virgin Mary or to make so much as a sign of the Cross. Do not pray for them," he concludes, impatiently it seems to us, "for they are buried in Hell."

Finally, the notary begs the authorities of La Guardia not to permit that the place where Juan Franco said that the Holy Child was buried should be ploughed over, but to see that it is left intact. Their Highnesses and the Cardinal of Spain, he adds, may desire to visit it, and he prays that God "may reveal to us the bones of the infant." It is expedient to mark the spot, he concludes, because, in view of the merits of such a place, he hopes that it may please God that the earth of it will work miracles.

The sentence is sent, it should be added, with order that it shall be read from the pulpit of La Guardia on the following Sunday, and this under pain of excommunication.

In Avila the popular feeling against the Jews as a consequence of this affair was so bitter that their lives were not safe, and it is on record that one was stoned to death in the streets. It became necessary for the Aljama of that city to petition the Sovereigns for protection, and M. Fidel Fita quotes a royal letter commanding such protection to be extended, with threats of rigour against any who should molest them.[218]

CHAPTER XXIV
EPILOGUE TO THE AFFAIR OF THE SANTO NIÑO

The evidence given by Yucé Franco as to whence the consecrated wafers had been obtained is hearsay evidence, and very vague even then. But it would appear that from Benito Garcia or Alfonso Franco the inquisitors have been able to obtain something more definite, for whilst the trial of the eight accused has been drawing to a close, the familiars of the Holy Office have been about the apprehension of the sacristan of the church of La Guardia.

On November 18, 1491—two days after the Auto—this sacristan is brought before the court at Avila, and admonished to tell the truth of this matter, being promised mercy if he will do so.

He states that about two years ago his uncle, Alonso Franco, besought him on two separate occasions to let him have two consecrated wafers, promising him a cloak and money and much else if he would so. Ultimately, in response to these requests, and in accordance with the instructions he received from Alonso, he delivered a consecrated wafer to Benito Garcia, who came for it on the other's behalf.

He remembers that it was winter-time, but he cannot recall the day or even the month. He explains that he took the Host from the pyx in the sanctuary of the Church of Santa Maria, having obtained the keys from the earthenware pot in which they were kept. He says that he begged Benito to tell him what it was wanted for, but that he could not induce him to say. He was assured, however, that no harm was intended.

He is able to fix the date more closely by remembering that the Francos were arrested about five months later.

Under further examination he declares that he believes in the True Presence, and always did, and that when he urged this upon Alfonso Franco and Benito Garcia they admitted that his act was a sin, but they assured him that it was not a heresy, and that no heresy was involved, and that for the sin his confessor would absolve him.[219]

One man who is alleged to have had a share in the affair of La Guardia escaped all mention at the time in the depositions of the accused, and was, consequently, entirely overlooked. This was one Hernando de Ribera, a man of a station in life very much above that of the others, and it is said that in consequence of this to him had been assigned the aristocratic role of Pilate in that parody of the Passion.

Not until nearly thirty years later was he arrested, self-betrayed, it is said, the man having boasted of his share in that affair. He was convicted of that crime, and also of flagrant Judaizing, for in the meanwhile he had accepted baptism to avoid expulsion from Spain when the decree of banishment of all Jews was published.

Now, whilst the publication by M. Fidel Fita of the records of the trial of Yucé Franco has shed a good deal of light upon the affair, it is not to be denied that much still remains to be explained, and that until such explanations are forthcoming—until the records of the proceedings against Yucé's co-accused are brought to light and we are able to compare them one with another—the affair of the Holy Infant of La Guardia must to a certain extent continue in the category of historic mysteries.

Meanwhile, however, in spite of the glaring contradictions contained in the evidence at present available, in spite of the incongruities which refuse to fit into the general scheme, we cannot hold that M. Loeb is justified of his conclusion that the Holy Infant of La Guardia—and consequently the crime with which we have dealt—never had any real existence.[220]

M. Loeb makes a twofold contention:

> (*a*) If the crime of La Guardia ever did take place, then upon the evidence itself, it was not ritual murder at all, but a case of sorcery in which Christians were concerned as well as Jews.

> (*b*) No such crime ever did take place.

He bases his somewhat daring final conclusion upon three premises:

> (*a*) The depositions of the witnesses, obtained under torture or the threat of it, are full of contradictions, of improbabilities, and of facts materially impossible.

> (*b*) The judges made no inquest to discover the truth.

> (*c*) The Inquisition is unable to fix the date of the crime; it did not verify the disappearance or discover the remains of any child.

The first of these premises is the most worthy of attention. The other two appear to us to overlook the fact that our present knowledge is confined to the record of the trial of one of the accused, and this one a youth who was guilty of participating in the crime in a comparatively minor degree.

No one is in a position to say that the judges made no inquest to discover the truth. All that we know is that it does not transpire from Yucé's trial that any such efforts were made. But then such efforts may not so much concern Yucé's trial as the trials of some of the ringleaders, and it is very possible that the records of the latter may divulge some such inquest. It is more than possible. The compiler of the résumé of seven of the trials distinctly shows that this was done.[221] He cites the fact that when Juan Franco had confessed that he and his brother Alonso buried the boy, the inquisitors took him to the place where he stated that the body had been inhumed, and made him point out the exact spot, "and they discovered the truth and demonstration of all this."[222]

This, of course, does not mean that the body was found. It simply means— as we are told—that the place indicated by Juan Franco presented the appearance of having lately served the purpose of a grave. The failure to find the body is undoubtedly one of the unexplained mysteries of this affair. But it does not justify the statement that no inquest was made—a statement which in itself implies that the inquisitors knew the whole story to be false, and therefore deliberately avoided inquiries which should expose that falseness.

The vagueness and confusion that appear to exist on the subject of the date when the crime was committed certainly call for comment.

The contradictions on this score appear to be flagrant, and it is impossible to reconcile the date of the crucifixion with that of Benito Garcia's arrest in Astorga. It seems to be established by Yucé that the crucifixion took place at the end of Lent 1488; and he and others tell us that about six months later they all assembled again to dispatch the Host to Zamora by the hand of Benito. Yet Benito is arrested in Astorga in May or June of 1490—more than eighteen months after setting out for Zamora—and the wafer is still in his possession, undelivered. That is what *seems* to be established. But it is possible that a very simple explanation may dispose of this discrepancy. We are not justified by our present knowledge in saying that the inquisitors were unable to dispose of it. We may not assume that there is not, in the records of the trials of the other accused, matter that will clear up this question.

The date supplied by the sacristan, for instance, does not seem to be so very inconsistent with that of the event in the inn at Astorga. He said, it will be remembered, that he had delivered the wafer to Benito some five months before the arrest of the Francos. This tends strongly to confirm the impression we have already formed that the wafer discovered upon Benito at the time of his arrest was not the one that he had set out to take to Zamora some two years earlier. The Host, together with the letter for Abenamias, may very well have reached its destination. If this is admitted—and there is nothing in the evidence to forbid its admittance—much that is irreconcilable in the depositions at once disappears.

M. Loeb, of course, has proceeded upon the assumption that it is pretended that the Host dispatched from La Guardia in 1488 and the Host found upon Benito at Astorga in 1490 are one and the same. It may appear to be the obvious thing to assume. Yet it is a hasty assumption, which nothing in the evidence before us will justify.

As for the other discrepancies which M. Loeb points out, when all is said, they refer to matters of detail, upon which mistakes are not impossible.

Benito states that the child's hands and feet were nailed to the cross in addition to being tied, whilst Yucé makes no mention of nails.

According to the statements of Yucé and of Juan Franco, it is the latter's brother who opened the veins in the boy's arms, whereas Ocaña said that this was done by Yucé. We have already drawn attention to the circumstances under which Ocaña so accused Yucé, and we have suggested the vindictiveness that may have inspired him.

Juan Franco confessed that he himself cut open the boy's side and drew out the heart, whilst Yucé's statement was to the effect that Juan had opened the wound and Garcia Franco had torn out the heart.

Mainly the evidence seems to say that the child bled to death. Yet Benito states that he was strangled(?), and Yucé in one of his statements says that they gagged him because he was crying. We have already suggested that by the expression "*lo ahogaron*" so much as "strangling" may not necessarily have been meant.

These are, after all, the principal discrepancies; and it is to be remembered that these men were referring to things done at least two years before; that confusion on the score of particulars is not only possible but more or less inevitable; and that, despite contradictions in these details, the main facts stated are always the same in the depositions of each. M. Loeb more than suggests that this unanimity was contrived by the inquisitors. He puts it forward as more than probable that the prisoners were left alone together on the occasions of the confrontations, to the end that they might agree upon the same tale.

There is not the slightest warrant for such an assumption. In the records the notary very clearly states that the inquisitors were present throughout those confrontations, and it is of importance to remember that these records were not prepared for publication, but were to be consigned to the secret archives of the Inquisition—so that any notion of a fraud having been deliberately perpetrated may once for all be dismissed as entirely idle.

But even were it not the recorded fact that the inquisitors were present at the confrontations, and that the prisoners were afforded no opportunity of coming to any understanding, it would still be extremely difficult to believe that they should have come to an understanding to get themselves all burnt.

M. Loeb's attempt to make this appear reasonable is the least convincing thing in a very able but quite unconvincing article. It certainly seems to display his own want of confidence in the general acceptance of such a situation.

"We could understand," he says, "that guilty men should come to an understanding to deny the crime committed, or to attenuate the fault, or to cast it upon others. But what should be the meaning of an understanding whose object, as would be the case here, is to make truthful avowals of a real crime? The accused would be taking unnecessary trouble. But all is explained if, on the contrary, they prepared confessions of a crime that was never committed."

M. Loeb has vitiated his argument by the absolute assumption that an understanding did take place. This we cannot admit upon the evidence before us. But if we do, is the position materially altered? M. Loeb says that "all is explained if they prepared confessions of a crime that was never committed." To our mind, nothing is explained by such a procedure. What possible object could have induced them to come to an understanding to make an uncommitted crime the subject of a unanimous confession that must infallibly send them to the stake? What possible advantage could they hope to derive from a falsehood of that description?

One of the chief obstacles to the rejection of the story as a fabrication is Yucé's confession to "the Rabbi Abraham" in the prison of Segovia. M. Loeb recognizes it, and although he makes a determined attempt to overcome it, his arguments are too arbitrary and do not materially affect the point even if they are admitted.

But if M. Loeb is entirely unconvincing in his attempts to prove that the crucifixion of the boy is a fable, nothing could be more convincing than his first contention: that even if we account the story true as contained in Yucé's *dossier*, the deed is not to be looked upon as ritual murder, but purely as an operation in magic.

It is a conclusion with which you must come to agree, although at first glance you may be tempted to form the opinion that the crucifixion of the child served both purposes. Some such opinion had been formed by the inquisitors when they asked why the boy had been crucified rather than put to death in some other fashion, since his heart was all that was required for the enchantment.

The answer was that crucifixion was chosen in derision and vituperation of the Passion of Jesus Christ. But this is a very different thing from ritual murder or "the hanging of Haman." If we turn to the actual vituperative phrases employed,[223] we find the expression of a desire to wound the Redeemer Himself, through that form of magic, common in all ages, known as *envoûtement*. Instead of the waxen or wooden effigy usually employed, a living body is used in this case. For the rest the immolation of a child plays its part in the magic ritual of other than Jews. We need mention but the notorious instance of the Black Masses celebrated by the infamous Abbé Gribourg in the eighteenth century.

There seems, indeed, no doubt at all that we are justified in rejecting the theory that the crucifixion of the Holy Child of La Guardia is to be accepted as an instance of Jewish ritual murder. So far we can accompany M. Loeb, but no farther. We cannot say with him that no such crime was ever committed. To convince us of that it would be necessary to show that the whole of the *dossier* we have considered is a forgery to serve the purposes of Torquemada. And this we have proof that it is not. Had it been that, had it been manufactured for popular consumption, it would not have lain concealed for four centuries in the secret archives of the Inquisition.

That Torquemada exploited the matter and turned it to the fullest account is admitted. But this merely shows him to be an opportunist; it is very far from proving him a forger. The very sentence was couched in terms calculated to excite—as it did—popular indignation against the Jews. Nor did the publication of the sentence end in La Guardia, whither copies were sent. We may infer that Torquemada scattered those copies broadcast through Spain, since we actually find a Catalan translation which was specially prepared for publication in Barcelona.

The cult of the Holy Child of La Guardia sprang up at once, and developed rapidly. Numerous shrines were set up in his honour, the first and chief of these being on the site of the house of Juan Franco, which had been razed to the ground. Here an altar was erected in the cellar of the house, on the spot where it was believed that the child's sufferings had begun; it was surmounted by a figure of a child pinioned to a column.

Over this subterranean shrine a church sprang rapidly into existence.

Another hermitage was erected near Santa Maria de Pera, on the spot where the child was alleged to have been buried, and yet another in the cave where he was believed to have suffered crucifixion. "In all times since," says

Moreno,[224] "the three sanctuaries have been frequented by those who come to pray to the Niño as to a saint."

The first of these sanctuaries was erected by 1501—at which date records of it are to be found. It was called the Sanctuary of the Holy Innocent, and Moreno adds that this has always received the approval of Popes and Bishops, and that plenary and partial indulgences have been granted to the faithful visiting these shrines.

The people of La Guardia elected him their patron saint, and a fast was appointed for the eve of his feast-day, which at first was March 25, but was afterwards changed to September 25. Moreno includes in his book the prayers prescribed and a litany to the Niño.[225]

But it is not without a certain significance that Rome—ever cautious, as we have already had occasion to say, in the matter of canonization—has not yet recognized the Holy Child of La Guardia as one of the saints of the Church.

Yepes chronicles four miracles performed by the child after his death, beginning with his mother's obtaining sight. All these, with other very interesting and purely romantic details, are to be found in that piously fraudulent work—the "Life of the Holy Child," by Martinez Moreno.

CHAPTER XXV
THE EDICT OF BANISHMENT

It was, as we have already suggested, the very opportuneness with which the trial and sentence of those concerned in the affair of La Guardia came to afford Torquemada an additional argument to plead with the Sovereigns his case against the Jews, which has led so many historians—prior to M. Fidel Fita's discovery—to reject the story as an invention. Another reason to discredit it lay in the circumstance that it was circulated in Spain together with a number of other stories that were obviously false and obviously invented expressly for the purpose of defaming the Jews and exciting popular indignation against them.

Meanwhile Ferdinand and Isabella pressed triumphantly forward on their conquering progress through Andalusia. Lucena, Coin, Ronda, and scores of other Moorish strongholds in the southern hills had fallen before the irresistible arms of the Christians; and the Sovereigns, aided by Jewish gold— not merely the gold extorted by confiscations, but moneys voluntarily contributed by their Hebrew subjects—pushed on to the reduction of Malaga, as the prelude to the leaguer of Granada itself, the last bulwark of Islam in Spain. This fell on January 2, 1492, and with it fell the Moslem dominion, which had endured in the peninsula, with varying fortunes, for nearly 800 years.

It might well have seemed to the Catholic Sovereigns that the conquest of Spain and the victory there of Christianity were at last accomplished, had not Torquemada been at their elbow to point out that the triumph of the Cross would never be complete in that land as long as the Jews continued to be numbered among its inhabitants.

He protested that the evils resulting from intercourse between Christian and Jew were notorious and unconquerable. He declared that in spite of the Inquisition, and in spite of all other measures that had been taken to keep Christian and Jew apart, the evil persisted and was as rampant as ever. He urged that the Jews continued unabatedly to pervert the Christians, and that they must so continue as long as they were tolerated to remain in the peninsula. Particularly was this notorious in the case of the Marranos or New-Christians, to whom the Israelites gave no peace until—by indoctrination or by the scorn and abuse they heaped upon them—they had seduced them back into error.

And in proof of what he urged he was able to point to the affair of La Guardia, to the outrage to the crucifix at Casar de Palomero, and to other matters of a kindred nature that had lately been brought to light.

He called upon the Sovereigns to redeem the promise they had made to give consideration to this matter—a consideration which, in answer to his earlier pleadings, they had postponed until the war against Granada should have been brought to its conclusion.

In the meantime the Jews themselves had fought strenuously against the banishment with which they saw themselves threatened. Eloquent had been their appeals to the Sovereigns. And the Sovereigns could hardly turn a deaf ear to the intercessions of subjects to whom they owed so much. For was it not the very Jews who had supplied the Spanish crown with the sinews for this campaign against the enemies of the Cross? Was it not owing to wonderful Hebrew administration—an administration gratefully surrendered to them—that the army of the Cross was equipped, maintained, and paid out of moneys that the Jews themselves had provided?

They found means to bring this to the attention of the Sovereigns, as a proof of the loyalty of their devotion, as a proof of their value to the Spanish nation. And the Sovereigns had other experiences of the loyalty and affection which had ever been manifested towards them by their long-suffering Hebrew subjects. When, for instance, their son, the Infante Don Juan was proclaimed in Aragon, after the Cortes of Toledo, the Jews had been foremost in the jubilant and loving receptions that everywhere met their Highnesses in the course of their progress through the kingdom of Ferdinand. Whilst the Spaniards were content to greet their Sovereigns with acclamations, the Jews went to meet them with valuable gifts.[226] Bernaldez tells us[227] of the splendid offering made to their Highnesses by the Aljama of Zaragoza. It consisted of twelve calves, twelve lambs, and a curious and very beautiful service of silver borne by twelve Jews, a rich silver cup full of gold castellanos[228] and a jar of silver—"all of which the Sovereigns received and prized, returning many thanks."

Loyalty so tangibly manifested, of which this is but an instance, must have some weight in the scales against fanaticism; further, it seems impossible that the Sovereigns should have been altogether blind to the possible jeopardizing of the industrial prosperity of the kingdom if those chiefly responsible for it were driven out.

So they had put off their decision in the matter, urging that the present war demanded their full attention. But now that the conquest of Granada was accomplished, they were forced to look the matter in the face. For Torquemada was giving them no peace. Hard-driven by his fanatical hatred of the Israelites, the Grand Inquisitor had resolved upon his course and was determined that nothing should turn him aside.

Constantly were his arguments—all founded upon the love of Christ—poured into the ears of the Sovereigns, and to prove the soundness of these arguments he was able to bring forward concrete facts—or, at least, matters upon which the courts of the Inquisition had pronounced—prominent among which would be the affair of La Guardia.

And what Torquemada was doing by the Sovereigns, the brethren of his order were doing by Spain. Popular indignation against the Jews, so easy to arouse, already inflamed by the outrage at Casar de Palomero and the crucifixion at La Guardia, was further and unscrupulously excited by false stories that were set in circulation. It was even alleged that the illness of the Prince Don Juan was the result of Hebrew infamy, and to explain this a foolish, wicked story was invented, put about and universally accepted.

Llorente quotes this story from the "Anonymo de Zaragoza."[229] It is to the effect that the prince coveted a golden pomander-ball worn by his physician, who was of a Jewish family, and this gewgaw the physician ended by relinquishing to his patient. One day, moved by youthful curiosity, the boy wished to see what the pomander contained. Opening it, he discovered an indecent and blasphemous picture, insulting to the divinity of Christ. The sight of it inspired the princeling with such horror and grief that he fell sick. Nor would he divulge the origin of his illness until the instances of his father succeeded in drawing the secret from him, whereupon "it was resolved to take proceedings against the physician and to sentence him to the fire."

This trivial, scurrilous, and obviously untruthful story would not be worth repeating did it not serve the purpose of showing the sort of rumours that were being propagated to the hurt of the Israelites.

Another story that was circulated alleged that in Valencia there had also been an attempt by a number of Jews to crucify a Christian boy. This is recorded in that scurrilous, infamous publication, "Centinela contra Judios," by Frey Francisco de Torrejoncillo. We have already referred to it more than once. It was first printed in 1676, and is the book of a friar of the Order of St. Francis, a disgraceful work which proves its author to have been as barefaced as he was barefooted. It is a collection of stupid lies and forgeries, and, it is scarcely an exaggeration to add, obscenities; it may be another instance of those frauds termed pious, but it is scarcely to the credit of a Church exercising, by means of the "Index Expurgatorius," a censorship of the press—to have permitted the circulation of a work of this order from the pen of a churchman.

This, however, is by the way.

The story here to be recorded is taken, Torrejoncillo tells us, from the "Sermon de la Cruz" by Frey Felipe de Salazar.[230] On a Good Friday evening a youth who was in a street of Valencia observed several men entering a house. Considering this to be strange—although no suspicious circumstance is mentioned—he approached the door and listened. He heard them say, "There seems to be some one at the door." Fearing that a brawl might be the result if he were discovered there when they opened, he drew his sword and fled. (How the drawing of his sword was calculated to assist his flight the author does not think it worth while to inform us.) As he was running he came upon a patrol, which seized him, demanding to know whither he was hurrying in this fashion with a naked sword in his hand. He related what he had witnessed, whereupon the officer, not only for the purpose of testing the truth of the story but also that he might ascertain to what end so many men should be assembling, went to the house and knocked.

The door was opened by a Jew, who began to make obvious excuses to him. Suddenly the officer heard a child's voice within the house, crying, "These men want to crucify me."

The Jews were taken, the house demolished, and on the site of it was built the Church of Santa Cruz.

In this collection of lies and forgeries are included the "letter of Christ to Abgarus," another letter of Pontius Pilate to Tiberius dilating upon the miracles of the Saviour, and a letter from the Jews of Constantinople to those of Toledo, which played an important part in this anti-semitic campaign.

It was the Cardinal-Archbishop Juan Martinez Siliceo who was alleged to have discovered this letter in Toledo. We are to suppose that he also found in Toledo the letter to the Jews of Constantinople to which this is a reply, for the chroniclers are able to supply us with the texts of both,[231] a circumstance which no one at the time appears to have considered strange.

The letter to Constantinople ran as follows:

"THE JEWS OF SPAIN *to* THE JEWS OF CONSTANTINOPLE

"Honoured Jews, health and grace.—Know that the King of Spain compels us to become Christians, deprives us of property and of life, destroys our synagogues and otherwise oppresses us, so that we are uncertain what to do.

"By the Law of Moses we beseech you to assemble, and to send us with all speed the declaration made in your assembly.

"CHAMARRO, Prince of the Jews of Spain."

To this the answer received from Constantinople was in the following terms:

"THE JEWS OF CONSTANTINOPLE *to* THE JEWS OF SPAIN

"Beloved Brethren in Moses,—We have your letter in which you tell us of the travail and suffering you are enduring there.... The opinion of the Rabbis is that since the King of Spain attempts to make you Christians, you should become Christians; since he deprives you of your goods and property, you should make your children merchants, that they may deprive the Christians of theirs; since you say that they deprive you of your lives, make your sons apothecaries and physicians to deprive the Christians of theirs; since they destroy your synagogues, make your sons clerics that they may destroy the Christian temples; since you say that you suffer other wrongs, make your sons enter public offices that thus they may render the Christians subject to them.

"Do not depart from these orders, and you will see that from oppressed you will come to be held of great account.

"HUSÉE, Prince of the Jews of Constantinople."

The matter of these letters—so very obviously forged—was freely circulated. Being accepted, public indignation was suddenly increased by fear. Imaginations were stimulated, and stories based upon these injunctions of Prince Husée became current, nothing being ever too flagrant for popular consumption. It was related that a Jewish physician in Toledo carried poison in one of his finger-nails, and that with this he touched the tongues of the patients he visited, thus killing them. Of another physician it was reported that he deliberately poisoned the wounds he was desired to heal.[232] And that there were many other such stories current is beyond all doubt.

What use, if any, Torquemada made of those forged letters and the stories that were their offspring, we do not know. But it would be strange if the circulation and acceptance of such matters displeased him, since they were plainly calculated to forward his aims and compel the Sovereigns to lend an ear to his insistent denunciations of the Jews.

Incessantly he preached the need for religious unity in a united Spain. Indeed, Spain, he urged, never could be united, never could deserve the blessing of Heaven, until all men in that land were the children of God, true believers in the Holy Roman Catholic Apostolic Faith. God had greatly favoured Ferdinand and Isabella, the friar continued. He had collected the various elements of the peninsula into one mighty kingdom, which He had subjected to their sceptre. Let them fuse those elements into a solid whole, rejecting all those who resist this fusion—and this for the honour and glory of God and of their own kingdom.

Before this terrific gospel of Religious Unity nothing could stand. Humanitarian considerations, principles of equity, indebtedness and gratitude are mere trifles to be swept away by that hurricane of religious argument.

The Sovereigns found themselves face to face with an issue of such a magnitude that no temporal considerations could be allowed to weigh. And to the pressure of Torquemada's fierce arguments was added now the pressure of public opinion, cunningly excited by his lieutenants. To the voice of God from the lips of the Grand Inquisitor was added now the *vox populi*— the voice of God from the lips of the people.

And so clamorous was this popular voice, so insistent were the accusations which it levelled against the Israelites, of ritual infamies and of seducing back to the Law of Moses their apostate brethren, that the Jews were warned of the storm that was about to break over their luckless heads.

Torquemada's demand was that they must receive baptism or go.

The Sovereigns hesitated still. In Isabella perhaps the voice of humanity was too strong to be entirely stifled by the dictates of bigotry.

But Torquemada's strength of purpose was the greater and more irresistible by virtue of its purity and singleness of aim. Obviously he was no self-seeker. Obviously he had no worldly ends to serve. What he demanded, he demanded in the name of the religion which he served—solely for the greater honour and glory of his God; and to sovereigns of the temper of Ferdinand and Isabella demands so inspired are not easily resisted.

And although it was clear that he sought no worldly advantage for himself, he did not scruple to use the prospect of the Sovereigns' worldly advantage as a weapon to combat their reluctance; he did not hesitate to dangle before their eyes temporal advantages that must result from the banishment of the Israelites. To arguments upon religious grounds he added arguments of worldly expediency, arguments which cannot have failed of effect upon the acquisitive nature of the King.

Never, urged the Grand Inquisitor, would Spain know tranquillity whilst she harboured Jews. They were predatory; they were untrustworthy; their sole objective was the satisfaction of their pecuniary interest—the only interest they knew; and their acquisitiveness would always dispose them to serve any enemy of the crown so that it should profit them to do so.[233]

But Torquemada was not the only advocate before the royal court. The Jews were there, too, pleading on their own behalf, with an eloquence that seemed for a moment on the point of prevailing—for the seductive chink of gold was persuasively intermingled with their protestations.

They urged their past services to the crown, and promised even greater services in the future; they swore that henceforth they would be more observant of the harsh laws formulated by Alfonso XI—that they would keep to their ghettos as prescribed, withdrawing to them at nightfall, and abstaining rigorously from all such intercourse with Christians as was by law forbidden. Last and most eloquent argument of all, they offered through Abraham Seneor and Isaac Abarbanel—the two Jews who had undertaken and so admirably effected the equipment of the Castilian army for the campaign against Granada—that in addition to giving this undertaking they would subscribe 30,000 ducats towards the expenses of the war against the Moslem.

Ferdinand's hesitation was increased by this offer. Ever in need of money as the Sovereigns were, the consideration of this gold not only tempted them, but it would undoubtedly have conquered them had not Torquemada been at hand. But for his violent intervention it is more than probable that the cruel edict of banishment would never have been promulgated.

The Dominican, learning what was afoot, thrust himself into their Highnesses' presence to denounce their hesitation, and to put upon it the name which in his opinion it deserved.

It is not difficult to picture him in that supreme moment. It is one of those rare occasions on which this being whom we have compared to a *Deus ex machina*, a cold stern spirit ruling and guiding the terrible organization of the Inquisition which he has himself established, steps forth in the flesh, a living, throbbing man.

You behold him pale, a little breathless in the excitement and anger by which he is possessed. His deep-set eyes glow sombrely with the fever of fanatical zeal and indignation. He draws his lean old frame erect. In his shrivelled, sinewy old hands he flaunts aloft a crucifix.

It is an intense moment. Everything contributes to it: the long-drawn duel between religion and humanity, between clericalism and Christianity, of which this is at last the climax; and nothing so much as the figure offered by the Jews. This *thirty* thousand is unfortunately reminiscent. It permits the Prior of Holy Cross to draw a very daring parallel.

"Judas," he cries, "once sold the Son of God for thirty pieces. Your Highnesses think to sell Him again for thirty thousand. Here you have Him. Sell Him, then, but acquit me of all share in the transaction."

And, crashing the crucifix upon the table before their startled Highnesses, he abruptly leaves the chamber.[234]

Thus Torquemada conquered.

The edict of expulsion was signed at Granada on March 31 of that year 1492—that glorious year in which Spain finally completed the erection of her monarchy upon the ruins of the old Visigothic kingdom, and in which the navigator Columbus laid a new world at the foot of the throne of the Catholic Sovereigns.[235]

CHAPTER XXVI
THE EXODUS FROM SPAIN

It was solemnly declared in the edict of expulsion that this decree was promulgated solely in obedience to the pressing need to cut off at the roots, once for all time, the evils arising out of the intercourse between Christians and Jews, since all other efforts hitherto undertaken with the same intent had proved fruitless.[236]

By this edict all Jews of any age and either sex who should refuse to receive baptism must quit Spain within three months, and never return, under pain of death and the confiscation of their property.

The cruelty of this expatriation calls for little exposition. Spain was the motherland of these Jews. For centuries it had been the home of their ancestors, and they held it in the affection implanted in the heart of each of us for the country which is his own. They must depart out of it, into exile in some foreign land, and the only terms upon which they could obtain immunity from that harsh decree was by the sacrifice of something dearer still, something as dear to them as honour itself. They must be false to the faith of their fathers and forswear the God of Israel.

That was the choice forced upon the Children of Judah—the choice which the arrogant Christian Church had been forcing upon all men from the moment that she had found herself mistress of the power to do so.

It was decreed that after the expiry of the three months allowed them in which to settle their affairs and be gone no Christian would be suffered to befriend or assist them, to give them food or shelter, under pain of being called to account as an abettor of heretics.

Until their departure the persons and property of the exiled were nominally under the protection of the Sovereigns. They were permitted to dispose of what property they possessed, and to take the proceeds with them in bills of exchange[237] or in merchandise, but not in gold, which it was forbidden to carry out of the country.

Little greater would have been the injury done them if their property had been confiscated outright. For being compelled to dispose of it at such short notice, and the buyers knowing that it must be sold, and eager to take advantage of these forced sales, what chance had the Jews of realizing anything that should approach its value? How could they avoid the pitiless Christian exploitation of their miserable position?

"The Christians obtained," says Bernaldez, "much property and many very rich houses and estates for little money; the Jews went about offering these, and could not find any buyers, so that they were forced to barter here a house for an ass, there a vineyard for a piece of cloth."[238]

From just this passage in the chronicle of an author whose detestation of the Jews we have earlier considered may be conceived how terrible was their distress, and how mercilessly was advantage taken of it by the Christians.

Photo by Donald Macbeth.

SANBENITO OF IMPENITENT.
From Limborch's "Historia Inquisitionis"

Amador de los Rios adds that entire ghettos entered into the sacrifice, and that, the Jews being utterly unable to dispose of such communal property, they were forced to make gifts of it to the municipalities that had shown them so little pity.[239]

Torquemada in his great zeal for the Faith was not content to leave matters there. His chief aim, after all, was not the expulsion of the Jews, but their conversion and the effacement of their creed. As a means to that end was it that he had wrung the edict of banishment from the Sovereigns.

Upon this campaign of conversion he now sent forth his army of Dominicans. He published an edict, with the royal sanction, in which he exhorted the Israelites to receive baptism, laying stress upon the fact that those who should do so before the expiry of the three months appointed for their emigration would be entitled to remain.

In every city, in every village, in every hamlet, in churches, in market-places, and at street-corners his black-and-white Dominicans sought by exhortation and argument to induce the Jews to receive the waters of baptism, thereby securing their well-being and prosperity in this world and their eternal salvation in the next. The preachers penetrated to the very synagogues in their zeal, and exerted themselves even in the Jewish temples, by the promises they held out of temporal advantage, to lead the Jews into the fold of Christianity. No place was sacred from the friars-preachers. In Segovia, when the hour of departure approached, the Jews spent three days in their cemetery weeping over the graves of their dead, which they were abandoning. And there were zealous Dominicans who intruded upon that sorrow, and seized the opportunity to preach conversion to that piteous assembly.[240]

But the response to all these sermons was only slight. If Torquemada's friars were preaching Christianity on the one hand, and attempting by argument and bribery to induce the Hebrews to embrace it, the Rabbis, on the other, were no less energetic in their efforts to encourage the Israelites to stand firm in their fidelity to their God, to resist the temptations of corruption, and to remember that even as God had delivered them out of Egypt and led them into the Land of Plenty, so in leading them out of Spain would He see that His children did not suffer loss of honour or of worldly goods.

Whether the Israelites believed or not, the great body of them remained staunch, and sooner than accept ease and advancement at the price of baptism, they firmly envisaged exile and the loss of their property, which the royal decree inspired by Torquemada rendered inevitable.

Bernaldez tells us that, notwithstanding the law against taking gold out of Spain, many of the exiles did take it in large quantities concealed about them—which is extremely probable. Not quite so probable is the common rumour which he reports, that they reduced many gold ducats to pellets with their teeth, and then swallowed them upon arriving at seaports or other places where they were to be searched, thus carrying the gold away in their stomachs. The women in particular, he says, were great offenders in this respect, and—again reporting the voice of common rumour—he informs us that some women contrived to swallow as many as thirty ducats each.[241]

The story of this swallowed gold evidently got abroad, to add to their affliction; and we are told that some who sailed from Cadiz to Fez, and who fell into the hands of Moors upon landing on the coast of Barbary, were not only plundered of their belongings, but were in several cases ripped open by these brigands in their quest for gold.[242]

Within the little period of three months appointed them, the Israelites sold or bartered what they could, and abandoned that for which they found no buyers. All boys and girls of the age of twelve or more they married, so that each nubile female should set out under the protection of a husband.[243]

The exodus from Spain began in the first week in July of 1492. Those amongst the exiles who were wealthy supported their poorer brethren, in pursuance of the custom that had ever prevailed in their ghettos. Many who had been very wealthy and masters of thriving trades abandoned their prosperity, and trusting to what Bernaldez terms "the vain hope of their blindness," they took the harsh road into banishment.

The parish priest of Palacios has left us a vivid picture of this emigration.[244] It is a picture over which Christianity must weep in shame.

On foot, on horseback, on donkeys, in carts, young and old, stalwart and feeble, healthy and ailing, some dying and some being born, and many falling by the way, they formed forlorn processions toiling onwards in the heat and dust of that July. On every road that led out of the country—on those that went southwards to the sea, or westwards to Portugal, or eastwards to Navarre—these straggling human droves were to be met, and they presented a spectacle so desolate that there was no Christian who did not pity them.

Succour them none dared, by virtue of the decree of the Grand Inquisitor; but on every hand they were exhorted to accept baptism and thus set a term upon their tribulations. And some, unable to endure more in their utter exhaustion and hopelessness, gave way and forswore the God of Israel.

But these were comparatively few. The Rabbis were at hand to encourage and stimulate them. The women and the young men were bidden to sing as they marched, and timbrels were sounded to hearten these wretched multitudes.

The Andalusians made for Cadiz, where it was their intention to take ship. Those of Aragon also turned towards the coast, repairing to Cartagena; whilst many Catalans sailed for Italy, where—singular anomaly!—a Catalan Pope (Roderigo Borgia) was to afford them shelter and protection in the very heart of the system that was oppressing and persecuting them.

Of those who arrived at Cadiz, Bernaldez says that at sight of the sea there was great clamour amongst them. Their imaginations fired by the recent sermons of the Rabbis, in which they had been likened to their forefathers departing out of the Egyptian captivity, they confidently expected to behold here a repetition of the miracle of the Red Sea, and that the waters would separate to allow them a dry-shod passage into Barbary.

Those who went westwards were permitted by King John of Portugal to enter his kingdom and abide there for six months upon payment of a small tax of one cruzado each.[245] Of these many settled in Portugal and engaged there in trade, which they were permitted to do subject to a tribute of 100 cruzados levied on each family.

It is no part of our present task to follow the Israelites into exile and observe the miserable fate that overtook so many of them, alike at the hands of the followers of the gentle Christ and at those of the Children of the Prophet. Many sages and rabbis were amongst those who abandoned Spain, and in their number was Isahak Aboab, the last Prince of the Castilian Jews, and Isaac Abarbanel, the sometime farmer of the royal taxes.

"The expulsion," writes this last, "was accompanied by pillage on land and sea; and amongst those who, stricken and sorrowful, set out for foreign lands, was I. With great trouble I contrived to reach Naples, but I was unable to find any repose there in consequence of the French invasion. The French were masters of the city, the very inhabitants having abandoned their Government. All rose against our congregation, expelling rich and poor, men and women, fathers and sons of the Children of Zion, and reducing them to the greatest ruin and misery. Several abandoned their religion, fearing lest their blood should be shed as water, or that they might be sold into slavery; for men and women, young and old, were being carried off in ships without pity for their lamentations, compelled to abandon their Law and continue in captivity."

France and England received some of the exiles, others went to settle in the Far East. Most wretched, perhaps, were those who landed on the coast of Africa and attempted by way of the desert to reach Fez, where there was a Jewish colony. They were beset by a horde of plundering tribesmen, who pillaged them of their belongings, treated them with the utmost cruelty and inhumanity, ravished their women under their very eyes, and left them stripped and utterly broken. Their sufferings had reached the limit of their endurance. The survivors sought baptism at the first Christian settlement they reached, and many of these returned to their native Spain, having thus qualified themselves for readmission.

There were many otherwise who, similarly unable to endure the hardships which they met abroad, broke down at last, accepted baptism and returned, or else returned clamouring for the baptism that should enable them to dwell in peace in the land of their birth.

For three years, says Bernaldez, there was a constant stream of returning Jews, who having abandoned all for their faith, had now abandoned their faith itself, and came back to make a fresh start. They were baptized in groups, all at once, by the sprinkling of hyssop over them.[246] Bernaldez himself baptized a hundred of them at Palacios, and from what he beheld, "I considered fulfilled," he writes, "the prophecy of David—'Covertentur ad vesperam et famen patiuntur ut canes et circundabunt civitatem.'"

The priest of Palacios estimates at 36,000 the Jewish families that accepted banishment,[247] which would represent some 200,000 souls. But Salazar de Mendoza and Zurita set the total exiles at twice that number,[248] whilst Mariana carries it as high as 800,000.[249] More reliable perhaps than any of these is the estimate left by the Jewish writers, who say that in the year 5252 of the Creation 300,000 Jews left Spain, the land in which their forbears had dwelt for close upon 2,000 years.[250]

These figures bring home to us the gravity of the step taken by the Sovereigns when they consented to the banishment of the Jews; and if anything had been wanting to make us appreciate the irresistible quality of Torquemada and of the fanaticism for which he stood, these figures would supply it.

The proposed expulsion must fully have been discussed in council before the edict was promulgated;[251] and it must have been obvious that Spain could not fail to be left materially the poorer if some 40,000 industrious families were driven out. It is unthinkable that king or councillor should not have raised the question of the inexpediency, of the positive danger attaching to such a measure. Yet certain it is that neither councillor nor king could stand against the stern, uncompromising friar, in whom they saw the representative of a God that was not to be trifled with—a God whom their conceptions transformed into some vindictive pagan deity.

Torquemada's crucifix so dramatically flung into the scales had definitely settled the question.

The Sultan Bajazet, who welcomed and sheltered not a few of the fugitives in Turkey, was overcome with amazement at this blunder of statecraft, so that he is reported to have asked whether this king were seriously to be taken for a great statesman who impoverished his kingdom to enrich another's.

What the Grand Turk perceived so readily, priest-ridden Ferdinand dared not perceive.

In banishing Jew and Moslem from her soil—for the Moor was soon to follow, though temporarily permitted to remain by virtue of the terms of the capitulation of Granada—Spain banished her merchants and financiers on the one hand, and her agriculturists and artisans on the other; in short, she banished her workers, the productive section of her community. It is accounted by many that she did so with the fullest consciousness of the consequences—an act of heroic sacrifice to principle and to religious convictions. And it may be that she accounted herself God-rewarded by the gift of a new world for this sacrifice to God.

The arts, the industries, manufactures, agriculture, and commerce have been bewailing for four hundred years the lack of hands to serve them. The New World proved but an illusory and transient compensation. Its gold could not furnish Spain with the workers that she lacked. On the contrary, it increased that lack. The New World repaid herself with interest for what she gave. In return for the gifts she poured into the lap of Spain she took to herself the very children of Spain, luring them overseas with the fabulous tales of riches easily to be acquired. Driven by this greed of gold, multitudes of families emigrated to increase the depopulation of their country. And when, in the course of time, those children of Spain in the New World had grown to a sufficient strength to claim their emancipation, they threw off the yoke of the motherland and distributed among themselves her vast possessions. They left her bare indeed, who by her own act was without home-resources, to realize perhaps at last what manner of service had been rendered her by the Prior of Holy Cross.

The Moors of Granada, meanwhile, had obtained from Ferdinand a promise that the Inquisition should not be set up in Granada within the following forty years, nor yet any prosecution instituted of Moriscoes (baptized Moslems) for the observance of Mohammedan customs.

The term, however, set too great a strain upon priestly patience. In 1526— long before the expiry of the period marked—the Holy Office crept slyly into Granada upon the pretext that it was requisite to watch the many suspected Marranos who had gone to reside there in the shelter of the immunity enjoyed by the Moriscoes. That it was the merest pretext is shown by the circumstance that already, as early as 1505, the Holy Office of Cordova had been moving in Granada and instituting there, when occasion arose, proceedings against Judaizers.

CHAPTER XXVII
THE LAST "INSTRUCTIONS" OF TORQUEMADA

The expulsion of the Jews may be considered the supreme and crowning work of Torquemada's life. It marks the high meridian of his achievement. Hereafter his career dwindles gradually in importance in a measure as it sinks slowly to its setting.

In Rome, meanwhile, in that year 1492, a new Pontiff—Roderigo Borgia—had ascended the throne of St. Peter under the title of Alexander VI, and from this Pontiff's hands Torquemada received his confirmation in the great office which he held—a confirmation which, being couched in the otiose terms of affection not uncommon in papal bulls, seems to have led many to believe that Alexander viewed Torquemada and the Holy Office of Spain with particular fondness. As a matter of fact, this Pope's attempts to curb the excessive rigour of the Grand Inquisitor were less lethargic—we dare not say more energetic—than those exerted by Sixtus IV and Innocent VIII; and it was Alexander VI who, weary of complaints, finally contrived the retirement of the Prior of Holy Cross.

But that was not yet. Before that came to pass, the scandals of secret absolutions sold and subsequently rescinded by the Holy See were now repeated. Vigorous appeals were made to the Holy Father against the procedure of the Grand Inquisitor, and the Holy Father, acting upon the advice of the Apostolic Court, dispatched his briefs of absolution. Torquemada, incensed once more by this fresh interference with his jurisdiction, made his appeal to the Sovereigns, and jointly with them laid his protests before the Pope, who complacently cancelled the briefs that had been paid for—or rather that part of the absolution which concerned the temporal courts. For the moneys received it could be shown that full value had been given, since these absolutions still held good in the tribunal of conscience. We are familiar by this time with the argument.

Torquemada's enemies in Spain were increasing now at an alarming rate. But, secure in the royal protection, this old man steadily and ruthlessly advanced along the path of intolerance, undismayed by ill-will. Conscious of the hatred he provoked, he may have gloried in the maledictions hurled against him by the persecuted, conceiving that the malevolence of the infidel would render his deeds the more acceptable in the sight of his God. But whatever the equanimity with which he may have confronted spiritual hostility, he took his measures to secure himself from its temporal manifestations. That he went in dread of attack is evinced not only by the fact that he was never seen abroad without his numerous escort of armed familiars, but further by the circumstance that he never sat down to dine without a horn of unicorn upon his table as a charm against poison.[252]

So arbitrarily and arrogantly did he widen the sphere of autocratic jurisdiction accorded him that soon he was usurping the functions of the civil courts, thereby provoking a still deeper resentment. He conducted the business of the Holy Office in such a manner that all other courts of the kingdom became subservient to it, and where the magistrates, resenting these encroachments, attempted to withstand him, or even to question his authority, they were—as had happened in the case of the Captain-General of Valencia—promptly charged with lack of zeal and even impeached as hinderers of the Holy Office. They were compelled to submit to humiliating penances, which in the case of magistrates entailed a total loss of dignity and prestige. And such was the ascendancy this man had gained by now that complaints or appeals to the Sovereigns were useless.

Meanwhile, however, and by his own act, his enemies at home had found two powerful mediators with the Pope, two powerful advocates to plead their cause before the Apostolic Court. These were Juan Arias Davila, Bishop of Segovia, and Pedro de Aranda, Bishop of Calahorra.

Torquemada's frenzied intolerance of men of Jewish blood was by no means confined to those who practised the Law of Moses. It extended to those who had accepted baptism and to their descendants, and it kept alive his mistrust of them.

Very markedly is this exhibited in the proceedings he instituted against the two bishops mentioned, notwithstanding the Papal decree which inhibited inquisitors from proceeding against prelates save by special pontifical authority.

The Bishop of Segovia—Juan Arias Davila—was the grandson of a Jew who had received baptism in the reign of Henry IV, and had held an honourable position at the court of that king by whom he had been ennobled. Considering the ecclesiastical eminence attained by his grandson—now a very old man—one would imagine that the latter should have been secure from inquisitorial attacks on the score of alleged offences committed by his ancestor against the Faith. But the terrible Torquemada contrived to rake up some matters against the long-deceased *converso*, accused him of having re-Judaized before his death, and instituted proceedings which must have resulted in the destitution, degradation and infamy of the bishop, his descendant.

"It sufficed," says Llorente on this subject,[253] "that a deceased Jew should have been fortunate and wealthy to seek cause of suspicion upon his faith and religion, such was the ill-will against those of Jewish blood, such the desire to mortify them, and such the covetousness to absorb their property."

To these proceedings Davila set up a stout resistance and made appeal to the Pope, whereupon Torquemada experienced his first serious check. The Pope ordered him to stick to the letter of the law, and to lay the matter before the Apostolic Court, as was due. Thither went the Bishop also, to defend his grandfather's bones from the accusation lodged. He was well received by the Pontiff, who ultimately gave him the victory over Torquemada, for when the case was tried his father's memory was cleared of all guilt.[254]

In the meanwhile, however, Davila had not only received a very kindly welcome at the Vatican, but, pending his trial, he was given a position of honour, and he was associated with Cardinal Borgia of Monreale (Alexander's nephew) when the latter went as papal legate to Naples, to crown Alfonso II of Aragon.[255]

Less fortunate was Pedro de Aranda, the other accused Bishop. In his case, too, the proceedings instituted were based upon the alleged Judaizing of his deceased father—a Jew who had been baptized in the time of St. Vincent Ferrer.

His case was tried at Valladolid, but the inquisitors and the diocesan ordinary disagreed in their findings, and in 1493 the Bishop, accompanied by his bastard son Alfonso Solares, set out for Rome, to present in person his appeal to the Pontiff. Him, too, the Pope received with the utmost kindliness. His Holiness issued a brief inhibiting the inquisitors, and relegating the case to the Bishop of Cordova and the Prior of the Benedictines of Valladolid.

The case being tried by them, a verdict entirely favourable to the Bishop was obtained, and his father's memory was acquitted of the charge preferred against it. But the tribulations of the living son were not permitted to end there. Torquemada would not suffer that his prey should escape so easily.

Already in 1488 the Bishop had been defamed by a suspicion of judaizing, and the Grand Inquisitor now pressed that he should be called to answer to that charge, forwarding the indictment under seal to Rome.

Pending the solution of the matter by the Apostolic Court, Alexander not only treated Aranda well, but heaped honours and favours upon him and his son. The Bishop was sent to Venice as papal legate, he was appointed Master of the Sacred Palace, whilst upon his offspring was conferred the position of apostolic prothonotary.[256]

But despite the papal favour which he enjoyed, and notwithstanding the fact that he called upwards of a hundred witnesses to testify in his defence, he was found guilty. It is said that his own witnesses helped to bring about his conviction. The Pontifical Court was obliged to sentence him to loss of all ecclesiastical dignities and benefices, to degrade him and reduce him to the lay estate, whereafter he was imprisoned in Sant' Angelo, and there he died a few years later.[257]

Notwithstanding the sentence of the Apostolic Court, Llorente finds it impossible to believe that Aranda was really guilty of Judaizing. "It seems incredible that it should have been so, considering that he had preserved the reputation of good Catholic for so long and with such applause that the Queen Donna Isabella should have named him President of the Council of Castile. His celebrating the Synodal Council in his bishopric argues zeal for the purity of religion and its dogmas. That the witnesses called should have deponed to any words or actions of his that were contrary to this does not signify as much as may at first appear, for we know, from a multitude of instances, that to fast on Sunday, to abstain from work on Saturday, to refuse to eat pork, to dislike the blood of animals, and other similar matters, sufficed as grounds upon which to declare a man a Judaizing heretic, and this notwithstanding that, as any one knows to-day, these are circumstances not at all at issue with a firm adherence to the Catholic dogmas."[258]

His sentence, however, was not pronounced until 1498. Until then he enjoyed, as we have seen, great favour at the Papal Court. Taking advantage of this, he and the Bishop of Segovia not only acted as mediators to lay their countrymen's grievances against Torquemada before the Pope, but, in their very natural resentment at the injustice of the prosecutions instituted against themselves, they went so far as to urge the Pope to depose the Grand Inquisitor from his office. And Llorente—who states this upon the authority of Lumbreras—adds that these petitions would, of themselves, have prevailed but for the royal protection which Torquemada continued to enjoy.[259]

But the complaints of the Grand Inquisitor's abuse of his power continued to pour into Rome. They multiplied to such an extent, they were of such a nature, and they were presented by Spaniards of such eminence at the court of the Spanish Pontiff, that thrice was Torquemada forced to send an advocate to defend him before the Holy See.[260] And in the end Alexander considered it necessary to take measures to circumvent the royal protection which continued to oppose the deposition of the Prior of Holy Cross.

Since to depose him were too aggressive a course to adopt towards the Sovereigns, with whom the Pontiff desired to preserve the friendliest relations, at least Torquemada's power must be curtailed. And so, by a brief of June 23, 1494, indited with all the craft and diplomacy of which Roderigo Borgia was a master, a brief in which he assures the Grand Inquisitor that "he cherishes him in the very bowels of affection for his great labours in the exaltation of the Faith," and charged with tender solicitude for Torquemada's failing health, the Pontiff puts forward these infirmities as a reason for assuming him no longer equal to discharge single-handed the heavy duties of his office. Therefore His Holiness considers it desirable to appoint him assistants who will lighten the labour of his declining years.

The assistants appointed by Alexander were Martin Ponce de Leon, a Castilian nobleman who was Archbishop of Messina, Don Inigo Manrique, Bishop of Cordova (nephew of the prelate of the same name who was Archbishop of Seville), Don Francisco Sanchez de la Fuente, Bishop of Avila, sometime Dean of Toledo and Councillor of the Suprema, and Don Alonso Suarez de Fuentelsaz, Bishop of Mondonedo, who had also held the position of inquisitor.

These assistants were equipped by the Pontiff with the amplest powers— powers as ample as Torquemada's own—so that they were in no sense subservient to the Prior of Holy Cross. The term "assistant" was a papal euphuism, serving thinly to veil the fact that Torquemada's autocratic rule was virtually at an end.

Such was the absolute equality of the authority of each of the five Grand Inquisitors now in existence, that it was explicitly set forth that any one of them had power singly to determine any matter, or singly to conclude any case that might have been initiated by one of the other four.[261]

But of the four assistants appointed only two accepted office jointly with Torquemada. These were the Bishop of Avila and the Archbishop of Messina, who at once took up their duties.

The Pope went a step further on November 4 following, when by a supplementary brief he appointed Sanchez de la Fuente (Bishop of Avila) to be Judge of Appeal in cases of the Faith. And from now onwards it is to Sanchez de la Fuente that the Pope addresses his briefs concerning the conduct of the affairs of the Holy Office. It was to him personally that Alexander gave orders that when a bishop was unable or unwilling to perform upon an offending cleric of his diocese the ceremony of degradation, this should be undertaken by the Bishop of Avila himself, or else by a bishop by him appointed.

Thus it would seem that Torquemada had virtually been superseded, and that Sanchez de la Fuente had been rendered his superior. If so, that superiority cannot have been more than nominal. In spite of it, Torquemada remained the guiding spirit of the Holy Office in Spain, the supreme arbiter and law-giver, as we shall see when we come to consider his last "Instructions," published in 1498.

In spite of these measures taken by the Pope with a view to softening inquisitorial severity and bringing it within more reasonable bounds, complaints to Rome seem to have continued unabatedly.

Photo by Donald Macbeth.

SPAIN AND PORTUGAL.
From Colmenar's "Délices d'Espagne."

Far from restricting inquisitorial jurisdiction—as was intended—the appointment of these assistant Grand Inquisitors appears to have widened it. They now went so far as themselves to sell and dispose of confiscated property—a matter which hitherto had been conducted by the officers of the royal treasury. And this was more than Ferdinand could stomach. Where humanitarian considerations, where arguments of political expediency had failed to curb his bigotry, acquisitiveness seems easily to have carried the victory. So that at last we see the King himself turning in appeal to the Pope against this despotism of a court upon which he had conferred the power to become mightier than himself in his own kingdom.

The response to his appeal was the bull of February 1495, commanding the inquisitors under pain of excommunication to desist from their course, and never to resort to it again save under royal sanction. The power to proceed against inquisitors in case of fraud or irregularity in this matter was vested in the famous Francisco Ximenes de Cisneros.[262]

This man, who has been called the Richelieu of Spain, had risen from very humble beginnings, as a barefoot friar-mendicant, to the very splendid eminence of Primate of Spain—in which office he had just succeeded Cardinal Mendoza, who died in that year (1495).

In the following year Torquemada made his exit from the Court, where for a decade he had been a figure of an importance second only to that of the Sovereigns themselves.

Crippled by gout, he withdrew to his monastery at Avila.[263] There he now dwelt in retirement, an emaciated old man in his seventy-sixth year, debilitated and racked with bodily infirmities, but with all his vigour and energy of mind unimpaired, his severity as uncompromising as of old, his conscience entirely at peace in the conviction that he had given of his best— indeed, his all—to the service of his God.

But even now his retirement can have been little more than physical. His attention continued focussed upon the Inquisition and engrossed by it. To the last do we find him actively directing the procedure of that tribunal of the Faith.

In the spring of 1498 he summoned the principal inquisitors of the kingdom to the monastery of St. Thomas of Avila, to the end that with himself they might concert the promulgation of further decrees to check abuses which had crept into the administration of the justice of the Holy Office, proving inadequate his enactments of 1484, 1485, and 1488.

These, the fourth "Instructions" of Torquemada, were published on May 25, 1498. They contain a good deal that seems calculated to soften the rigour of the earlier decrees, yet much of this is more or less illusory.

Let us very briefly consider the sixteen articles of which they consist.

The first three provide: (I) that of the two inquisitors appointed to each court one shall be a jurist and the other a theologian, and that they shall not proceed other than jointly to decree prison, torture, or publication of witnesses; (II) that the inquisitors shall not permit their officers to bear weapons in those places where the bearing of weapons is forbidden; (III) that no one shall be arrested save upon sufficient proof of his guilt, and that all cases be disposed of with dispatch and not delayed in the hope of discovering increased justification to sentence.

This last clause merely repeats an earlier one that we have already seen, and from this repetition we are led to suppose that the former expression of the same command had not received proper attention and obedience. The stipulation that no arrest should be made save where there was sufficient proof of guilt is not as generous as it sounds. It is dependent upon what the inquisitors would consider "sufficient proof"; this is revealed by the jurisprudence of the Holy Office: the accusation of a spiteful or malevolent person, or a delation wrung from some wretch under torture, would be accounted "sufficient proof" to justify the arrest and its sequel. To abolish the inequitable character of this it would have been necessary to have rescinded the decree which accounted "semiplenal proof" sufficient ground for taking action.

Very merciful in its terms is Article IV, which sets forth that in proceedings against the dead the inquisitors must absolve promptly where complete proof of crime is not forthcoming, and not delay in the hope of obtaining further proof, as legal delays are very injurious to the children, who are unable to contract marriage whilst such matters are *sub judice*. But it comes a little late in the day. It comes when the great harvest from the wealthy dead has been safely garnered. Besides, no conditions imposed could mitigate the horrible rigour of the enactment to exhume and burn the bones of the dead together with their effigies, and to reduce the children or grandchildren to destitution and infamy, even when the person convicted was known to have died penitent and comforted by the sacraments of the Church—in consequence of which, by their own Faith, the inquisitors believed him to be saved.

Article V provides that when the tribunal shall be short of money for salary, no further pecuniary penances be imposed than would be the case if the court had funds in hand.

Conceive, if you can, the notions of equity prevailing in a tribunal which needed to have it decreed that fines were to be governed by the offence committed, and not by the court's need of money at the time!

Similarly illumining is Article VI, which sets forth that imprisonment or other corporal penances must not be commuted to fines, and that only the inquisitors-general shall have power to dispense an offender from wearing the *sanbenito* and to rehabilitate the children of heretics so that they shall have liberty in the matters of apparel and employment.

As Llorente points out,[264] the very existence of this decree shows of what abuses of power the inquisitors were guilty for the purpose of increasing their already considerable profit.

Article VII is thoroughly imbued with the inquisitorial spirit of mercilessness. It warns inquisitors to be cautious in the matter of admitting to reconciliation those who confess their fault after arrest, since, considering how many years have passed since the institution of the Inquisition, the contumacy of such offenders may be taken as established.

On the subject of Article VIII, which enjoins inquisitors to punish false witnesses with public pains, Llorente is particularly interesting in a commentary:

"Properly to understand this article, it is necessary to realize that there were two ways of being a false witness: one by calumniating, another by denying knowledge of heretical words or deeds upon which a person might be questioned in the course of proceedings against an accused. I have seen many records of proceedings against those of this second class, but very rarely (*rarissima vez*) any against those of the first. Nor could it be easy to prove that a calumniator has borne false witness, for the unfortunate accused would have to guess his identity, and though he were to guess correctly the court would not admit it."[265]

Article IX provides that in no tribunal shall there be two persons who are related or one who is the servant of another, even though their respective offices should be entirely different and separate.

Articles X, XI, and XVI are calculated to increase the secrecy of inquisitorial proceedings. The first makes provision for the secret custody of all documents and for punishing any notary who shall betray his trust; the second enacts that a notary must not receive the depositions of witnesses save in the presence of the inquisitor; the last decrees that after the witnesses shall have been sworn by the inquisitors in the presence of the fiscal, the latter must withdraw so as not to be present when the delations are made.

The remaining four articles are concerned with such matters as the setting up of courts of the Inquisition where these have not yet been established, the submission of difficult questions that may arise to the Suprema for decision, the provision of separate prisons for women and for men, and the stipulation that officers of the court shall work six hours daily.

In addition to the foregoing sixteen articles, he promulgated in that same year special instructions concerning the *personnel* of the Holy Office. They speak for themselves, and very vividly suggest the abuses they were framed to suppress.

For governors of prisons and constables he decreed that they must permit no one to visit the prisoners with the exception of the persons appointed to bear them food, and that these must be bound by oath to preserve the "secrecy" inviolate, and to examine all food to ascertain that no written matter is concealed in it. Food, it is added, shall be conveyed to the prisoners by persons specially appointed for that duty, and never by a constable or gaoler.

All officers are to be sworn to preserve inviolate secrecy upon all things they may see or hear.

Receivers are commanded that in the event of the acquittal of a person whose property has been sequestered, they must restore the property according to the inventory drawn up at the time of effecting the sequestration—but if there are debts to be satisfied by such a person, these may be paid by order of the inquisitors without awaiting the consent of the debtor.

If amongst confiscated property there should be any that is in litigation, the matter is to be judicially decided; and if it is found that any property which should have formed part of a confiscation shall have passed into the hands of third parties, action is to be taken to recover it.

Confiscated property is to be sold after thirty days, and the receivers are not to purchase any under pain of greater excommunication and a fine of 100 ducats. Each receiver is authorized to give vouchers for property up to the value of 300,000 maravedis.

For the inquisitors themselves it is provided that upon assuming office they shall be bound by oath to discharge their duties well and faithfully and to observe the secrecy; that no inquisitor or officer of the Inquisition shall receive any gift of whatsoever nature from a prisoner, under pain of loss of office and a fine of twice the value of the gift plus 100,000 maravedis, whilst any who shall have knowledge of such matter and fail to divulge it shall be subject to the same penalty.

Inquisitors are to make oath never to be alone with a prisoner, and neither an inquisitor nor any officer of the court shall hold two offices or receive two salaries. Lastly, in any district where the Inquisition's tribunal is established, the inquisitors must pay for their own lodgings, and must never receive any hospitality from *conversos*.[266]

We have seen Torquemada's efforts strained to obtain the fullest possible control over subjects of inquisitorial jurisdiction in Spain, and to establish himself the sole arbiter in matters concerning heresies there committed. And we have seen his frequent conflicts with Rome in consequence of what he accounted undue interference on the part of the Holy See in affairs which he considered purely within his own province. Despite repeated protests which had resulted in the annulment of absolutions granted by the Apostolic Court, the Holy See had ever continued to receive those who fled thither from Spain in quest of a reconciliation that was procurable in Rome upon terms far easier than were accorded by Torquemada's delegates.

Never, however, had the fugitives to Rome been so numerous as they were now in the reign of Alexander VI. Never before had so many Judaizers—who were liable, if discovered in Spain, to perpetual prison or the fire—sought at the hands of the Pontiff the absolution which, subject to penitence and penance, the Holy Father was willing and ready to accord them.

On July 29, 1498, an Auto de Fé was held in Rome in the vast square before St. Peter's, when 180 Spanish Judaizers came to be reconciled to the Church.[267]

It is worth while to take a glance at this, and to mark the difference between the Act of Faith in the very heart of Christendom, and the spectacles provided under the same title by Spanish bigotry and fanaticism.

There were present the Governor of Rome, Juan de Cartagena, the Spanish Orator at the Vatican, the Apostolic auditors, and the Master of the Sacred Palace, whilst the Pope himself surveyed the scene from the balcony above the steps of St. Peter's.

The penitents received the *sanbenitos*, which were put on over their ordinary garments, and arrayed in these they entered St. Peter's. There all were assembled and reconciled, whereafter they were taken in procession to the Church of Santa Maria della Minerva. In this temple they put off their *sanbenitos*, and each one withdrew to his home without further bearing the insignia of shame and infamy.[268]

The view taken by Torquemada of a Pope who so little understood what the former considered to be the duties of Christ's earthly Vicar is to be gathered from the attitude of the Sovereigns in the matter of these reconciliations, and their protests—protests which, beyond doubt, would be inspired by the Grand Inquisitor.

Alexander advised the Sovereigns in reply—by a brief of October 5—that in according these absolutions one of the pains imposed upon the penanced was that they must never return to Spain without the special sanction of the Catholic Sovereigns.[269]

In this manner, clearly, there was no infringement by the Pontiff of the power relegated to the Spanish inquisitors, since as long as the penitents remained abroad they were beyond the jurisdiction of the Holy Office of Spain. As for the prohibition to return being a part of the penance imposed, it was surely supererogative, for we cannot think that any of those who had so fortunately obtained absolution would easily incur the risk of coming within reach of the talons of a court that would disregard, or else find a way to cancel or circumvent, the Roman reconciliation.

But by the time the brief reached Spain, Frey Tomás de Torquemada, the arch-enemy of the Jews, had breathed his last in his beautiful monastery of St. Thomas at Avila.

He passed away in peace, laying down the burden of life and sinking to sleep with the relief and thankfulness of the husbandman at the end of a day of diligent, arduous, and conscientious toil. His honesty of purpose, his integrity, his utter devotion to the task he had taken up are to be weighed in the balance of historic judgment against the evil that he wrought so ardently in the unfaltering conviction that his work was good.

His name has been execrated and revered at once. He has been vituperated as a fiend of cruelty, and all but worshipped as a saint; and there is bias in both judgments—both are no better than gratifications of prejudice.

Perhaps Prescott is nearest the truth when he says that "Torquemada's zeal was of so extraordinary a character that it may almost shelter itself under the name of insanity."[270]

Garcia Rodrigo speaks of the barbarians of the nineteenth century who desecrated the monastery of St. Thomas, and whose "revolutionary hammers" smashed so many of the sepulchral and other marbles. He turns the medal about for us when he pours his fierce invective upon anti-religious fanaticism and speaks of these broken marbles as evidences of "perversity, intolerance, and want of enlightenment."[271]

The anti-religious fanaticism and intolerance must be admitted. But it must be admitted that they are the inevitable fruits that fanaticism and intolerance produce. Men reap as they sow. And what but thistles shall be yielded by the seed of thistles?

The same author inveighs against the political fanaticism of Spanish Liberalism, which in the hour of reaction sought fiercely for the bones of the first Grand Inquisitor. He denounces it indignantly for disturbing the peace of sepulture. In the main we share his feelings; and yet can we avoid perceiving here a measure of retributive justice? Can we fail to see in this fanatical act the vengeance of humanity for the almost obscene violation of a thousand graves by that same Grand Inquisitor's fanaticism?

He was laid to rest in the chapel of his monastery, and his tomb bore the following simple inscription:

HIC JACET REVERENDUS P. F. THOMAS DE TURRE-CREMATA
PRIOR SANCTÆ CRUCIS, INQUISITOR GENERALIS
HUJUS DOMUS FUNDATOR. OBIIT ANNO DOMINI
MCDLXLVIII, DIE XVI SEPTEMBRIS.[272]

But his work survived him. His spirit—through his enactments—continued for three centuries after his death to be the guiding spirit of the Inquisition, executor of the stern testament he left inscribed upon the walls of his monastery—

PESTEM FUGAT HÆRETICAM.

BIBLIOGRAPHY

Ariz, Luys: "Historia de Avila." Alcalá, 1607.

Babut, Charles E.: "Priscillian et le Priscilliantisme." Paris, 1909.

Bernaldez, Andrés: "Historia de los Reyes Catolicos." 1870.

Bleda, Jaime: "Coronica de los Moros de España." Valencia, 1618.

Burchard, Johannes: "Diarium sive Rerum Urbanarum Commentarii" (Ed. Thuasne). Paris.

Castillo, Hernando del: "Historia General de Santo Domingo." Valladolid, 1612.

Colmenar, Juan Alvarez de: "Delices d'Espagne." Leyden, 1715

Colmenares, Diego de: "Historia de Segovia." Madrid, 1640.

"Copilacion de las Instrucciones hechas, etc." Madrid, 1576.

Didron, A. N.: "Iconographie Chrétienne." Paris, 1835.

Douais, C.: "Les Hérétiques du Midi au XIII Siècle."

Emeric, David: "Histoire de la Peinture." Paris, 1842.

Eymericus, Nicolaus: "Directorium Inquisitorum." Romæ, 1578-79.

Fita, Fidel: in "Boletin de la Real Academia de la Historia," vols, v., vi., ix., xv., xvi., xvii., and xviii.

Frazer, Jas. Geo.: "The Golden Bough." London, 1900.

Guidonis, Bernardus: "Practica Inquisitionis." Paris, 1886.

Lecky, W. E. H.: "Rationalism in Europe." London, 1865.

Limborch, Phillippi a: "Historia Inquisitionis." Amstelodami, 1692.

Llorente, Juan Antonio: "Anales de la Inquisicion de España." Madrid, 1812.

Llorente, Juan Antonio: "Historia Critica de la Inquisicion de España." Madrid, 1822.

Llorente, Juan Antonio: "Memoria Historica." Madrid, 1812.

Loeb, Isidore: in "Revue des Etudes Juives," vols. xv., xviii., xix., and xx.

Mariana, Juan de: "Historia General de España." Madrid, 1849-51.

Marin, Julio Melgares: "Procedimientos de la Inquisicion." Madrid, 1886.

Marineo, L.: "Cronica d'Aragon." Valencia, 1524.

Mendoza, Salazar de: "Cronica de el Gran Cardinal." Toledo, 1625.

Mendoza, Salazar de: "Monarquia de España." Madrid, 1770.

Moreno, Martin Martinez: "Historia del Martirio del Santo Niño de La Guardia." Madrid, 1786.

Paramo, Ludovicus a: "De Origine et Progressu Sanctæ Inquisitionis." Madrid, 1598.

Pulgar, Hernando del: "Chronica de los Reyes Catholicos." Valencia, 1780.

Pulgar, Hernando del: "Claros Varones de Castilla." Madrid, 1789.

Rios, José Amador de los: "Estudios sobre los Judios de España." Madrid, 1848.

Rios, José Amador de los: "Historia de los Judios de España y Portugal." Madrid, 1875.

Rodrigo, Francisco Xavier Garcia: "Historia Verdadera de la Inquisicion." Madrid, 1877.

Rule, W. H.: "History of the Inquisition." London, 1874.

St. Hilaire, Rosseeuw: "Histoire d'Espagne." Paris, 1845.

Torrejoncillo, Francisco de: "Centinela contra Judios." Pamplona, 1720.

Trasmiera, Diego Garcia de: "Epitome de la Vida de Pedro de Arbués." Madrid, 1664.

Zuñiga, Diego Ortiz de: "Anales de Sevilla." Madrid, 1677.

Zurita, Geronimo: "Anales de la Corona de Aragon." Madrid, 1852.

Milton Keynes UK
Ingram Content Group UK Ltd.
UKHW020752200524
442968UK00006B/772

9 789357 961806